GOD'S CHURCH FOR GOD'S WORLD

GOD'S CHURCH FOR GOD'S WORLD

Faithful perspectives on mission and ministry

Edited by T. A. Woolford and A. C. Young

INTER-VARSITY PRESS
36 Causton Street, London SW1P 4ST, England
Email: ivp@ivpbooks.com
Website: www.ivpbooks.com

First published 2022

British Library Cataloguing-in-Publication Data
A catalogue record for this book is available from the British Library.

ISBN: 978–1–78974–224–4
eBook ISBN: 978–1–78974–220–6

1 3 5 7 9 10 8 6 4 2

Set in Minion Pro 11.5/15pt
Typeset in Great Britain by CRB Associates, Potterhanworth, Lincolnshire
Printed in Great Britain by Ashford Colour Press Ltd, Gosport, Hampshire

Produced on paper from sustainable sources

*Inter-Varsity Press publishes Christian books that are true to the Bible and that
communicate the gospel, develop discipleship and strengthen the church for its mission
in the world.*

*IVP originated within the Inter-Varsity Fellowship, now the Universities and Colleges
Christian Fellowship, a student movement connecting Christian Unions in universities and
colleges throughout Great Britain, and a member movement of the International Fellowship
of Evangelical Students. Website: www.uccf.org.uk. That historic association is maintained,
and all senior IVP staff and committee members subscribe to the UCCF Basis of Faith.*

Contents

Contents

Part 3

GOD'S CHURCH IN GOD'S WORLD: TRAJECTORIES AND FUNDAMENTALS

Contributors

The Reverend Sophie Bannister Sophie is the Vice-Chair of the Junia Network and Assistant Priest at St John the Baptist, Spalding. She trained at Ridley Hall, Cambridge, and Oak Hill, London.

Dr Ros Clarke Ros is Associate Director of the Church Society, Course Leader of the Priscilla Programme and leader of the Co-Workers network for complementarian women in Anglican ministry in the UK. She is the author of *Forty Women* (IVP, 2021).

The Reverend Canon Dr Andrew Goddard Andrew is Assistant Minister at St James the Less Church, Pimlico, and teaches ethics at Ridley Hall, Cambridge, and Westminster Theological Centre. He is also a member of the Church of England Evangelical Council (CEEC) and has written extensively on the Anglican Communion and on sexual ethics.

The Reverend Sam Haigh Sam serves as the Vicar of Preston Minster, a Holy Trinity Brompton (HTB) church plant. He trained at Ridley Hall, Cambridge.

The Right Reverend Julian Henderson Julian is the Diocesan Bishop of Blackburn and President of the Church of England Evangelical Council. He trained at Ridley Hall, Cambridge.

The Right Reverend Sophie Jelley Sophie serves as the suffragan Bishop of Doncaster, in the Diocese of Sheffield. She trained at Wycliffe Hall, Oxford.

The Reverend Charles Lamont Charles is the Vicar of St Andrew's, Wimbledon, in the Diocese of Southwark. He trained at St John's College, Nottingham, following theological studies at the University of Nottingham.

The Reverend David McCarthy David is the Rector of St Thomas' Church, Edinburgh, and a trustee of GAFCON UK. He trained at New College, Edinburgh.

The Reverend Rachel Marszalek Rachel is the Vicar of All Saints, Ealing, and a lay ministry tutor at St Mellitus College. She trained at St John's College, Nottingham.

The Reverend Esther Prior Esther is the Vicar of St John's Egham, Vice-Chair of CPAS Patronage Trustees and a member of the Church of England Evangelical Council. Esther came to England from Zimbabwe for her theological education in 1999. After two curacies, she has served as a school chaplain, a young offenders prison chaplain and a team vicar in Farnborough.

The Reverend Dean Aaron Roberts Dean is the Rector of Bedwas, Machen, and Michaelston-y-Fedw, and Vicar of Rudry in South Wales. He trained at Trinity College, Bristol. He has sat on numerous committees within the structures of the Church in Wales, including the Governing Body, where he sat for two terms as a co-opted member. He currently sits on the Executive Committee for the Evangelical Fellowship in the Church in Wales, and also represents the Church in Wales as an observer at the Church of England Evangelical Council. Dean also sits on the Council of Reference for the Church Pastoral Aid Society and is the Chair of Trustees for the Parish Trust, which he founded in 2019.

The Reverend Dr Peter Sanlon Peter has a PhD in Doctrine from Cambridge University and is the author of *Simply God* (IVP, 2014) and *Augustine's Theology of Preaching* (Fortress Press, 2014). Having been an incumbent, he seceded from the Church of England in 2019 to found an independent Anglican church in Tunbridge Wells.

The Right Reverend Keith Sinclair Keith served as the suffragan Bishop of Birkenhead until 2021. Presently, he serves as the National Director of the Church of England Evangelical Council. He trained at Cranmer Hall, Durham.

The Right Reverend Charles Howell 'Rod' Thomas Rod has served as the Bishop of Maidstone since September 2015. He trained at Wycliffe Hall, Oxford.

The Reverend Dr Thomas Woolford Tom is the Vicar of All Saints' Church, New Longton, in the Diocese of Blackburn, and Tutor in Theology at Emmanuel Theological College. He has a PhD in History from the University of Cambridge.

The Reverend Adam Young Adam is Associate Minister at All Saints' Church, North Ferriby, and a padre attached to the Yorkshire (North and West) Army Cadet Force. He studied Theology at Wycliffe Hall, Oxford, before going on to train for ministry, and is currently an OMF Appointee.

Introduction

THE REVEREND DR THOMAS WOOLFORD AND
THE REVEREND ADAM YOUNG

The fifteenth Lambeth Conference – the traditional gathering of leaders from the worldwide Anglican Communion every ten years – was due to meet in 2020. At the time, no one could have imagined how much the world would have changed within just a few years, nor expected that it would not actually convene until, the Lord willing, 2022. The theme of this conference was set as 'God's church for God's world: walking, listening and witnessing together.' Despite all the global upheaval and change due to the COVID-19 pandemic, natural disasters and continuing conflicts since it was first put forward, some truths remain eternal. God is still God, the church is still his church – the bride of Christ – and the world is still his world.

Perhaps more than at any previous time – though that is quite debateable – the Anglican Church is divided and fractured. For many, it is quite difficult even to agree on what the 'Anglican Church' means. It is likely that many bishops from around the world will not attend this Lambeth Conference. Church attendance in the West is plummeting and churches are facing incredibly difficult choices about the future, with regard to buildings, finances and ministry. Current moral questions around gender and sexuality continue to tear apart not only the international Anglican Communion but also individual national churches within it, including the Church of England. The COVID-19 pandemic has shown us that life as we know it is much more frail and fleeting than we ever imagined was possible. The very idea that the government would force national church closures would have seemed laughable not so long ago, and the need to completely reinvent how outreach and ministry are done to adapt to this has presented new challenges.

It is in this context that the truth of our church being God's church for God's world is most vital. For all our struggles and failures, for all the challenges we face at present and in the future, we belong to God; we are his church. He is the one in charge, he is the one who sustains, he is the one who preserves his truth through the ages, he is the one who still works the miracle of changing unbelieving hearts of stone into hearts of flesh that beat for him alone. This world is still his world, his good creation, his chosen place of redemption and resurrection, the place he loved enough to enter into and die on a cross for. We are God's church and we have a mission to fulfil in God's world: we are to exist for God's glory and, by extension, for the salvation of his world.

Walking and listening together

Amid all the divisions and challenges of our time, now is an exciting time in Anglicanism. The idea of walking, listening and witnessing together as God's church for God's world has been manifested among evangelicals in a fresh way. Global movements such as the Global Anglican Future Conference (GAFCON) have united evangelicals – and others – across the worldwide Communion in an exciting and radical manner. The challenges facing gospel ministry and the proclamation of biblical truth have galvanized those who hold dear the role to witness the Scriptures and the Anglican Formularies. The evangelical essence of the Anglican Formularies – the Thirty-nine Articles of Religion, the 1662 Book of Common Prayer and the Ordinal – has brought a renewed interest in them and what helps make Anglicanism . . . well, Anglicanism. It is no small thing that the Jerusalem Declaration, created by GAFCON in 2008 as a statement of unified faith, contains as its point 4:

> We uphold the Thirty-nine Articles as containing the true doctrine of the Church agreeing with God's Word and as authoritative for Anglicans today.

Meanwhile within the Church of England, the more recent challenges of the push to affirm same-sex marriage have united evangelicals from across the width of that spectrum in a fresh way. The work of the Church of England Evangelical Council, a body founded by the late John Stott that exists to promote and maintain orthodox evangelical theology and ethics at the heart of the Church of England, has been more public and outward-looking. It has been working hard to unite evangelicals from the more generally complementarian reformed side of the church, such as the Church Society (which itself has been working hard to bring together its constituency), with the more generally egalitarian charismatic New Wine. It has also brought a more focused and unifying voice to issues in human sexuality by producing the video *Beautiful Story* and many other resources for engaging biblically with these topics. This is not to say that all has been rosy and easy; divisions do remain within evangelicalism over how to navigate issues that raise questions of 'Should I stay or should I go?' and where the red lines are drawn and why.

Witnessing together

In the past ten years since the previous Lambeth Conference, there has been a lot of walking and listening together among Anglican evangelicals globally and within England. There has also been *a lot* of witnessing. While the general trend for churches within England has been one of downward growth, many evangelical churches have been growing and thriving. Others have been faithfully ministering to and discipling the faithful. There has been an explosion in church planting by large churches and networks such as Holy Trinity Brompton (HTB) and New Wine-affiliated churches, as well as structures outside the Church of England, such as the Anglican Mission in England (AMiE), a parallel Anglican province in relationship with the Anglican Church in North America (ACNA) and many of the global south GAFCON churches. The struggles of many non-evangelical churches have also opened the door to what might be called 'turn-around ministries', which many evangelicals have leapt to in an attempt to witness faithfully to a dying church, and minister into that congregation a gospel-centred ministry that had likely not been there before.

Along with this church-planting fervour, in recent years there has been an increased focus on reaching the unchurched parts of England, such as many of the most deprived areas of the nation – a demographic in which, historically, there has been less of an evangelical presence from the Church of England. The Junior Anglican Evangelical Conference has also been working hard to foster young vocations and help those exploring, training, entering and starting their ministry. Meanwhile, ministries such as the Junia Network have been active in resourcing and promoting ordained ministry among evangelical women, while more complementarian offerings, such as the Priscilla Programme, have been resourcing women who serve their local churches in voluntary ministries. The importance of the laity – those who are not ordained – has also been increasingly coming to the fore among evangelicals, and the work of the Church Pastoral Aid Society (CPAS), the Church Society, Church of England Evangelical Council (CEEC) and others has been promoting and speaking into this afresh.

Together going forwards

Yes, there is much that is exciting and worth celebrating happening in God's world through God's church! There remain faithful orthodox evangelical Anglicans in England, and they are walking, listening and witnessing together more than ever before. Evangelicalism within the Church of England is diverse and there are many disagreements that remain about the role of women in ministry, the continuation of the spiritual gifts, strategy and focus, matters of soteriology. There is, though, also an exciting unity and fresh willingness to put aside secondary issues in order to protect and promote the first-order issues of the gospel, sin and salvation.

That unity has global implications, because it is also a unity with the global Anglican Church, which remains, primarily, conservative on these issues and seeks to resist revisions. Traditionally, the Church of England has always been the centre of global Anglicanism, the Archbishop of Canterbury the first among equals, the mother church the locus of global unity. As these traditions are tested in a way that they have never been before, it is not exaggerating to say that what happens among evangelicals in the Church of England has global implications for the Anglican Communion.

This book hopes to bring together testimony, story and reflection from across evangelical Anglicanism in England. United around the gospel, we seek to explore the key issues we are facing and share our thoughts and ministries – share what God has been doing among us. Together, we hope to give a glimpse of the vibrant work of God's church in England.

Not everyone who has contributed to this book will agree with everyone else on all things, and that includes those of us who have edited it. We all, though, love Jesus and seek his glory, and we all recognize the importance of God's church and his love for his world. We are all evangelicals who can happily subscribe to the CEEC's Basis of Faith, and it is in our evangelical faith that we acknowledge afresh our core unity.

Part 1: God's church for God's world: what is happening to the Church of England?

Part 1 is an overview of the broad situation in England. We begin, in Chapter 1, with Andrew Goddard exploring how the Anglican Communion has changed over the years. Beginning with the early eighteenth century, he explores the growth of a sense of global Anglicanism by tracing the creation of structures such as the first Lambeth Conference in 1867 and the central consultative bodies, as well as defining events, such as the writing of the Chicago–Lambeth Quadrilateral. In more recent times, he considers the formation of GAFCON in response to revisionism among some Anglican churches with regard to issues concerning sexuality. Finally, Andrew explores the complexity of what is and is not 'Anglican' in the light of this history.

In Chapter 2, Thomas Woolford considers his own journey, from thinking that the Church of England was simply 'the best boat to fish from' – a common idea among evangelical Anglicans – to an understanding of the importance of the catholicity of the Church of England as a convictional Anglican. He explains how true catholicity is biblical, historical and evangelical. The catholic faith handed down to the saints is biblical and traditional, creedal and canonical, listens to those who have gone before and is open to being in the conversation with those around us today. Thomas then considers the challenges but also, especially, the benefits of being in a broad church such as the Church of England, as well as the importance of not focusing only on our own little flock of sheep but also serving, loving and caring for the whole flock of believers across England.

It is one thing to think of how clergy serve with conviction and whether they should stay or go on a theological level but, ultimately, it is the laity they serve. In Chapter 3, Ros Clarke introduces us to this vital topic by considering the biblical basics of lay ministry in the Church of England and the radical vision of J. C. Ryle in this regard. She explores the role of the laity in the church – local, regional and national – and the incredible influence they can wield by serving their local church and participating intentionally in the larger structures of the deanery and diocese.

Of course, a diocese comes with a bishop. One of the four defining points of Anglicanism within the Chicago–Lambeth Quadrilateral is episcopacy. In Chapter 4, Adam Young introduces the history and purpose of bishops within the Church of England, from the Reformation onwards. Then, four serving bishops explain their understanding of what it means to be an evangelical bishop in the Church of England today. These evangelical bishops show a remarkable common unity of vision, despite being at different points in their episcopacy – fairly new or recently retired – or having different roles in the hierarchy – diocesan, suffragan, flying – and coming from different parts of the evangelical spectrum on issues such as women in ministry and the gifts of the Spirit today.

Part 2: God's people in God's church: stories and perspectives

In Part 2, we look at stories from across the country and the evangelical spectrum to see the gospel unity, common themes, unique challenges and shared testimony of the work of Jesus today in his church and world.

In Chapter 5, Sam Haigh explores the culture shock he experienced when he entered theological college. He then reflects on the importance of exegetical preaching and the lessons he has learnt through his work with Holy Trinity Brompton (HTB) – how we must have an audacious faith that expects God always to do immeasurably more than we ask or imagine. From Alpha, HTB, church planting and turn-around ministry at Preston Minster, Sam challenges us to think big, even as we address the challenges of our time face on.

Charles Lamont, in Chapter 6, shares with us his testimony of God's work revitalizing St Andrew's Wimbledon amid all the very real challenges a minister faces taking on such a radical turn-around ministry as an evangelical. He brings home to us the importance of discipleship, mentoring and training, as well as answering questions on how issues concerning human sexuality – especially in a more revisionist setting – can have an impact on the basic work of mission.

Coming from Zimbabwe, Esther Prior became a Christian and longed to serve and minister in God's church, but had no idea just how deep the divisions relating to charismatic gifts and the ordination of women can go. In her time at Bristol, she would wrestle with these and, here, in Chapter 7, she shares her understanding of the biblical witness of women in ministry, especially in light of 1 Timothy 2:9–12. Shortly after her ordination, Esther attended the GAFCON conference, where the divisions between evangelicals on this matter were more than apparent. Mutual flourishing, for both complementarians and egalitarians, was the promise and commitment from the Church of England and, in this chapter, Esther handles openly and frankly the very real challenges, pains and struggles that this walking together brings on all sides.

Staying on this theme in Chapter 8, Sophie Bannister introduces us to the work of the Junia Network and explores the current challenges and opportunities for ordained women in the Church of England. Sophie shares with us the testimony of a large number of women, their stories of calling and ministry.

Turn-around ministry is never easy and requires the most generous help of the Holy Spirit. Rachel Marszalek, in Chapter 9, explores what this can look like by sharing with us her ministry at All Saints Church in Ealing. She considers the strategies, hurdles, challenges and joys of such a ministry, as well as the parallels it has with the wider challenges and situation of the Church of England as a whole.

Part 3: God's church in God's world: trajectories and fundamentals

In Part 3, we turn our eyes to the situation outside of the Church of England, in more ways than one. We begin, in Chapter 10, with the evangelical situation in the Church in Wales, as Dean Aaron Roberts shares his curacy experience with us. Unlike in England, in Wales evangelicalism has, at best, been an influential minority. Today, it remains but a small fraction of active ministry in the church and faces many challenges and hurdles.

David McCarthy, in Chapter 11, then shares with us his story of ministry within the Scottish Episcopal Church (SEC), as it changed its teaching on marriage in the years following the Windsor report of 2004 through to officially changing its teaching on marriage in 2017. His chapter includes not only a recounting of the journey of the SEC but also his own journey, ultimately, out of it, along with that of the vast majority of his congregation at St Thomas' Church.

In Chapter 12, Peter Sanlon, who left the Church of England for the Free Church of England in 2019, helpfully reminds us that, for well over a century, 'Anglicanism' has been something much broader in its meaning than simply referring only to those in direct communion with the Archbishop of Canterbury. Peter introduces us to the history of the Free Church of England, his own journey with that denomination and the internal issues it is facing currently. He also examines other 'alternative Anglicanisms' within England.

Appendices

What harmonizes the diverse evangelical voices of this book is a common faith and heritage, shared biblical convictions and emphases. Because of this, we felt that it would be helpful to include in this volume the historic confession that binds us all together as Anglicans: the Thirty-nine Articles of Religion from 1571. We have also included the Jerusalem Declaration from GAFCON, which sets out the tenets of orthodoxy underpinning its subscribers' shared Anglican identity. Finally, we have included the CEEC's Basis of Faith, to which all contributors can happily subscribe, and IVP's Statement of Faith.

We hope that this book will both excite and challenge, provoke and be a reason for rejoicing among evangelical Anglicans. We are glad to see the work God's church is already doing in God's world through evangelical ministry, and all live in the hope that there is much more to come, for God can do immeasurably more than we ask or imagine. It is our prayer that you, too, will be inspired and led to offer up your own prayers of both thanksgiving and longing petition for God's church in God's world.

Part 1

GOD'S CHURCH FOR GOD'S WORLD: WHAT IS HAPPENING TO THE CHURCH OF ENGLAND?

1

A changing Communion

THE REVEREND CANON DR ANDREW GODDARD

I have to confess that I was an evangelical Anglican for many years before I really began to recognize the existence, never mind the importance, of the Anglican Communion. I suspect that the same could be said of many evangelicals in the Church of England.

For me, the penny began to drop back in 2002, shortly after I joined the staff at Wycliffe Hall in Oxford. To mark the college's 125th anniversary, we held a conference on 'The future of Anglicanism', which brought together Anglicans from across the globe. For the first time, I was in a significant gathering of Anglican leaders (mainly evangelicals) from Africa, Australia, New Zealand, South-East Asia, North America, the West Indies and South America.

At the time when we met, the tensions and divisions within the Communion were already appearing: New Westminster Diocese in Canada agreed to bless same-sex unions, and it was announced that Rowan Williams would be the next Archbishop of Canterbury, leading to protests from some conservative evangelicals in the Church of England because of his previous statements on sexuality. Those tensions would erupt a year later with the consecration of Gene Robinson as Bishop of New Hampshire, and the first authorized same-sex blessing in New Westminster. By then, I had been on a steep learning curve about the nature of global Anglicanism, working with others to help the Primate of the West Indies present a paper on these issues to the Communion's leaders.

In the years since that conference, most evangelicals in the Church of England have been on a similar learning curve, becoming much more aware of Anglicanism outside England and the significance of the wider Communion. The Communion now has forty-one member churches (known as provinces), with two more in formation, and five other extra-provincial churches (such as the Falkland Islands). These are located in more than 165 countries and the Communion claims to comprise tens of millions of Anglican Christians. Nevertheless, understanding of its history and structures, and even of its recent struggles and divisions, remains a mystery to many. This chapter seeks to respond to that wide-spread ignorance and lack of clarity by offering, with the delayed fifteenth Lambeth Conference now happening, a short, simple guide to the history of the constantly changing identity and structures of the Anglican Communion.

As with so much in relation to the Anglican Communion, determining when it began is itself far from easy. Some might point to the first ever Lambeth Conference, gathered by Archbishop Longley just over 150 years ago, in 1867. There the gathered bishops sought 'Unity in faith and discipline . . . among the several branches of the Anglican Communion' (Resolution IV). The earliest known use of the term, however, is two decades earlier. It appears in November 1847, in a letter from the Mis-sionary Bishop in the Dominions and Dependencies of the Sultan of Turkey – a title that captures the combination of missionary endeavour and English imperialism which gave birth to the Communion. Bishop Southgate wrote of 'The Anglican Branch of the Church of Christ', high-lighting that the Communion has always sought to locate itself within the wider, one, holy, catholic and apostolic church. He also referred to 'the Anglican Church', describing 'the three branches of the Anglican Com-munion . . . the English, the Scotch, and the American'. That threefold distinction points to the longer history behind the Communion as we know it.

The Scottish branch arose in the late seventeenth century when, follow-ing the Glorious Revolution, the national, established Church of Scotland abolished episcopacy and embraced Presbyterianism. This led to the cre-ation of the Scottish Episcopal Church, distinct from the Church of England. It would, nearly a century later, play a crucial role in what would become the Anglican Communion when, in November 1784, it estab-lished the third branch, referred to by Southgate. Following American Independence, former churches of the Church of England in the USA sought their own bishop, but one could not be consecrated within the

Church of England, due to the requirement to swear allegiance to the Crown. It was the Scottish bishops, therefore, who consecrated Samuel Seabury as Bishop of Connecticut, the first bishop from and for the American church and the first 'Anglican' bishop to serve outside the British Isles. Here, then, is another, even earlier, possible date for the birth of the Communion.

Three years later, in 1787, following changes in English law, two more Americans were able to be consecrated as bishops by English bishops and then, in 1789, the Protestant Episcopal Church in the USA was formally constituted. Its origins included its separation from the state and the different place of bishops (and lack of Archbishops) within its formation. Its distinctive constitution and canons expressed a different understanding of church polity, shaped by a political vision similar to that underlying the new US Constitution. All this represented a major development within the emerging family of churches related to the Church of England. Some of these historic mutations, built into the DNA of American Anglicanism from its birth, have, arguably, contributed to the Communion's subsequent evolution and its more recent difficulties.

While recognizing this expansion beyond England, it is also important to remember that those branches distinct from the Church of England were, strictly, not even in full communion with it for many decades. The Acts of 1786 and 1792 relating to the American and Scottish churches made it clear that their members of clergy could not minister in the Church of England. This continued into the middle of the next century. So, for example, a private Act of Parliament was required in 1843 to enable Henry Caswall, ordained in the American Church, to be able to hold a benefice in England. Only after further Acts of Parliament in 1864 and 1874 were ministries in the two countries interchangeable.

In the eight decades that followed the formation of the American Church, before the Communion took visible and structural form at the first Lambeth Conference, we can trace its gestation as a result of evangelistic and missionary enterprise, which was interconnected, normally, with British imperial expansion. An important formative influence on the American Church was the Society for the Propagation of the Gospel in Foreign Parts (known as SPG, later USPG). Founded by the Reverend Thomas Bray in 1701, and often connected with the work of SPCK (which

Bray also led when serving as the Bishop of London's representative in the American colonies), its more catholic tradition would give birth to, and shape, much more than the Episcopal Church in the USA (to which it sent more than 300 missionaries, including John Wesley, before American Independence). Through the eighteenth and nineteenth centuries, it played a major part in the birth and/or growth of Anglican churches in many other parts of what would later become provinces within the Anglican Communion, including the West Indies, Canada, West Africa, India, Japan and Burma/Myanmar.

Nearly a century after the SPG started, in 1799, evangelical Anglicans founded the Society for Missions to Africa and the East, which would become the Church Missionary (from 1995, Mission) Society (CMS). Starting in Sierra Leone, its work spread rapidly, particularly through much of Africa (it was important in Nigeria, Kenya, Uganda, Tanzania, Rwanda, Sudan and Congo) but also in Asia (India, Pakistan, Sri Lanka) and Australia and New Zealand. In contrast to the SPG, and reflecting its evangelicalism, the CMS was less tied into existing ecclesiastical and episcopal structures. Under the leadership of Henry Venn, it sought to establish self-supporting, self-governing and self-propagating ('Three Self') churches. That vision and the significance of the CMS's work has led to Venn being described as 'a father of the worldwide Anglican Communion'.

These two missionary movements were instrumental in the appearance of an international 'Reformed Catholic' church, which was an earlier designation than that of the 'Anglican Communion' for identifying the spread of the pattern of faith established in England post-Reformation. Their emphasis was weighted differently between the 'Reformed' and the 'Catholic' aspects, as seen in, among other things, their different visions for the relationship between mission and episcopacy. This 'Reformed Catholic' church, however, was very much (apart from the American Church) the Church of England overseas. When the United Church of England and Ireland (with Wales as part of the Church of England) was established in 1800, it had only two overseas dioceses, both in Canada. A further eight were added over the next four decades (two more in Canada but also Calcutta, Madras and Bombay, Barbados and Jamaica, and Australia) and became seen as a new branch: 'the Colonial Church'.

In the decades that followed, more 'missionary bishops' would be consecrated for the colonies and sent out from England. Alongside this, from the 1830s, the American Church, via its Domestic and Foreign Missionary Society (founded in 1821), began to send missionaries overseas to places such as Liberia, Argentina, Greece, China (for which they consecrated their first ever missionary bishop outside the USA in 1844) and Japan.

In this context of global expansion, it is easy to forget what a radical and controversial step it was for the Archbishop of Canterbury to call together at Lambeth in 1867 those 151 serving and retired bishops 'in visible communion with the United Church of England and Ireland'. The background for this initiative within the Church of England was the revival of church councils apart from Parliament. The Convocations of Clergy began to meet for genuine deliberation again in the 1850s and 1860s, after over a century of inactivity, and 1851 had seen the first calling of a diocesan synod in Exeter. Abroad, there had been an appetite for such a development for some time, with calls for an international gathering of bishops from the bishop of Vermont in 1851 and the Provincial Synod of Canada in 1865. There had also been major theological controversies. Most notable were the publication of *Essays and Reviews* in England in 1860, giving voice to radical, liberal theological views and the dispute in Natal surrounding Bishop Colenso's deposition, which also related to scriptural authority, as well as his more accommodating stance regarding polygamy. Nevertheless, the innovative and unprecedented step was not universally welcomed by some English bishops. Most significantly, the Archbishop of York – and many bishops from his province – refused to attend. Alan Stephenson's history of the conferences also notes that, when Longley circulated a programme and possible declaration, 'Evangelical bishops . . . were not a little alarmed at the Declaration and its reference to the first four Great Councils and what they considered its inadequate attitude to the Bible, the Reformation, and the Thirty-nine Articles'.[1]

It was also not clear exactly what was being convened. Longley adamantly repudiated the idea that it was 'a synod' (terminology some were happy to use to describe what they sought) and significantly noted that it would do nothing 'in direct opposition to the authority of the Crown'. Nevertheless, the gathering's discussions and resolutions (deliberately not called 'canons'), revealed a desire for greater consultation and coordination between the 'several branches of the Anglican Communion' and even the development in future of 'due and canonical subordination of the synods of the several branches to the higher authority of a Synod or Synods above them' (Resolution IV).

At the time, however, it wasn't even clear that there would be another such gathering. There was certainly no sense that this innovation would become the important instrument in the development of the idea of an Anglican Communion that it is today.

The second conference was called by Archbishop Tait in 1878, just over a decade after the first gathering. This established the frequency of episcopal meetings that has become the pattern. There were still only 173 bishops to invite and only about 100 accepted the invitation and did attend. Further Lambeth Conferences occurred in 1888, 1897 and 1908. They followed a similar pattern, of gathering from around the world in England for several weeks of worship, discussion in groups focused on various themes, agreeing resolutions on a range of theological, ecclesiological and ethical matters, and issuing an encyclical letter to the churches.

Despite a slowly growing number of bishops representing churches from outside the UK, Canada or the USA, the Conferences remained dominated by white Englishmen and Americans. Samuel Crowther, the first black Anglican bishop, a Nigerian converted through the work of CMS, was consecrated in 1864, but he did not attend a conference until 1888. It would take a century before the cultural variety and ethnic diversity of the churches represented was reflected in the composition of attendees at the conference.

By meeting every ten years, a developing sense of shared identity was developed and articulated. Thus began the process that Owen Chadwick famously described in 1992:

> Meetings start to gather authority if they exist and are seen not to be a cloud of hot air and rhetoric. It was impossible that the leaders of the Anglican Communion should meet every ten years and not start to gather respect; and to gather respect is slowly to gather influence, and influence is on the road to authority.[2]

Particularly important to this growing sense of shared identity was the decision in 1888 to affirm what has become known as the Chicago–Lambeth Quadrilateral. Originating in the work of American priest William Reed Huntingdon, this adapted an 1886 resolution of the American bishops. It set out four agreed articles as the basis for finding church unity, although these are often also taken to provide a definition of the characteristic features of Anglican identity.

1 The holy Scriptures of the Old and New Testaments, as 'containing all things necessary to salvation' and as being the rule and ultimate standard of faith.
2 The Apostles' Creed, as the baptismal symbol; and the Nicene Creed, as the sufficient statement of the Christian faith.
3 The two sacraments ordained by Christ himself – baptism and the supper of the Lord – ministered with unfailing use of Christ's words of institution and of the elements ordained by him.
4 The historic episcopate, locally adapted in the methods of its administration to the varying needs of the nations and peoples called by God into the unity of his church.

It soon became clear that some additional structure would be required in order to nurture the developing common Anglican identity and facilitate communication across the distant provinces between the decennial conferences. In 1897, the conference therefore asked the Archbishop of Canterbury to create 'a consultative body . . . for information and advice'. This Consultative Committee first met in 1901, although without the Americans, who (in an early sign of their different ecclesial identity and caution about any limitations being put on their autonomy) declined to participate. Only one of the nine episcopal attendees was then serving outside England. Restructured in 1908 as the Central Consultative Body (CCB), with wider colonial representation but the American Church still absent, this would continue to evolve and become an important episcopal, predominantly primatial, group. Increasingly, it acted almost as a standing committee of the Lambeth Conference, with American representatives attending from the 1930s.

Following the horrors of the First World War, the 1920 conference (then comprising more than 250 bishops) built on the Chicago–Lambeth Quadrilateral to issue its famous 'Appeal to All Christian People'. Based on its opening confession that 'God wills fellowship', this would become a foundational statement of an Anglican vision of ecumenism. The question of the character of the fellowship embodied and sought among Anglicans within this quest for wider unity was also addressed by the Encyclical Letter. It included words that are worth quoting at some length as they are perhaps even more powerful a century later than they were at the time:

The more our minds are filled with the hopes of seeing the universal fellowship in full and free activity, the more zealous ought we to be to improve and strengthen in every way the fellowship of our own Church. This is one of the most direct and obvious methods of preparing for reunion . . . Because our Church has spread over the world and still more because we desire to enter into the world-wide fellowship of a reunited universal Church, we must begin now to clear ourselves of local, sectional, and temporary prepossessions, and cultivate a sense of what is universal and genuinely Catholic, in truth and in life . . . The fact that the Anglican Communion has become world-wide forces upon it some of the problems which must always beset the unity of the Catholic Church itself. Perhaps, as we ourselves are dealing with these problems, the way will appear in which the future reunited Church must deal with them . . . The Lambeth Conference . . . does not claim to exercise any powers of control or command. It stands for the far more spiritual and more Christian principle of loyalty to the fellowship. The Churches represented in it are indeed independent, but independent with the Christian freedom which recognizes the restraints of truth and of love. They are not free to deny the truth. They are not free to ignore the fellowship. And the objects of our Conferences are to attain an ever deeper apprehension of the truth and to guard the fellowship with ever increasing appreciation of its value. If the Conference is to attain such objects, it must be because it is itself a fellowship in the Spirit.[3]

Discerning the nature of that fellowship was a particular concern of the next conference, in 1930. Drawing on the report of one of the conference's committees, it passed no fewer than thirteen resolutions relating to the 'Anglican Communion', giving much sharper definition than ever before to its nature. Having affirmed that 'the true constitution of the Catholic Church involves the principle of the autonomy of particular Churches based upon a common faith and order', the bishops approved, in Resolution 49, a statement on the 'nature and status of the Anglican Communion', which became, over time, a definitive statement of the ecclesial identity of the 'Anglican Communion'.

The fundamental identity of the Communion is that it is:

a fellowship, within the one Holy Catholic and Apostolic Church, of those duly constituted dioceses, provinces or regional Churches in communion with the See of Canterbury.[4]

These churches are then held to have three characteristics in common:

a. they uphold and propagate the catholic and apostolic faith and order as they are generally set forth in the Book of Common Prayer as authorized in their several churches;
b. they are particular or national churches and, as such, promote within each of their territories a national expression of Christian faith, life and worship; and
c. they are bound together not by a central legislative and executive authority but by mutual loyalty sustained through the common counsel of the bishops in conference.[5]

Here, we find helpfully named the various strands of Anglican Communion identity. There are the emphases on the Anglican recognition of the wider church, of which it is but a part, and the shared historically based links to Canterbury within the fellowship. The centrality of catholic and apostolic faith and order tied to common prayer, the importance of diverse adaptation to local context and the balance between autonomy and interdependence in the decision-making processes are also key. These are the strands that, in recent decades, have increasingly unravelled and become frayed.

Due to the Second World War, the 1930 conference would be the last full corporate expression of the Communion for nearly twenty years. The bishops did not gather again until 1948, although the CCB met several times during the 1930s and in 1944, 1946 and 1947. At the post-war conference, presided over by Geoffrey Fisher, the bishops began a process that would accelerate in the following debates: seeking to establish new structures to enable communication, consultation and coherence in a growing and increasingly diverse Communion. It welcomed plans to create new provinces in Africa, proposed a Communion Advisory Council on Missionary Strategy (ACMS), urged a Central College, and began work to hold 'a congress representative of the Anglican Communion' (similar to that held back in 1908 and eventually held in 1954 in Minneapolis). A 'Primates' Committee' also met to advise the Archbishop and, following the conference, the CCB was reconstituted, with each primate an ex officio member.

This trajectory continued at the 1958 conference, with reform of the CCB so that it included representatives of sixteen provinces and, significantly, was staffed by a full-time secretary. The number and identity of the provinces illustrates how different the Communion was then compared to now. There were four from the UK; the four provinces of the USA, Canada, Australia and New Zealand; and eight others (just three from Africa – South Africa and the new provinces of West Africa and Central Africa – plus the West Indies, China, Japan, the Middle East and a single province covering India, Pakistan, Burma and Ceylon).

Following this decision, the first Executive Officer of the Anglican Communion, Bishop Stephen Bayne from the USA, was appointed in 1960. Herein lie the origins of what would become the increasingly influential Anglican Communion Office (ACO). He played a vital role, particularly in the 1963 Toronto Congress, which brought together clergy and laity as well as bishops. It set out a new vision of 'Mutual Responsibility and Interdependence in the Body of Christ' (MRI) that became central to the Communion's self-understanding and development. There appears to have been a growing recognition in this period that the political 'winds of change' that Harold Macmillan had spoken of back in 1960 in relation to decolonization would need to blow also through the imperially formed ecclesial structures of Anglicanism. There was, too, with the

20

expansion of international air travel, a growing Communion-wide ministry for the Archbishop of Canterbury, with Fisher visiting many of the provinces for the first time.

These early attempts at an institutional expression of the Communion took a major and distinctive leap forwards at the 1968 conference. It proposed the creation of an Anglican Consultative Council (ACC), with formal functions, constitution, offices (including a Secretary General) and membership. Each of the member churches was to be represented by a bishop but also by a member of the clergy and/or the laity – the first non-episcopal participation in the Communion's formal structures. By bringing together dozens of Anglicans for over a week, every two years, and with an annual Standing Committee, this development was to greatly intensify the inter-provincial connections within the Communion. It also ended the episcopal dominance, even monopoly, within Communion structures.

The ACC's first meeting was held in 1971 in Kenya – the newly created national African province – and twenty-two member churches were represented. That meeting also voted on the most contentious issue of the time within the Communion. It made the significant decision, by the smallest of majorities and against the vote of its President, the Archbishop of Canterbury, to accept any province's decision to ordain women as priests and committed itself to 'use its good offices to encourage all Provinces of the Anglican Communion to continue in communion with these dioceses'. Nearly half a century later, only a relative handful of provinces of the Communion still do not permit women priests.

By the time of the next Lambeth Conference, in 1978, the ACC had met two further times, there were more provinces and a number of provinces had ordained women priests. That conference sought a way through the threatened divisions over the issue in order to hold the Communion together. It also learned from the then Archbishop of Canterbury, Donald Coggan, that he was formalizing and extending a more ad hoc pattern that had developed: he intended to start convening meetings of the Communion's primates on a regular, likely twice-yearly, basis. This decision established the Primates' Meeting as the fourth of what would soon become known as the 'Instruments of Unity' (later 'Instruments of Communion') alongside the Archbishop of Canterbury, the Lambeth

Conference and the ACC. From the start, its relationship to the ACC was unclear and contested. Over the years, these two bodies have struggled to establish a clear relationship with each other and they (and their respective forms of authority) have come to be viewed quite differently across the Communion. Broadly speaking, the historic, Western, more liberal provinces have favoured the ACC, while the growing, more conservative, global south provinces have (with the support of resolutions from Lambeth Conferences) looked to the primates to exercise enhanced authority, especially in relation to defining the boundaries of Anglican diversity and safeguarding faith and order.

The 1978 Lambeth Conference was also the first conference directly to address the issue of homosexuality. This was already becoming contentious in a number of Western Anglican provinces, as openly gay and lesbian people were being ordained and some sought to bless same-sex unions. It reappeared on the conference agenda ten years later in 1988. Then an attempt by an American bishop (later revealed to have been in various gay relationships himself while married) to affirm the rights of homosexuals was strongly resisted by other, especially African, bishops. This was the first Lambeth Conference to embody the new geographical and theological shape of the Communion. The number of African bishops present, who numbered only 80 in 1978, had more than doubled to 175. Nigeria, represented as a separate province for the first time in 1988, would continue to grow, sending 59 bishops in 1998 (and, currently, has around 160 bishops). It was also in 1988 that the bishops (pressured by the American Church) voted to acknowledge that provinces could ordain women as bishops. Although a highly contentious development at the time, it has now been implemented in most of the provinces with only a minority having never chosen a woman to serve as bishop.

Another important feature of this changing shape of global Anglicanism has been the emergence of what has become known as the 'global south'. Growing numbers of local (often evangelical) leaders in South-East Asia and various African provinces were developing innovative forms of mission and ministry. This led to the ACC sponsoring an 'Anglican Encounter in the South' gathering in Kenya in 1994, which brought together Anglicans from twenty-three different provinces under the chairmanship of the Nigerian Primate. Another important contributory factor was the work of the Evangelical Fellowship in the Anglican Communion (EFAC), which had been set up by John Stott back in 1961. EFAC, along with Stott's Langham Scholarships, helped to nurture and connect leaders in what was then called the two-thirds world and built relationships between the historic Anglican churches and the new ones. Following the Kenya meeting, a second gathering in Kuala Lumpur in February 1997 issued a 'trumpet call' with Scripture, evangelism and mission at its heart. It also published a statement on sexuality arising from concerns about the direction of the Communion under the influence of the American Church. Here, for those with eyes to see, was one of the first signs of the storm that would engulf the Communion from the 1998 Lambeth Conference onwards.

Disputes over sexuality have riven the Communion for the past twenty-plus years. Triggered by Resolution I.10 at the 1998 Lambeth Conference and the reactions to it, they have raised awareness of the Communion and its importance, not least in England. That resolution, overwhelmingly supported by the bishops, reaffirmed a traditional Christian sexual ethic in a concerted attempt by both Western conservatives and the many global south bishops to prevent a more affirming, or at least permissive, stance towards same-sex relationships. Hopes that this would put a brake on developments and divisions, particularly in the American church, proved unfounded.

In early 2000, two Communion primates (South-East Asia and Rwanda) consecrated two American priests to serve as bishops in what was called the Anglican Mission in America (AMiA). When, in 2003, the General Convention of the Episcopal Church (TEC) elected Gene Robinson – a gay priest in a same-sex relationship – as Bishop of New Hampshire, further fractures developed. A Primates' Meeting, hurriedly convened by the then Archbishop of Canterbury Rowan Williams, warned the imminent consecration would 'tear the fabric of the Communion at its deepest level', but this powerful prophetic image was ignored. As a result, further splits occurred in North America, and yet more global south provinces offered oversight to breakaway congregations and consecrated new bishops to serve in the USA.

In late 2004, the Lambeth Commission on Communion, commissioned by the primates a year earlier, published the Windsor report. This set out a vision of life together as a communion of churches building on the vision we've seen set out in earlier Lambeth Conference resolutions and more recent work, such as the 1997 Virginia report. It also proposed a way forwards together based on apologies for, and moratoria on, contentious actions, such as same-sex blessings, same-sex-partnered bishops and cross-provincial interventions. It soon became clear, however, that these recommendations were not going to be accepted. Furthermore, not one of the Instruments of Communion was able or willing to implement them and address the problems effectively. This was despite the fact that these matters dominated regular and fractious Primates' Meetings in 2005, 2007 and 2009. The attempt to find a short-term resolution having failed, attention then turned to the proposed medium- and long-term solution in the Windsor report: the development of a new Anglican Communion Covenant. It was hoped that this would draw people together in shared commitments and agreed procedures for managing disagreements.

Work began on the covenant in 2007 and its second draft was considered at the last Lambeth Conference in 2008. That conference was markedly different from its predecessors on two counts. First, hundreds of bishops refused to attend because of the failure to resolve the conflict and to discipline the American and Canadian Churches for their unilateral actions. Those bishops (and others) instead attended a new gathering – the Global Anglican Future Conference (GAFCON) – which brought together many conservative Anglican leaders in Jerusalem, just before the Lambeth Conference. That meeting issued the Jerusalem Declaration as the basis for their fellowship and made clear their belief that being a faithful Anglican and being in communion with the see of Canterbury were now to be viewed as distinct categories. Second, the Lambeth Conference took the form of an indaba, with small group conversations, and, for the first time, there were no resolutions expressing the mind of the bishops gathered in common counsel.

The covenant was finally published at the end of 2009. It gave clear expression to the self-understanding of the Anglican Communion as this has developed since at least the 1920 conference. It attempted to balance provincial autonomy with interdependence and mutual accountability of the provinces, asking member churches to join together to embrace its affirmations and commitments. Although a number of provinces expressed their support, more provinces either ignored or rejected it. GAFCON supporters and other conservative provinces saw it as too weak and 'toothless'. In contrast, others were concerned that it was too centralizing and controlling and would be used to punish and marginalize churches that were innovating. Its rejection by the dioceses of the Church of England in 2012 effectively ended any chance that it could provide the pathway forward for the Communion. Since taking up office in 2013, Justin Welby has made no effort to revive it and, unlike his predecessor, never clearly articulated and commended its vision of Communion life.

Taking reconciliation as one of the priorities for his ministry as Archbishop of Canterbury, Welby has sought to move the Communion on from these conflicts and decisions and the impasse reached by the Windsor and covenant processes. After visiting all the primates in their own countries, he called a meeting in January 2016 – the first attempt to gather all the primates since 2011 when, following the precedent set at Lambeth 2008, a significant number of primates had refused to attend. Remarkably, Welby succeeded in gathering them all (although Uganda left after a few days), in part by also inviting the primate of the new conservative province in North America (ACNA) to attend. ACNA, although not part of the Anglican Communion and, in origin, a breakaway from the Episcopal Church, is the American Anglican Church, recognized by many Communion provinces, GAFCON and the global south. In what many experienced as a miraculous work of the Spirit, the Communion primates expressed their 'unanimous desire to walk together'. However, now faced with the TEC's 2015 acceptance of same-sex marriage, they also recognized that there remained 'significant difference between us' and 'huge strains on the functioning of the Instruments of Communion'. In recognition that 'such actions further impair our communion', it was agreed that for a period of three years, the TEC would 'no longer represent us on ecumenical and interfaith bodies, should not be appointed or elected to an internal standing committee and that while participating in the internal bodies of the Anglican Communion, they will not take part in decision making on any issues pertaining to doctrine or polity'. This development suggested to some that, despite the failure of the covenant, its controversial proposal of 'relational consequences' for unilateral and divisive actions was now being applied.

In the years since that meeting, the reactions to it and the implementation of its decisions have varied. The Archbishop of Canterbury and many others have stressed the language of 'walking together', the growing trust and honest communication among Communion leaders and the need to move on from the bitter divisions of the past two decades. Others, particularly within GAFCON (which met again in Jerusalem in 2018), have highlighted the continuing differences, strains and impairment, protested that the agreed consequences have not been followed through and, in some cases, continued to absent themselves from Communion gatherings. The decision by Archbishop Welby to invite all Communion bishops to Lambeth (including those in same-sex marriages, in contrast to his predecessor's decision in 2008 not to invite Gene Robinson) has fuelled these concerns, with hundreds of bishops, especially from the provinces of Nigeria, Uganda and Rwanda, again deciding not to attend.

In late 2019, the global south, meeting in Cairo, published its own detailed proposals for a covenantally structured 'Global South Fellowship of Anglican Churches', which are now being implemented. Their covenant comprises doctrinal declarations (though with no reference to GAFCON's Jerusalem Declaration), relational commitments and, significantly, 'conciliar structures for a global ecclesial body'. These structures are 'for addressing "Faith and Order" issues, establishing the limits of diversity, holding one another accountable to a common dogmatic and liturgical tradition, and making decisions which carry force in the life of the Global South Fellowship of Anglican Churches'. Questions remain as to how this will become an ecclesial reality and how it relates to the vision developing within GAFCON. Nevertheless, it represents a serious attempt to re-establish a coherent ecclesiology for the Anglican Communion in continuity with the past and with clear theological boundaries. This is something that, since the stalling of the covenant, has largely disappeared from the statements of the established instruments.

As we approach the 2022 Lambeth Conference, much remains unclear about the present and future structures and ecclesial identity of the Anglican Communion. Some will argue that we have entered a new phase and detailed political and institutional questions should not be a major concern. What matters, they say, is that there continue to be flourishing relationships and genuine 'bonds of affection' between Anglicans around the globe. This is evident in long-standing connections between numerous dioceses and their leaders. These involve financial and other support, partnership together in a shared mission – shaped by the Communion's Five Marks of Mission – and a variety of fruitful Communion networks (Environmental, Inter-Faith, Peace and Justice and others), despite the tensions within the formal instruments.

These positive signs of life in communion continue to offer hope and show that God has not abandoned the churches of the Communion. It would be wrong, however, to downplay the seriousness of the challenges that remain. The history sketched here illustrates how the Communion, over many decades, developed a deepening understanding of how God was at work within it. Also, how it sought to establish its common faith and order as a fellowship of churches within a wider vision and hope for greater Christian unity. As part of this, there evolved structures which embodied that understanding and encouraged deeper communion. In recent decades, various actions have undermined those structures and seriously impaired communion. The attempt in the Windsor report and the covenant to rise to these challenges, rearticulate that vision, renew the existing instruments and recover what has been weakened, or even lost, appears to be no longer being pursued.

More recently, a growing tendency has developed to define the Anglican Communion in rather limited legal, even bureaucratic, terms, as simply those churches in full communion with the see of Canterbury or listed on the schedule of the Anglican Consultative Council. This masks the more complex reality of the pattern of impaired and broken relationships of communion that now exist. Many provinces within the Communion are not in communion with other provinces but are in full communion with alternative, overlapping 'particular or national' provinces that they recognize as more faithfully Anglican, even though those are not in communion with Canterbury. It must not be forgotten that the classic 1930 definition was a *theological* account which also spoke of characteristic features of the Communion as a fellowship of churches located within the broader catholic church. It is the loss of these shared characteristics that reveals the changing nature of the Communion and the crisis it still faces. The decision that the TEC (and, subsequently, the Scottish Episcopal Church) should not represent the Communion ecumenically or participate in Communion decisions on doctrine or polity effectively acknowledged that not all Communion churches now recognizably 'uphold and propagate the catholic and apostolic faith and order'. That is because what some viewed as simply 'a national expression of Christian faith, life and worship', other churches viewed as a departure from Christian faith, life and worship. These deep differences then further transformed the Communion because of actions that showed a disregard for 'mutual loyalty sustained through the common counsel of the bishops in conference'. Potentially more serious are the pattern of many bishops declining invitations to the Lambeth Conference (if the next conference after 2022 is in 2032, it will then be thirty-four years since bishops from some major provinces have attended) and the changing structure of the Lambeth Conference itself (to being shorter, not generative of resolutions and now including spouses in a joint rather than separate conference). These may even have removed any future possibility of the Communion expressing such common episcopal counsel in the way that it did for more than a century. Were the Church of England, following the 'Living in love and faith' process, itself to act in ways that other provinces viewed as undermining these historic characteristics, it is likely that the continuing bond of 'communion with the see of Canterbury' would be damaged or even destroyed.

Alongside this, however, new movements, structures and visions of what it might mean to be a global communion of churches have appeared. Both GAFCON and the wider, reconstituted Global South Fellowship of Anglican Churches arise from the new branches of the Communion's provinces that, in many cases, have only gained their own autonomy in the past half century or so. Many of these churches were born out of, and shaped by, evangelical Anglicanism. GAFCON, through its emphasis on confessional Anglicanism, is reaffirming the importance of catholic faith, which, it believes, the Communion has failed to safeguard. The Global South Fellowship of Anglican Churches, through its new covenantal structure, is reaffirming the importance of catholic order, which the Anglican Communion's covenant also sought to do, but failed to achieve, to re-establish, in continuity with the Communion's historic self-understanding. A major question likely to face evangelicals in England in the coming decade is, 'How can we participate in these new movements and structures and how can we learn from them and embody their insights within the Church of England?'

Notes

1 A. M. G. Stephenson, *The First Lambeth Conference, 1867* (Church Historical Society; London: SPCK, 1967), p. 34.

2 O. Chadwick, Introduction, in R. Coleman (Ed.), *Resolutions of the Twelve Lambeth Conferences 1867–1988* (Toronto: Anglican Book Centre, 1992), p. xvii.

3 *Conference of Bishops of the Anglican Communion: Holden at Lambeth Palace, 5 July to 7 August 1920: Encyclical letter from the bishops, with the resolutions and reports* (London: SPCK, 1920), pp. 13–14 (available online at: <https://archive.org/details/conferenceofbish00lamb/page/n3/mode/2up>).

4 Lambeth Conference, 1930, Resolution 49 – The Anglican Communion (available online at: <https://anglicancommunion.org/resources/document-library/lambeth-conference/1930/resolution-49-the-anglican-communion.aspx>).

5 Lambeth Conference, 1930, Resolution 49 – The Anglican Communion (available online at: <https://anglicancommunion.org/resources/document-library/lambeth-conference/1930/resolution-49-the-anglican-communion.aspx>).

2

Keeping evangelicals catholic and the catholic church evangelical

THE REVEREND DR THOMAS WOOLFORD

For 500 years, 'the hotter sort of Protestant' has wondered if it is time to leave the Church of England. Each generation has faced its crisis: the question of wearing a surplice (sixteenth century), whether one can acquiesce with episcopal rather than presbyterian polity (seventeenth), the bureaucratic restraints on extra-parochial revival preaching (eighteenth), doctrinal drift towards ritualism (nineteenth) and accommodation of liberalism (twentieth). None of those issues evangelicals have faced within the Church of England, as it happens, has gone away – though none of the worst fears evangelicals had at the time has been realized either. Each is also just an arbitrary selection of one from each century from many controversies that have exercised evangelical consciences within the established church through its history. Crises come and crises . . . well, *stay*; but also dissipate a bit.

Yet, here we still are. It's easy to imagine that *this* is the biggest crisis the church has ever faced. Objectively, it isn't. The fourth-century church, to use Athanasius' famous phrase, woke up and found itself Arian, confessionally denying Christ's deity. As crises go, that will take some topping. In today's Church of England, I'm pretty sure we're two or three decades past the high watermark of creedal unorthodoxy. Not never, but very seldom do we hear clerical denials of the Trinity, the virgin birth or the bodily resurrection. It's certainly not fashionable and unheard of among the current bishops.

While such an historical perspective, not to mention faith in God's providence, ought to prevent us lapsing into panic or despair, because evangelicals feel perennially beleaguered (often with good cause), they – we – also need to be perennially reminded of why we bother. Specifically, why we persevere in worshipping and ministering within the Church of England, when the grass in exclusively evangelical denominations or independency so often seems quite a bit greener.

An earlier generation of Anglican evangelicals made the case on pragmatic grounds: 'the Church of England is the best boat to fish from', they would say. They were almost certainly right – the established church provided 'free' evangelistic opportunities through weddings, baptisms and funerals; plenty of links with schools and community groups; prominent, central public buildings; and a kind of cultural inertia that made the parish vicar the default, trusted and respected source of pastoral care and spiritual advice. Such advantages amply outweighed any drawbacks, whether they were institutional bureaucracy, internal politics, rules we'd rather not keep or procedures we don't much care for. But as society has become increasingly secular, such inbuilt missional benefits have diminished. Perhaps in some local contexts, in some of these ways, we will still retain an advantage over our free church brothers and sisters, but the 'cons' column is certainly starting to look relatively longer as we compare it to the diminishing number of 'pros'. If that's the case, we are likely to see a number of serving ministers leave the Church of England as they assess the tipping-point to have been reached. If the Church of England is still the best boat to fish from now, it may not be for much longer. Something other than evangelistic pragmatism is needed to convince evangelicals to remain within the Church of England.

Part of my own pilgrimage from a pragmatic to a convictional Anglicanism was reading John Stott's essay, 'Pursuing truth and unity'.[1] Stott sketched four features of the Church of England that he described as reasons for his remaining within the national church. It is, he wrote, an *historical* church, organically connected with believers on these shores all the way back to the second century. Second, it is a *confessional* church, with robustly biblical doctrinal standards in its Book of Common Prayer, Thirty-nine Articles and Ordinal. Third, it is a *national* church, 'with a responsibility to be the nation's conscience, to serve the nation and to bring Christ to the nation.'[2] Fourth, it is a *liturgical* church, enshrining, protecting and imparting scriptural truth through participatory worship.

The second half of Stott's essay, recognizing the discomfort felt by evangelicals in the Church of England due to 'an assault on traditional Christian doctrine and morality',[3] counselled against the easy options of secession on the one hand ('to pursue truth at the expense of unity') or conformity on the other ('to pursue unity at the expense of truth').[4] Stott urged the reader to eschew 'both ways of easing tension and escaping conflict' and commended instead the painful, long-term and difficult option of 'comprehensiveness without compromise' – the pursuit of truth and unity simultaneously, in strained dialogue. None of Stott's reasons for sticking with the Church of England were pragmatic; they were convictional – theological, ecclesiological.

I was convinced by Stott's reasoning and I think his argument still ought to be sufficient to encourage evangelicals to continue to worship in and contend for the Church of England two decades later, when the attack on traditional Christian teaching (from within and without the church) has made more ground. But I wish to develop a minor theme in Stott's essay and make it the major theme of mine as I make my case for evangelicals not only reluctantly to continue in but also heavily invest themselves in the Church of England. That is the theme of *catholicity*. I will argue that evangelicals should remain in the Church of England for *catholic* reasons. Specifically, the Church of England helps to keep evangelicals catholic, and evangelicals help to keep the catholic Church of England evangelical. If 'evangelexit' were to occur, it would inevitably be into churches that are less catholic than the Church of England. That would be to the detriment of the spiritual health of the evangelical Anglican movement itself and of the nation as a whole.

'Catholic' is not a dirty word

As something of a church historian, I tend to operate with a definition of 'evangelical' taken from the Reformation: an evangelical is someone who believes, on the basis of Scripture alone, that people may be saved by God's grace alone, through faith alone in Christ alone, to the glory of God alone. These five 'alones' (in Latin, *solae*) summarize the doctrinal guiding principles of the sixteenth-century Reformers, were the clarion calls of the eighteenth-century revivalists and remain the touchstone of evangelical faith and piety today.

'Catholic' is a term that requires more explanation. For many people, the word 'catholic' is associated with the Pope and pilgrimage, candles and ciboria, images and incense, the mass and transubstantiation, ceremony and vestments. That is to say, for the last 500 years, 'catholic' has become synonymous with *Roman* Catholic doctrine and practice. To describe the Church of England as the truest expression of evangelical catholicity sounds, therefore, like a rehash of the anachronistic and quite inaccurate cliché that the Church of England is a via media between Roman Catholicism and Protestantism.

Historically and theologically, however, nothing about true catholicity compromises any of the fundamentals of the evangelical faith. The word 'catholic' comes from the Greek '*kata holos*', which means 'in accordance with the whole'. Catholicity means *wholeness* – a 'thick' concept of wholeness applied to the Christian faith, life and Church. It is in this *wholeness* sense that, when we recite the creed, we confess our belief in 'one, holy, *catholic* and apostolic church'. It is in this wholeness sense that the English Reformers claimed (and we today still claim) that the Church of England is part of the *catholic church*. 'Catholic' is not a dirty word: it is a wonderful, sacred word and concept that evangelicals should treasure, protect and prosper by; and I believe the best way to do so in England is to worship and minister within the Church of England.

The catholic canon and creed

Evangelicals are Bible people. We believe the Bible to be God's word written: inspired and infallible, living and active, authoritative and powerful, clear and sufficient. Everything we believe, we believe because the Bible teaches it. Evangelical Anglicans draw inspiration from the Church of England being wedded by law to the teaching of Scripture (Canon A5, see Article 6). No evangelical could countenance being a member of, much less ministering within, an ecclesial body that was not formally biblical in its faith.

Being 'biblical' in one's doctrine, however, while necessary, is not sufficient. That may seem a shocking thing for an evangelical to say, but allow me to explain. I'm not saying that 'capital-T Tradition', as preserved, developed and interpreted by the magisterium of the Church, has coequal authority with Scripture, as a Roman Catholic would. And I am also far from suggesting that 'reason' has an autonomous role in establishing what we ought to believe and teach, as a liberal Christian might. Instead, what I am saying is that 'just reading the Bible' has proven insufficient as a bulwark against heresy and error since the beginning of the Christian church. The Arians of the fourth century 'just read the Bible', and it is the claim of their modern-day successors, Jehovah's Witnesses, that they do the same. Throughout church history, it has been the claim of modalists, universalists, Unitarians, Socinians and all sorts of other false teachers that all they are doing is simply reading and expositing the Scriptures.

Ever since the second century, the church has found that, to protect and propagate the Christian faith, she has had to not only enjoin disciples to read the Scriptures but also had to explain *how* they should read the Scriptures; to define or summarize *what it is the Scriptures actually say*. In fact, the question, 'What are the Scriptures?' could not be answered neatly in isolation from the question, 'What do the Scriptures say?' In the early centuries of the Christian church, canon and creed developed together. It could hardly have been any other way. For nearly three centuries, the Christian religion was illegal. The various scattered churches across the known world all kept their own libraries of writings for their readings and homilies – typically possessing a copy of one or two of the Gospels, several letters by Paul and other apostles, and one or two other early Christian writings, such as letters by church leaders who had known an apostle (Clement and Polycarp, for example), the Didache (instructions on worship and church leadership) or the popular visionary book *The Shepherd of Hermas*. The underground nature and wide dispersion of the early church meant that copying, distributing, comparing and compiling the apostolic writings that eventually comprised the New Testament canon was extremely difficult and risky. This process could be properly conducted only once Christianity was legalized (from AD 312), with a stable twenty-seven book New Testament canon emerging in the second half of the fourth century. For more than 300 years, then, it could not have been 'the Bible' as we now know it that held the churches together. Instead, it was the 'Rule of Faith'. The Rule of Faith (which transmogrified at some

34

unknown early juncture into what we know as 'the Apostles' Creed') functioned as a summary of the common teachings of the churches founded by apostles and, in the West, was recited by candidates for baptism. The Rule also served as a yardstick against which teachers and teachings were measured – against which, therefore, Gnostic, Docetic, Ebionite, Adoptionist and other early heresies (and associated writings) came up short.

By the 320s, even the Rule of Faith was insufficient to safeguard the integrity of the true Christian faith. A Libyan presbyter called Arius could subscribe to the Rule without crossing his fingers behind his back, yet, at the same time, deny that Jesus Christ was God. To cut a long and complicated story short, the bishops at the Council of Nicaea (summoned by the Emperor Constantine to deal with the controversy surrounding Arius' views) found it necessary to pen a much longer creed, with extra-scriptural language (such as '*homoousios*', meaning 'the same substance'), in order to define the Christian faith in such a way that Arius and his allies could *not* subscribe to it. Similar modifications, additions and definitions were required to exclude other heretical beliefs at ecumenical (whole church) councils in 381 (Constantinople), 431 (Ephesus) and 451 (Chalcedon), resulting in what we call the Niceno–Constantinopolitan Creed (commonly called the Nicene Creed) and the Chalcedonian Definition, which have ever since defined the bounds of orthodoxy, particularly regarding the Trinity and the doctrine of Christ. The bare words of Scripture had proven insufficient – because of human sin and error – to define the Christian faith.

The true Christian faith, then, has always been no less than 'biblical', but has also been something *more* than nakedly 'biblical': it has been *catholic*. Heretics have always claimed that their beliefs are biblical and have always been able to mount some sort of scriptural case for their errors. The catholic faith is the *right kind* of biblical. All this means, in essence, is that the catholic faith (that which is summarized in the catholic creeds) expresses, in summary, the true, core message of the Scriptures when read, considered and synthesized as a consistent, divinely authored whole. 'Biblical' heresies strain intolerably the meaning, consistency and coherence of the Scriptures in a way that the catholic faith does not.[5]

History reveals, then, a creed-and-canon symbiosis, in which the inspired canon of Scripture and the credal summary of the Christian faith developed in dialogue. A sense of the essence of the apostles' gospel (Rule of Faith) was a plumb line by which certain 'would-be Scriptures' were ruled out (alongside other criteria), while credal statements were accepted and professed only on the basis of their agreement with the acknowledged prophetic and apostolic writings. What are we to make of this creed-and-canon symbiosis, particularly as evangelical Protestants who believe in the authority of Scripture alone in defining matters of faith?

We need not accept the Roman Catholic argument that the church as an institution directly invested with Christ's authority determined the canon of Scripture. We should retain our Protestant belief that the word of God created, sustains and rules the church of God – not the other way around. At the same time, however, we surely have to 'dial up' what we believe and confess about the role of the Holy Spirit in providentially guiding the early church in its decision making. Concerning the canon, the Spirit both authenticated his own authored works in the hearts of true believers and superintended the church's leaders and representatives in their discussion of the matter. It was the corporate experience of the church as a whole that those twenty-seven books – and those alone – made their hearts burn within them (Luke 24:32) as they read and meditated on them. Once the canon was settled, it was no longer controversial: the Spirit saw to it, for the sake of seventeen-and-counting centuries' worth of new Christians, that the fourth-century church got it right. Now, if we grant the Spirit's superintending providence over the production of the catholic canon, then, given the symbiotic relationship we have discussed, we must surely grant the Spirit a similar superintending providence over the writing of the catholic creeds. To put it plainly, the Niceno–Constantinopolitan Creed is divinely inspired. Certainly, it is inspired in a *different* – derivative and indirect – way from Scripture: the content of the prophetic oracles and apostolic epistles was not decided through committee decisions via debate and compromise. We have nothing to fear here: in saying that the Spirit inspired the canon and the creed, we are far from diluting, let alone denying, the supreme, indeed sole, *ultimate* authority of the Bible. We are just expounding what that actually means in terms of God's gracious involvement in our history, by which he has led and preserved his church. Scripture's ultimate sole authority, then, does not (and the history of orthodox Christianity tells us it *cannot* and *must not*) rule out all other sources of authority. We should be able to affirm that the catholic creeds have a *real authority*, able to command the consent of all believers. That authority is not independent of the Bible, it *is* the authority of the Bible, repackaged as a set of foundational propositions – propositions about who God in Scripture is revealed to be and what God is revealed in Scripture to have done. The catholic creeds simply ensure that we have *the right kind* of biblical faith.

The catholic conversation

To the catholic canon and the catholic creed, we can add what we might call the catholic *conversation*. To be conversant in the catholic conversation is to accord a measure of foundational *authority* to the Church Fathers and to swim in the current of the Great Tradition flowing from the springs of their work. The Fathers are those theologians from the late first to the late fifth centuries whose thought provided the theological scaffolding for all subsequent Christian theology. Justin, Basil, Jerome, Hilary, Cyril, Gregory are not just the quaint names of your grandfather's contemporaries, but towering minds, whose apologetics, commentaries, polemics and systematics were indispensable to the intellectual defence and propagation of the faith of the church in its early centuries.

While the Fathers' work is properly foundational, the catholic conversation continued through the Middle Ages. It is a matter of regret that many evangelicals acquiesce in the popular conceit that the 'Dark Ages' – a period of ignorance, credulity and intellectual turgidity – interposed for a millennium between the end of the western Roman empire and the beginning of the Renaissance. Even if that were true in other fields (and it isn't), it is scandalously erroneous concerning theological developments. Among the prime contributors to the catholic conversation between the pen being put down in Chalcedon (451) and the hammer being picked up in Wittenberg (1517), are such luminaries as Gregory the Great, Thomas Aquinas, John Duns Scotus, William of Ockham, Anselm of Canterbury, and Bernard of Clairvaux. Their writings, together with those of the Fathers, comprise the Great Tradition.

There's no space here to summarize the contributions of Athanasius, Augustine, Aquinas and so on: the point here is that to be a catholic Christian is to be openly and gratefully dependent on their work. It mattered a very great deal to the Reformers to be able to demonstrate patristic and scholastic precedence for their own arguments: they cited the Fathers and Doctors of the church thousands of times (none more than Augustine) in order to show that Protestant doctrine was no novelty, but the recovery of ancient teaching.

We are, of course, not obliged to submit our faith to everything the Fathers and medieval theologians taught. Indeed, that is impossible, as they frequently disagreed among themselves. To have a catholic faith in this regard is, therefore, not blindly to follow, say, Jerome's interpretation of Daniel, nor even necessarily to stand full square with Gregory of Nazianzen's understanding of the Trinity. Rather, it is to adopt a certain *posture* towards what we believe and why we believe it. It is to be perturbed to find oneself on the other side of a debate to Augustine. It is to consult Cyril on a Christological question with which one is wrestling. It is to weigh carefully how Chrysostom preached this passage from the book of Hebrews. It is to confer with Aquinas on the attributes of God. It is instinctively to doubt (though not a priori rule out) every 'new' doctrinal construct or scriptural interpretation for which we can find no patristic anticipation or scholastic formulation.

This posture is, essentially, one of *humility* – one that admits we who happen to be alive in this one location at this one moment in time do not have a monopoly on Christian wisdom. To profess a catholic faith is to imagine oneself taking part in a Bible study or theological debate to which Athanasius and Jerome contribute as contemporaries – even as the chairs of the meeting who introduce and shape the discussion. None of this is to venerate capital 'T' tradition at the same level as Scripture itself, but it is to value and receive 'lower-case t' tradition as the Spirit's good gift to us.

The catholic conscience

While creed, canon and conversation have described the propositional side of the catholic faith, the concept of catholicity also applies to the ethical: there is a catholic *conscience*. If, following Vincent of Lérins (d. 445), we define the catholic faith as, 'What has been believed everywhere, always, and by all',[6] we can easily see how catholicity impinges on moral matters such as those currently being debated in the Church of England. The blessing of same-sex unions ought to be rejected not only on scriptural grounds (though, as evangelicals, those are our ultimate and, strictly speaking, sufficient grounds) but also on *catholic* grounds: it has *everywhere*, *always* and *by all* been believed that there are only two 'honourable estates' – celibate singleness and chaste, heterosexual monogamous marriage. The revisionist, therefore, needs to argue not only that Scripture does *not* preclude blessing same-sex unions but also that God's Spirit has – for some strange and unspecified reason – kept the whole Church from seeing this for 2,000 years. The common retort regarding the church's historical acquiescence in slavery actually *strengthens* our case: slavery was most certainly *not* accepted everywhere, always and by all – it was much controverted in every century until evangelicals finally won the argument in the nineteenth. Slavery was never catholic, but the traditional sexual ethic was and is. Catholicity applies as much to orthopraxy (right doing) as it does to orthodoxy (right believing); to uphold the catholic faith means also to uphold the catholic life.

The catholic cultus

Catholicity refers not only to faith (creed, canon, conversation) and morals (conscience) but also to the pattern of worship (cultus). You will recall from earlier in this chapter, I mentioned that a catholic approach to the church is one shaped by the most expansive notion of 'wholeness'. This wholeness extends not only across space but across time also:[7] a catholic-minded Christian regards the faithful departed as current, rather than former, members of the church. We therefore have a responsibility, a moral obligation arising from Christian love, to honour our 'parents' in how we treat what they have handed down to us. This will mean a default conservatism in matters of worship: we are consciously cautious regarding change, as we respect previous generations' practices and seek the wisdom therein. This was, in fact, the approach adopted by the English Reformers. When reforming the church, they did not imagine a blank plot on which they constructed an entirely new ecclesial edifice. Instead, they took the church as it was and, guided by Scripture, removed any gospel-denying accretions, reforming the ambiguous or obscure so that it served gospel proclamation and edification more effectively. Latin liturgies were translated and tweaked, good prayers copied and pasted, rites and ceremonies realigned but not abolished, clerical vesture simplified but not eradicated. While the Church's worship was thoroughly Protestantized, it was done in such a way that congregants could recognize organic links with what had gone before. Tradition was not sacrosanct and absolutized as in the Roman conceit, but nor was it held in contempt, as in the anabaptist estimation. The preface to the Book of Common Prayer explained that many of the 'sundry Alterations proposed unto us' by some of the reformist agitators had been rejected because they were held to be 'secretly striking at some established doctrine, or laudable practice . . . *of the whole Catholick Church of Christ'.*[8] As both a *catholic* and reformed church, tradition was to be accorded a secondary, derivative authority; respected and retained as much as was possible in good conscience.

The English Reformers' catholic instinct likewise lay behind the Church of England's retention of episcopacy. It is rare for someone to claim that the New Testament lays out a blueprint for church polity and holy orders. Instead, we must extrapolate from biblical principles and patterns. Historically, the early church soon adopted a stable threefold order of ministry (deacon, presbyter, bishop). Biblically, I believe that the early church was justified in doing so, as episcopacy most closely resembles the way in which the apostles led the church. One sees in the New Testament groups of congregations having a particular formal relationship with one senior church leader (Romans 15:22); a council of apostles and their delegates assembling as equals to decide doctrine and practice and enforce it in their various jurisdictions (Acts 15); and particular men being given a regional remit to ordain presbyters and ensure sound teaching (Titus and Timothy are explicitly cited as proto-bishops in the Canons of 1606).[9] But even if the positive biblical case is not strong enough to *require* episcopal government, the negative biblical case was not and is not strong enough to require *abolishing* it.

The catholic connection

Consideration of the office of the bishop paves the way for a discussion of a sixth element of catholicity: connectionism. All Christians believe in the unity of the church as the mystical Body of Christ, but a catholic ecclesiology seeks to translate that eschatological faith into temporal, practical expressions of it. One of the singular advantages of episcopal polity is its institutional connectionism.

The New Testament describes the emergence of a network of churches, the links between the members of which were not merely bonds of fondness and fellowship (though scarcely less than that) but also the fact that they were related to one another through the supra-congregational authority of the apostles – as both planters and overseers, severally and as a single band (Acts 15). Those church leaders who fancied themselves as independent of the apostles' external oversight were chastised in the most severe terms (3 John: 9–12). The contention of those who believe in the apostolic origins of episcopacy is that the office of external authority over groups of churches did not cease with the death of the apostles but was handed on to their delegates (such as Timothy and Titus) – the proto-bishops of the following generation. Regardless of whether this was indeed the germ of the episcopal polity that was firmly established by the end of the next century or not, it is certain that the early church continued and cherished institutional unity, mediated by the supra-congregational loci of churchly authority. Through the bishops, the Jesus movement, despite persecution, which made communication both difficult and dangerous, was able to remain *one* church across its thousand outposts, united in faith and coordinated in mission.

There are many practical benefits to having a connectional church polity with a source of authority external to each local congregation. When functioning well, such a system provides checks and balances against the doctrinal drift or eccentric idiosyncrasies of individual churches, and against the unchecked, egregious moral failure or tyrannous rule of unaccountable ministers.

Such connectionism is properly seen as not only a matter of wisdom but also one of obedience. Jesus emphatically wanted and prayed for his church to be *one* (John 10:16; 17:21). What did he mean by 'one'?

Evangelicals characteristically refer Jesus' desire for oneness to spiritual and/or eschatological oneness: the invisible church (now) and eschatological church (in the future) will be one, for Christ has one Body and one Bride. For many evangelicals, therefore, the unity that the New Testament so clearly demands is spiritual only: we talk of 'gospel unity' to refer to the affinity for and sometimes missional cooperation with 'like-minded churches'. Christian unity is a heavenly and end-time hope rather than an earthed, present-time reality. We are therefore connected only to other churches that think and act like us and only by loose, voluntary – albeit affectionate – association: a convenient, easy, opt-in form of unity. To coin a phrase, 'even the gentiles' have unity like that.

In the opposite Roman Catholic view, the oneness of the church is entirely visible and temporal: the one true church today is identical to the one eschatological church. Oneness is therefore defined primarily institutionally: it includes precisely and only those in formal ecclesial communion with the Pope as the earthly head of the church in succession to St Peter.

For a reformed catholic, however, the 'evangelical' view discussed above is guilty of an under-realized eschatology, while the latter Roman view is guilty of an over-realized eschatology. The truth lies in the middle. The oneness of the church will surely only be perfectly revealed and realized at the eschaton (the final event in the divine plan, the end of the world), but it is to be as fully – tangibly – expressed, pursued and protected as much as humanly possible in the current age. This will mean a difficult, costly, inconvenient and tense kind of unity; a unity that will always be more or less strained. That, after all, is what we observe in the New Testament: church unity strained almost to breaking point over serious matters theological, missional and ethical. Church unity that required conference, compromise and intervention. Half of the content of the New Testament epistles are concerned to teach, correct and rebuke so that congregations would not split internally, nor splinter off from the rest of the church. The apostles and the Fathers prioritized unity between the disparate churches in this way because they believed, with justification, that Christ had charged them to preserve one catholic and apostolic church. The formal connectionism through creed and canon, bishops, synods and councils, was the practical outworking of this catholic outlook.

The catholic circumference

With a catholic connectional ecclesiology goes a catholic *circumference*. By this term I mean to denote how it is that a catholic-minded Christian answers the questions, 'Who is a Christian?' and 'Who are the members of the church?'

To be absolutely clear, the eschatological church of the redeemed at the end of the world will comprise all of and only regenerate, unfeigned, true believers in Jesus Christ. Those who outwardly professed a faith that, inwardly, they lacked will not be members of Christ's Body in the New Creation. That said, let me now establish 'the catholic circumference': *all the baptized are (to be considered) Christians and members of the Church.* This differs from a baptistic ecclesiology, by which only those who are conscious of a moment they first exercised saving faith in Christ and whose articulated belief and lived-out life make that profession 'credible' can be called and treated as Christians, potentially eligible for church membership. The catholic circumference is much wider and simpler: it is coterminous with baptism.

It is easy for evangelicals to be attracted to the baptistic view. Evangelicals have always been 'the keener sort' of Christian: we take our faith seriously, partake of good spiritual disciplines regularly and (seek to) let it have an impact on how we live out our lives day by day. This can lead to (justified) frustration with those who profess to hold the same faith, but are lax in church attendance, personal evangelism, prayer and reading of the Scriptures, and the generous and sacrificial giving of money and time to the church. The way in which a baptistic approach makes church membership an earned *privilege* rather than a *right* by virtue of baptism is, therefore, appealing. A consistent baptistic set-up makes a lot of sense, considering what we know church *should* be like (and are frustrated to find it unlike that): a community, covenanted together in love, sacrificially giving of self and resources to the fellowship, while pursuing corporate holiness. In a baptistic model properly executed, there would be no 'passengers' in church membership.

Why, then, is a catholic circumference – membership conferred completely and simply by baptism – to be preferred? First, because it is appropriately circumspect about our ability to discern the hidden counsel of God. A baptistic ecclesiology, by seeking a 'credible' profession and expression of faith, is attempting to conform the formal membership roster of the visible church to the membership of the invisible church. The catholic circumference, however, operates on the basis that we cannot read names from the 'Book of Life', so doesn't try to. Instead, it concedes that, as Jesus taught, the wheat and the tares will grow together in the church until the Lord's harvest on the last day. Peering into people's hearts to test genuineness of faith is, frankly, God's job then and not an earthly minister's now. Second, if the church's first calling is to be the bastion of *grace*, then it is inappropriate for its membership to have to be earned by soundness of doctrine, godliness of life and seriousness of commitment. The church is a hospital for sinners, not a museum for saints. There is a place for discipline, of course, but discipline is not what *constitutes* the church. Rather, it serves to ensure the spiritual health of the already constituted church. The catholic circumference, whereby all who simply receive the promise of God in Christ conferred in baptism are counted as true members, better represents the economy of the gospel of grace.

Keeping evangelicals catholic

It is my contention that remaining in the Church of England is good for evangelicals on catholic grounds.

Of course, all evangelicals share the same (catholic) canon of Scripture, but evangelicals in the Church of England are kept in closer contact than our free church friends with the catholic creeds (which we swear to uphold and are obliged to recite every Lord's day) and the catholic conversation (which is an intrinsic part of the theological method in which we are trained). We're deeper into the stream of the Great Tradition, and that makes it less likely that we'll be swept up in an eddy off to some dead-end brook of theological or missional faddism. It gives us a much wider, historical vista from which to discern what is essential to the faith, what is allowable and what is indifferent to it. It prevents us from a biblicism, both naive and proud, that absolutizes one possible (or even probable) interpretation by humbling and appropriately relativizing our own convictions in dialogue with hundreds of years' worth of prayerful study. The catholic conscience also gives us another weapon with which to resist ethical revisionism: the Spirit has surely not misled the church in its reading of Scripture for two millennia. The catholic cultus not only connects us with previous generations of believers but also prevents potential excesses. Unorthodox innovations cannot predominate in a Church of England church for long: we are constantly summoned back – by law! – to robustly biblical liturgies, the systematic reading of Scripture, the regular administration of the sacraments and to reverent, ordered worship. If straightjackets feel restrictive, it's important to remember that, without them, the insane and violent could seriously hurt themselves and others.

The comprehensiveness of the Church of England, however, in terms of the disparate beliefs held by its members and taught by its ministers, is more difficult for evangelicals to embrace. A much tighter confessionalism, treating the Thirty-nine Articles of Religion in the way a conservative Presbyterian denomination treats the Westminster Standards, we reason, would surely be preferable. Though I firmly believe all the Thirty-nine Articles, I'm not so sure.

In this I follow others who, when writing about church identity and membership, have found a pair of concepts borrowed from set theory to be enlightening. A 'bounded set' is defined by its boundaries: it yields a clear binary 'in' and 'out' categorization. A 'centred set', however, is defined by its centre: it measures direction and distance, yielding an incremental range for the 'near' and 'far'. The ecclesiological genius of the Church of England is its quality of being both a bounded and centred set at the same time. Its boundary is the catholic creeds; its centre is the Articles and Prayer Book. This perspective enables one to make sense of the combination of comprehensiveness and particularity that is, I believe, unique to our church. All who worship and minister within the Church have to acknowledge, and at least acquiesce to, the components of its confessional centre; those who cannot countenance bishops and baby baptisms will, sooner or later, have to find a different church home. Moreover, at the moment of ordination, all the church's ministers are at least 'facing' the centre as they swear to draw their 'inspiration and guidance' from the historic formularies. The definition afforded by this centre is rightly precious to evangelicals: it assures them that the church's official, confessional centre is 'the Protestant Reformed religion'. At the same time, however, in the Church of England, the centre is not the boundary. There is a distance between the Articles in the centre and the creed at the boundary that accounts for the diversity of theology and practice ('tradition' or 'churchmanship') that subsists within the same church. It is anachronistic to imagine that this breadth is new. Indeed, there have been both 'church papists' and credobaptists in the pews and pulpits since the reign of the first Elizabeth. Certainly, over the past 450 years, in various moments of political or numerical strength, one or other of these impulses has attempted to alter (or should that be 'altar'?) the centre – but none has succeeded. Sixteenth-century low church Puritan attempts to edit the Prayer Book were largely fruitless; nineteenth- and early twentieth-century Anglo-Catholic efforts were eventually defeated also. No liberal assault on the Articles or official liturgy (including in *Common Worship*) have got very far either. The distribution of weight between the centre and various points on the boundary has, it seems, been well-balanced enough to prevent a permanent and decisive slide to a new pivot.

J. C. Ryle (one of my heroes) may have bewailed how the Church of England was, in the late nineteenth century, in danger of becoming 'a kind of Noah's ark, within which every kind of opinion and creed shall dwell safe and undisturbed', but what he was concerned to avoid was the 'throwing overboard *all* Articles and creeds'.[10] I make no defence of *that* kind of ark, in which 'there is no creed or standard of doctrine', but the metaphor of the Church of England as a kind of Noah's ark in which 'every kind of opinion *that confesses the catholic creeds (boundary) and acknowledges the privileged and official place of the Articles and Prayer Book (centre) shall dwell safe and (relatively) undisturbed*', well is that such a bad thing?

Those evangelicals who, like me, are determined to remain in the Church of England prize the Reformed Protestant centre, and my ministry as a theological educator and as a presbyter will consist in calling the church back towards this centre. However, we evangelical Anglicans ought also to prize the catholic circumference. We've no need to be embarrassed about it – in fact, it should be our boast. The Church of England's 'mere Christianity' approach to membership (all the baptized) and profession (the Apostles' and Nicene Creed) *is a good thing*. Yes, it means that we rub up – uncomfortably, no doubt – against Anglo-Catholics, pseudo-Lutherans, wannabe Eastern Orthodox, pre-millennial Pente-costals and liberals in our dioceses, deaneries and congregations, but why on earth should we expect to be part of a *comfortable* Church? Why should we expect everyone to believe all the right things and behave in all the right ways? We should know better than that – we've read the New Testament.

This brings us back to the question of Christian unity. Evangelicals often undervalue unity in the pursuit of doctrinal and ethical purity. To be an evangelical in the Church of England, however, means always being confronted with the tension between the two, forced into forms of unity that we would not freely choose – and that is *good* for us. Being institu-tionally united with Anglo-Catholics, middle-of-the-roaders and liberals (not to mention with those evangelicals with whom I disagree about a raft of secondary issues) is painful, costs time and energy (particularly in synods and committees) and involves many compromises and fudges. We're obliged to navigate a strained, tense, inconvenient Christian unity. A Christian unity with people *not* like us – folk who are dissimilar demographically, culturally and theologically. A Christian unity that is stubbornly and intensely *practical*: institutional, political, financial, structural, strategic, geographical, sacramental, missional. Such a chal-lenge is good for us as Christians. It means that we're bearing with one another. It means that we're making sacrifices for the good of another or for the good of the whole. It means that we're holding some things firmly but other things lightly. It means that we are less susceptible to being siloed off into an evangelical subculture, ignorant of our own blind spots and cut off from the spiritual and missional resources of the wider church that could potentially bless and prosper our ministry.

If 'evangelexit' should occur, the kinds of unity that we'll pursue and practise will be much narrower, lighter, easier and more pleasant than they are presently. It will be on our chosen terms; it will be with the retention of all sorts of vetoes, firewalls and break-clauses. If it gets emotionally difficult, theologically argumentative or politically demanding ('distracting', we'll call it), we'll unhitch whatever regional, denomin-ational or network-based 'unity' we had claimed to form and go it alone or start something else a bit nicer. That should worry us – it simply isn't the 'feel' we get from the New Testament and sub-apostolic Church. In contrast, resolving to stick it out in a difficult, mixed, tension-filled broad church is a form of spiritual discipline for evangelicals. Our circumstances demand that we wrestle with, work hard for and constantly weigh up a kind of broad Christian unity that we might not have chosen, but which God, by his providence, has handed down to us.

The catholic circumference also helps evangelicals to process what it is that they are about in parish ministry. We mentioned earlier the missional advantages that go with being part of the established Church. Though these opportunities may be getting fewer and further apart, they are still precious and full of promise for the evangelistically minded pastor. They only make sense within a catholic circumference model, however. Parish priests are given a duty of care ('cure of souls') for all the baptized in the parish, together with their friends and families. This means that even those who might never, as an adult, have darkened the door of our church buildings still have a claim on our time. The fact that people still somehow know that and still turn to the vicar at times of great sadness and challenge (family breakdown, addictions, poverty and homelessness, bereavement), as well as at times of joy and celebration (weddings, christenings), is a great privilege and evangelistic opportunity that flows organically out of the catholic circumference of our ecclesiology. Week by week we look and work hard for opportunities to speak of Christ to unbelievers. The legacy of the reformed catholic ecclesiology of the English Reformers means that, in considerable numbers, unbelievers still come to us, because they recognize that it is, in some sense (a sense they do not fully understand) *their* church and *their* vicar. Unbelievers do not have the same attitude towards the local Congregational church, because it does not regard them as, in any way, members – they have no investment in nor claim on that church's time. Correspondingly, unsolicited opportunities for evangelism and discipleship are much rarer in gathered churches.

Keeping the catholic church evangelical

While there are spiritual and missional advantages to evangelicals of worshipping and ministering within the Church of England, that is only half the story. For while the Church of England helps to keep evangelicals catholic, evangelicals also have a responsibility to help keep the catholic Church of England evangelical.

To be a catholic Christian is to recognize that it's not all about *us*. It's not all about us as evangelicals; and it's also not all about us as a local church. The local church is extremely important in God's economy. It is the front line in the spiritual battle, an outpost of the inaugurated eschatological kingdom. However, while in a Congregationalist ecclesiology the local church is *ultimate*, in a catholic ecclesiology it is *penultimate*. The catholic church is primarily *one* and secondarily *many*: each parish church is a 'franchise' of the catholic Church. A catholic ecclesiology, therefore, both radically decentralizes the local congregation (it is but one small part of the visible catholic church) and fundamentally dignifies it (in any small parish chapel, *the* church of God, that very entity called of God throughout the ages and destined to be the Bride of Christ, is extant). A catholic ecclesiology, therefore, demands that one's ecclesial identity and loyalty is not *primarily* found in a specific local, gathered congregation and only derivatively, through membership of that particular body, with the church as a single entity, but precisely the other way around. One is a member of the church catholic, to whom one primarily owes love, prayer and devotion, and, therefore, one has a secondary (though very real) bond of affection and loyalty to that *branch* of the one church where one regularly receives the Word taught and broken.

But putting things this way round – putting the one church at a national and regional (diocesan) level first and the local church second – will affect both our priorities now and strategies for the future. What will it mean to seek *a* healthy Church over and above *many* healthy local churches? It may mean persevering more with official diocesan channels when seeking to plant a church rather than pursuing the project largely independently, only seeking the bishop's rubber stamp at a late stage (with an ultimatum that we'll do it anyway). Navigating through the official channels will be slower and likely involve difficult compromises, but the work will be more coordinated at a regional level and the church will have more resources at its disposal and more secure long-term prospects, free from the sort of 'viability' calculations that have to be made by independent would-be church planters, which make planting into deprived areas difficult and rare. If evangelicals are involved in petitioning the bishops with such plans and proposals, they have unparalleled chances to start new and lasting gospel work, in principle, anywhere in the country.

A second way that evangelicals can discharge their catholic responsibility is by serving on deanery, diocesan and general synods. If we are invested, above all, in the health of *the whole* Church in England, not just the particular local expression of it that we are members of or for which we are responsible, then serious investment in the instruments that pertain more widely than my parish alone is a valuable pursuit. It is my *business* to oppose, for instance, ethical revisionism, even in another minister's parish, *because I am a reformed catholic*: I have a love for, duty to and a stake in the whole Church of God in England. Of course, there is an impact on parish-level ministry whenever evangelicals devote some of their time to diocesan or national roles and causes, but if our first love and loyalty are for the catholic Church rather than the particular congregation in our cure, then at certain seasons for certain persons, that will prove entirely appropriate.

This instinct to privilege the overall health of the church may have important implications, in terms of how we might navigate the current crisis. Some moot the possibility of a third province as a way to get past the impasse between revisionists and traditionalists on matters to do with sexuality. Such a province, coterminous with the provinces of Canterbury and York together, and itself in communion with Canterbury, would likely be sufficient to safeguard traditionalists' consciences from the encroachments of liberal doctrine and practice. I think, though, that we should be cool about the possibility, not enthusiastic, for it is not really a *catholic* solution. If we evangelicals were to sue for it and get it, might it not be a dereliction of the duty of the orthodox as *catholic* Christians, betraying a sect mentality that prioritizes the holiness and purity of *part* of the church at the expense of the soundness of the whole? As reformed catholics, we owe it to this, the Church of England – our portion of the catholic Church – to be the brakes and conscience of that body, seeking its reformation by the Holy Spirit and Scripture, even if it is at great personal cost. We are to be the preservative salt that prevents, for as long as possible and as much as possible, the putrefying of the whole – if necessary, by sheer intransigence. As it happens, a third province may prove to be the least bad option, but let us at least call for it (should it be necessary) to be provided for revisionists who petition for inclusion therein. At least that way, we orthodox evangelicals might retain our preservative function for the undecideds, for whom inertia might prove decisive.

Faith, hope and love

My purpose in writing this chapter has been, in the first place, to convince evangelicals that 'catholic' is not a dirty word. It is, properly understood, a gospel word; a word of faith, hope and love. Faith, because we believe in the comprehensiveness of the mystical Body of Christ and in the oneness of the gospel that avails for *all* believers in *all* the world in *all* ages. Hope, because this wholeness across space and time is part of an inaugurated eschatology: we protect and prosper catholicity *now* because it is the shape of our inheritance *to come*. The catholic church is both the glorious destination to which we're headed together and, therefore, the fitting path for our pilgrimage. Love, because to prize catholicity is to bear with others, compromise for others, sacrifice for others – and others who are very different culturally, demographically and theologically. Catholicity is difficult and costly: love is the only sufficient motive and efficient power to help us achieve it.

I then argued that the Church of England represents the best way for evangelicals in England to be catholic – resolutely creedal, conversant in the Great Tradition, shaped by a venerable shared moral vision, co-worshippers with our forebears, intractably connected to a greater whole, embracing the baptismal circumference in pastoral responsibility and the evangelistic opportunities that it presents. Finally, I've charged evangelicals with their catholic responsibility to put the health of the whole church first and of its local expressions second. That will often mean frustration, pain and compromise – but that's exactly what the New Testament leads us to expect.

Pragmatic arguments will soon be insufficient to keep evangelicals in the Church of England. It's only going to get messier and more difficult within the church in the next several years, and the missional opportunities that come with the territory are likely to continue to dry up. We evangelicals must persevere with and press within the Church of England for scriptural, *catholic* reasons, however –because it's both good for us and for the church we love for us to be here.

Notes

1 J. Stott, 'Pursuing truth and unity', in C. Chartres (Ed.), *Why I am Still an Anglican* (London: Continuum, 2006), pp. 7–15.

2 Stott, 'Pursuing truth and unity', p. 9.

3 Stott, 'Pursuing truth and unity', p. 10.

4 Stott, 'Pursuing truth and unity', p. 13.

5 That is why such heresies inevitably precede or follow revisions to the canon, whether deletions (from Marcion to the Jesus Seminar), additions (from the Gnostic gospels to the Book of Mormon) or (ingenious) radical retranslations and reconstructions (from Arius to modern-day revisionists).

6 Sometimes the Vincentian canon is described as a three-fold test of ecumenicity (everywhere), antiquity (always) and consent (all).

7 For this reason, it is inappropriate to replace the word 'catholic' with 'universal' in the creed, as some churches do, as 'universal' refers only to extension in space.

8 'Preface', in B. Cummings (Ed.), *The Book of Common Prayer*, Oxford World's Classics (Oxford: Oxford University Press, 2013), p. 210.

9 G. Bray, *The Anglican Canons: 1529–1947* (Woodbridge, Suffolk: Boydell Press, 1998), Book II, section 6, p. 473.

10 J. C. Ryle, *Principles for Churchmen* (London: William Hunt and Company, 1884), pp. xxiii–xxiv.

3

Laying claim to the Church of England

DR ROS CLARKE

When I became a Christian in 1990, women could not be ordained as priests in the Church of England. That changed during my last year as an undergraduate student in 1994 and, in the years since then, various people have suggested to me that I should consider ordination. I've certainly thought about it, but I've never felt that it was the right thing for me. That is partly because of my conviction that ordained ministry is not what God wants for women in the church, but it is also because of my strong conviction that laypeople are no less significant in the church's life and ministry than ordained people.

Perhaps ordination leads to a clearer, more well-trodden path within the Church of England but, as a layperson, I've found that there are very many ways in which we can be involved in, and significantly influence, the Church of England. I have served as a parochial church council (PCC) member and PCC secretary; I am currently an elected lay member of both the deanery and diocesan synods, and I have recently been elected to the General Synod; I have been on the paid staff of a couple of churches; I was employed for two years by the Diocese of Lichfield, in an online role; and I now work as Associate Director of the Church Society, an organization with the aim of contending to reform and renew the Church of England in biblical faith.

Laypeople matter to the church. Indeed, laypeople *are* the church. It is easy to overlook their significance in the Bible's teaching about the church, and easy to underestimate their importance in the work of the Church of England today. In this chapter, I want to look briefly at what the Bible has to say about the role of laypeople in the church, then turn to consider the history of lay involvement in the Church of England. The way in which laypeople are involved in almost every part of the current structures of the denomination will be considered in more detail, along with some examples of the kinds of impact laypeople can have on the Church of England now and for the future.

Lay ministry: service and leadership

In those days when the number of disciples was increasing, the Hellenistic Jews among them complained against the Hebraic Jews because their widows were being overlooked in the daily distribution of food. So the Twelve gathered all the disciples together and said, 'It would not be right for us to neglect the ministry of the word of God in order to wait on tables. Brothers and sisters, choose seven men from among you who are known to be full of the Spirit and wisdom. We will turn this responsibility over to them and will give our attention to prayer and the ministry of the word.'
(Acts 6:1–4)

The elders who direct the affairs of the church well are worthy of double honour, especially those whose work is preaching and teaching.
(1 Timothy 5:17)

These two New Testament texts demonstrate a distinction made between kinds of leadership in the early church. There is the kind the Twelve in Acts 6 describe as 'ministry' (the Greek word simply means 'service') and the kind Paul in 1 Timothy calls 'eldership'. These latter people 'direct the affairs of the church' and are considered worthy of double honour. People in both kinds of leadership require the Spirit and wisdom as they fulfil their responsibilities.

Those responsibilities, however, are different. In Acts 6, we're told that some are set apart for the ministry of the Word, while others are not. In 1 Timothy 5, there are some elders whose work is preaching and teaching, and some whose work is not. Not all church leaders have a teaching ministry. Some are called to serve in practical ways and to take on responsibilities other than teaching and preaching, but in the New Testament, such people are still honoured as leaders in the church.

Today, of course, very few people are set aside for teaching ministries without having to take responsibility for any practical matters in the church. The division between ordained and lay service in the Church of England does not neatly separate into teaching ministry versus practical responsibility, even if the clergy might sometimes wish it did! Nevertheless, there is clearly biblical precedent for recognizing leaders in the church whose primary ministry is not Bible teaching. In the contemporary Anglican church, those leaders will usually be laypeople.

We should note that most laypeople will not be leaders at all. Most will simply serve as faithful foot soldiers in their local churches by living in obedience to Christ, loving their neighbours, sharing the good news of the gospel and praying faithfully in whatever circumstances the Lord has called them. In the body of Christ, we need many more of these hands and feet than those who lead them.

But we do need some to lead. We need those who are called to ordained ministry, to be set apart for the ministry of the Word and sacrament. And we need some who are called to lay leadership, just as in the New Testament, taking on responsibility for directing the affairs of the church, together with the teaching elders.

The changing role of laypeople in the Church of England

In the late nineteenth century, the first Bishop of Liverpool, J. C. Ryle wrote a Church Association tract on the position of the laity in the Church of England.[1] One of the most striking things about the tract is just how much has changed within just a hundred years or so. He ended by calling for the following five changes to be made regarding the involvement of laypeople in the Church of England:

No English Convocation ought ever to be sanctioned without an equal representation of the laity.

The Convocation was the forerunner of General Synod and, at the time Ryle was writing, Convocations consisted only of clergy. In 2019, the General Synod consisted of 49 bishops, 197 clergy and about 260 laypeople.

> No Diocese ought to be governed by a Bishop alone without the aid of a Lay Privy Council.

Today, all dioceses have bishop's councils, which consist of a mix of clergy and laypeople, elected by the diocesan synod.

> No parochial clergyman ought ever to attempt the management of his parish or congregation without constantly consulting the laity.

In Ryle's day, PCCs did exist, but they were optional, though churchwardens were not. Now every parish has to have a PCC, elected by and consisting solely of laypeople.

> No appointment to a living or cure of souls ought ever to be made without allowing the laity a voice in the matter.

Clergy appointments used to be made directly by the patrons. These days, while patrons do still play a part, every parish has to appoint two lay representatives to have their say in the appointment of any new incumbent. There are also lay representatives formally involved in the appointment of all diocesan bishops and Archbishops.

> No system of ecclesiastical discipline ought ever to be sanctioned which does not give a principal place to the laity.

This has not been implemented. Church discipline by excommunication can only be done by the bishop, and clergy discipline is also in the hands of the bishop.

In the last century, increasing amounts of power and influence have been given to laypeople throughout the Church of England. Ryle would surely have been pleased to see that. I think, however, that he would have been disappointed by the way evangelicals have largely squandered the opportunities that they could have given us. It is still true that the house of laity at the General Synod tends to be more conservative than the house of clergy on theological and moral issues, but laypeople have not often been the positive force for good in the Church of England that Ryle imagined they would be.

Yet, the most powerful force for change in the Church of England is its laypeople. They have the right and the power to hold the church accountable to its founding formularies, to refuse the revisionist agenda and to contend for the gospel in synods and on committees, in parishes and dioceses. Laypeople have the right to defend the Church of England as a true expression of the church of Christ in England.

We have the right to defend the church because, as laypeople, we *are* the church. It is always hard for members of a body to hold its leaders to account, but it is our responsibility to do so and, because of the way the Church of England is now structured, it is now easier than ever for us to do so. If we are concerned for the future of the Church of England, I think the single most important thing we should be working and praying for is the mobilization of its faithful laypeople up and down the country.

The role of laypeople in the Church of England today

The contemporary Church of England is a large and extraordinarily complex structure, comprising three different hierarchies, across four or five different levels. There are clergy, synods and staff, functioning in parishes, deaneries, dioceses, provinces and the national church.

Laypeople are involved in all of these hierarchies, at almost every level.

Clergy

The process of appointing every incumbent, every diocesan bishop and every Archbishop in the Church of England requires the input of laypeople. Rural or area deans may be appointed without consulting laypeople, and other clergy appointments may also be made directly by bishops or incumbents, though usually there will be some consultation with laypeople on these appointments. In addition to the appointment process, all incumbents, bishops and Archbishops must regularly consult with a council that includes laypeople.

Synods

The parish synod, or PCC, consists of the clergy of the parish, lay readers and other licensed lay ministers, churchwardens, any members of the General Synod, diocesan synod or deanery synod who are on the roll of the parish and representatives of the laity elected at the annual PCC. In most parishes, this means that laypeople significantly outnumber clergy on the PCC.

Laypeople are elected to the deanery, diocesan and General Synod and comprise approximately half of all members of these synods. At the General Synod, measures dealing with the government of the church and its institutions, and canons determining doctrine and the form of worship must be passed separately by all three houses (bishops, clergy and laity), so that lay members may block any changes to these, even when they are approved by the bishops and clergy. Laypeople thus hold very significant powers in the synodical government of the church.

Staff

Most administrative staff at all levels are laypeople, while those holding pastoral roles in parishes and deaneries or working as diocesan and national officers are a mix of clergy and laypeople.

Given the complexity of this structure, the question as to how decisions are made and implemented in the Church of England is not a straight-forward one! More or less any of these people or groups can initiate a discussion or make a decision that can lead to change.

Clergy-led initiatives, for example, may be introduced by an Arch-bishop or bishop and pushed out into the parishes. Alternatively, parish clergy can try new ideas in their parishes that, if successful, may be imitated and multiplied across deaneries, dioceses or further afield. Some matters are the sole responsibility of clergy, according to canon law, and certain other matters will naturally fall within the general remit of the pastor-teacher – prayer, mission, evangelism and so on. On other issues, the clergy may work together with other staff or officers, and members of the clergy may, of course, submit proposals to synods.

It is synods where the most significant power for change is found. Church of England synods at every level are asked to make all kinds of decisions – about budgets and buildings, staffing and pensions, the ministry of ordained women, liturgy and doctrine. Even decisions about practical matters, such as finance, need godly wisdom and gospel priorities to be divined, but some synodical debates are much more obviously theological. A PCC might be asked to consider passing a resolution concerning the ministry of a female incumbent or a woman bishop, for example. The General Synod could debate new liturgy for same-sex marriages or transgender baptism.

Laypeople, often with no formal theological training, have significant responsibility for making both practical and theological decisions in the synodical structure of the Church of England.

One further role given to synods and their subcommittees is that of holding paid staff to account. In parishes, additional staff (that is, not the incumbent or the curate) are most often employed by the PCC, which agrees the job description and terms of employment. They may not always be involved in day-to-day management of the employee, but they will have overall responsibility for ensuring that the staff member is acting appropriately in a role, according to the needs of the church. In a diocese, typically there will be a good number of paid staff and a more formal HR department. Nonetheless, they are still accountable to the diocesan synod, which usually exercise that accountability through the Board of Finance, the Bishop's Council and the Board of Education.

It may sometimes feel as though diocesan staff, national officers and even paid workers in a parish church are the people driving the agenda of the church. However, the system says otherwise and, as lay members of the church, we have both the right and the responsibility to hold them to account, to ensure that their work follows Christ's agenda for his church.

How laypeople can make a difference

There are many ways in which lay leadership makes a significant difference within the Church of England, including the following.

Finance

Money can be used to hinder gospel ministry or to enable it to flourish. Lay people serving as PCC treasurers, on diocesan boards of finance or General Synod finance committees, as well as in paid roles in finance departments, can have a huge impact, in terms of freeing up resources for gospel work or preventing it from being used for church growth.

Appointments

Parish representatives, members of vacancy-in-see committees and the Crown Nominations Commission (CNC) all have a role in appointing clergy to their posts. Anyone can write to the CNC to make suggestions for diocesan bishops and Archbishops. Lay members of synods and lay staff members may also be involved in other appointments of diocesan officers, parish workers and national church staff.

Jane Patterson, a lay member of the General Synod for the Diocese of Sheffield, writes about her experience:

> In 2010, as I stepped down as churchwarden in a large conservative evangelical church, my vicar asked me to consider standing for election to the General Synod. Having no synodical experience, I went on a day trip to York with a friend to see how it works, to inform my decision making. We were shocked! In a debate which seemed to be about pension provision for clergy who might leave the Church of England as a matter of conscience if the women bishops legislation was passed, one woman said, speaking of those who hold a complementarian view of the role of women, 'the writing has been on the wall for twenty years, they should just go.' My friend and I exchanged glances . . . I said, 'OK, I will stand.'
>
> I have literally had to 'stand' numerous times – either to indicate a desire to speak and sometimes being called to speak or to support the use of the synodical rules to influence the debate for the promotion of the gospel. Standing has meant voting, knowing that the electronic records are published and will be scrutinized by others. It has also meant sitting around the table during meetings of the Crown Nominations Commission, with the Archbishops and other members, some of whom have had a very different theology,

'discerning' who should be nominated to the vacant see, when there is no shared understanding of episcopacy. Mostly the conversations have been cordial, but sometimes they have been aggressively antagonistic, and followed by comments in Christian newspapers, and even a procedural challenge to my re-election for a second term.

Before standing, I would not have imagined that I would be called a heretic by a senior member of the clergy in a diocesan synod debate, but, yes, it really did happen one Saturday morning in 2014 in Sheffield.

I am still standing, by the Lord's grace and through his power, although, at times, with knees shaking and feeling unable to walk, but not alone, and in partnership with brothers and sisters in the gospel.[2]

Jane is a layperson, contending for the gospel in the process of making the most senior appointments in the Church of England. We should pray for her, but we should also pray for many more laypeople like Jane, willing to stand for Christ in this way.

Debates and decisions

Laypeople on synods can propose motions, ask questions, contribute to the debate and exercise the right to vote. Sometimes a single comment from a layperson can change the whole tone of a debate. Gracious, gospel-hearted, articulate and well-taught laypeople are very difficult for a synod to ignore.

I want to show you a couple of relatively recent examples of when the power of laypeople made a significant difference. The first comes from the Diocese of Hereford, where the diocesan synod passed this motion in 2017:

That this synod request the House of Bishops to commend an Order of Prayer and Dedication after the registration of a civil partnership or a same-sex marriage for use by ministers in exercise of their discretion under Canon B4, being a form of service neither contrary to, nor indicative of any departure from, the doctrine of the Church of England in any essential matter, together with guidance that no parish should be obliged to host, nor minister conduct, such a service.

Result: the synod voted with forty-one in favour, eighteen against and four abstained.

The Bishop of Hereford explained that this motion came to the diocesan synod from three deanery synods, because of requests that had been made by same-sex couples. The motion had its origins, then, in parishes. Clergy were receiving requests from same-sex couples to have a church service after the registration of their civil partnership or marriage. They brought the matter to their deanery synods, which passed motions to raise the matter at their diocesan synod, which then passed the motion quoted above. Sufficient numbers of laypeople voting against this motion could have stopped it at either the deanery or diocesan synod.

New liturgy isn't a matter that parishes, deaneries or dioceses can implement independently, but the diocesan synod can call on the House of Bishops to act, as it did in this case, claiming that such liturgy need not indicate any departure from the established doctrine of the church. The House of Bishops, however, determined that this motion should be debated at the General Synod where, once again, laypeople would have the power to block it.

It seems likely that this motion, and a private member's motion with identical wording, will not be debated by the General Synod, because of the COVID-19 pandemic and because it will have been superseded by the 'Living in love and faith' process. That said, as you consider the origin and progress of this kind of motion, which could have ended with an extremely serious change to the church's doctrine and practice, I hope it shows just how much influence, and the responsibility, laypeople can have.

There is a direct line of influence from the person in the pew through to real and significant change in the church's doctrine and liturgy. Of course, there are, quite rightly, checks and balances to ensure that one person's quirk isn't going to change the whole church. There is also, sadly, potential for the system to be manipulated and abused. Nonetheless, it is a system by means of which all communicant members of the Church of England can vote for their representatives on their PCC and deanery synod. Those deanery synod representatives then vote for their representatives on their diocesan synod and the General Synod. The people we elect as our representatives are tasked with making important decisions on extremely weighty matters, so we must take our responsibility in electing them very seriously.

Here's a second example, again, something that began in a deanery synod, this time in my own diocese, the Diocese of Lichfield. This is a motion that the Oswestry Deanery Synod put forward to our diocesan synod in 2019:

Recognising the importance of vocations to both lay and ordained ministries for the future of the Church, Oswestry Deanery Synod is aware that some fail to pursue their vocations because the training offered is unsuitable for their churchmanship or too distant. Therefore, Oswestry Deanery Synod requests the diocese to affirm a thorough commitment to vocations, discipleship and enabling evangelism across the entire diocese by:

1 undertaking a review to:

(a) consider additional training providers who can offer and accommodate a comprehensive and wide range of church traditions and churchmanship;

(b) reduce the environmental impact and disadvantage of long journeys to training candidates in remoter parts of the diocese by:

(i) exploring alternative training options such as distance learning;
(ii) assessing the feasibility of collaborating with neighbouring dioceses and provinces to allow those pursuing vocations to choose where is most suitable and convenient for them

(c) report findings to Diocesan Synod within 12 months

and

2 where practicable, to undertake diocesan training events and roadshows in remoter parts of the diocese.

This motion is asking for provision of training for lay and ordained people in the diocese to be more accessible geographically and, further, to include a wider range of church traditions and churchmanship. In the debate at diocesan synod, lay readers as well as curates and others spoke about their experiences of training that had not been appropriate and had been hard to access.

The diocesan staff who spoke during the debate were clearly opposed to the motion and defensive in their response to it, but the elected synod passed the motion. Staff who are responsible for training in the diocese will, therefore, now have to review their provision and report back. The synod has agreed that training in the diocese should respect a wide range of church traditions, people should have the power to choose the training most appropriate for them and it should be possible to seek appropriate alternative training beyond diocesan boundaries.

In this example, laypeople, as well as clergy, who had been elected to the diocesan synod, were exercising their power and responsibility to hold paid diocesan staff to account by bringing this motion to the synod. As a result, decisions about training providers and pathways may need to be changed and more people will be able to access training appropriate for their ministry.

The need for lay leaders

Occasionally I have been a member of a church where the PCC elections were hotly contested but, in my experience, most churches struggle to find enough people to fill the places on PCCs and on deanery synods. It is a different story with respect to diocesan synods and the General Synod, where there will usually be more candidates than positions available. There are plenty of people wanting to have their voice heard and to get their agenda on the table in those instances.

If evangelical laypeople aren't willing to engage, the result will be that there will still be laypeople, but it will be only liberal laypeople and Anglo-Catholic laypeople. It will sometimes be laypeople who do not know Christ at all, but who merely see an opportunity to gain a certain kind of power and status for themselves or, worse, actively to disrupt the church from its gospel work.

If no evangelical laypeople are willing to contend for the true gospel in our synods and on our committees, the simple truth is that the liberalization of the Church of England will continue unhindered. Ungodly appointments will continue to be made, worldly priorities will be set, evil will be called good, good will be called evil and the church will, at some point, cease to be a true church. It will be no good evangelicals on that day crying that no-one listened to us, that we were ignored and overlooked, that we had no say. We do have a say and we must take the opportunities that are built into the current structures of the Church of England that allow us to speak and to have our voice heard.

As laypeople, we must not wash our hands of our responsibility for the church. This is our church. We are the church.

Not everyone will be called or have the gifts necessary to take on this kind of lay leadership, but I don't think the qualifications are particularly restrictive. We need godly men and women, those who are 'full of the Spirit and wisdom' to step forwards. We need people who will show up and vote. We need some who understand the structures and processes, others who understand the policies and politics, some who understand the finances and yet more who can communicate those things clearly, to help all of us to engage well and vote wisely.

We need people who are able to give some of their time. PCCs generally meet monthly, deanery synods bimonthly, diocesan synods three times a year and the General Synod twice a year. The General Synod lasts several days, but it is possible to claim costs for travel, accommodation and loss of earnings.

We need people who are able to step up now. As I write this, the results of the 2021 General Synod elections are coming out and the need for people in every house – including the laity – who will oppose any revisionist proposals arising from the 'Living in love and faith' process is urgent.

We need people to step up in every generation because institutions are not static. The Church of England has changed a lot in the last century and it will continue to change in the future. It is up to all of us – clergy and laypeople alike – to ensure that those changes are towards greater gospel faithfulness for the sake of God's glory and for the good of future generations. This is Christ's church and, as laypeople, we must not hesitate to lay claim to it, in his name.

Notes

1 J. C. Ryle, 'Church reform: The position of the laity', Church
   Association Tract 191 (available online at: <www.churchsociety.org/
   wp-content/uploads/2021/05/c_a_tract_191.pdf >, accessed November
   2021).

2 First published in L. Gattis, *Fight Valiantly* (Watford: Church Society,
   2019), pp. 217–218.

4

Moving diagonally:
the bishops' chapter

ADAM YOUNG TALKS WITH SOPHIE JELLEY,
JULIAN HENDERSON, ROD THOMAS
AND KEITH SINCLAIR

Introduction by Adam Young

If you were to travel back in time to the Synod of Dort in 1618–1619, something of an ecumenical council of the Reformed churches, you would spot something rather odd. On the right was a man sitting on a large chair – almost like a throne – with a fancy canopy placed above it. No-one else in the room has been given such an honour. The man under the canopy, of course, was the then Anglican Bishop of Llandaff, George Carleton (1559–1628). Though the Church of England was not the only Protestant Reformed church to keep a form of episcopacy, it was certainly the most prominent one – and clearly the divines at Dort did not see episcopacy as something inherently un-Reformed. To this day, episcopacy is central to Anglican identity – hence, it is one of the four points of the Chicago–Lambeth Quadrilateral.

This begs two questions. First, why did the Church of England keep its bishops at the time of the Reformation and, second, what did it think bishops were supposed to do?

The keeping of episcopacy during the English Reformation was driven more by practical considerations than deep theological ones, though both played a role. Reforming an entire nation from the top down in a monarch-led reformation was a very different affair from reforming the structure in a single city and attracting wide popular support for it. Bishops, already intimately tied into the structure and mechanics of the state, were obvious candidates for implementing and protecting the fledgling reformation while keeping what was actually reformed on the cautious and conservative side. Neither Archbishop Cranmer (1489–1556) nor Archbishop Whitgift (1530–1604) saw episcopacy, or any form of church polity, as directly commanded by Scripture and so didn't feel the need to push for its reform.

For the Reformers, what makes a church a true church had nothing to do with bishops or orders –episcopacy is not part of the esse (essence) of the church. That is why, in Article 19, we are told simply that the visible church of Christ is a congregation of the faithful in which the pure Word of God is preached and the sacraments are correctly administered. There is no mention of bishops. No English Reformer claimed that episcopacy alone was the single divinely instituted form of church government till Bishop Thomas Bilson took that step in 1593. Indeed, it seems likely that some Presbyterian ministers were given the cure of souls of Anglican parishes even into the early 1600s, despite the official line being that they should be ordained by a bishop.

All of that, though, is not to say that the Reformers at that time thought episcopacy to be detrimental to the *bene esse* (good and well-being) of the church. They saw biblical precedent for it in the twelve apostles and the seventy disciples, in the role of Paul regarding Timothy and Titus, and of Timothy and Titus themselves in terms of their areas of responsibility. The preface to the Ordinal is quite clear that episcopacy has an apostolic origin. Men such as Anglican theologian Richard Hooker (1554–1600) saw episcopacy as the most scriptural form of polity, without 'de-churching' other polities. The Anglican Reformers valued the long-standing historic nature of episcopal government as well as the hard authority and public leadership it gave to the church. It was the reaction against Anabaptists and, later, the Puritans, influenced by Theodore Beza of Geneva (1519–1605), that ultimately led to a hardening on this point among Anglicans and an emphasis on proving the biblical and historical nature of the episcopacy to the exclusion of other forms of governance.

The question remains, however: what was to be the core ministry of the bishops in a Protestant Reformed church? In the Ordinal service for the consecration of bishops, we find the key markers of episcopal ministry. The opening collect prays for the bishops that they might 'diligently preach thy Word, and duly administer the godly discipline thereof'. The primary ministry of the bishop, then, is to preach God's Word and, from that beginning, to exercise discipline within the church; to pastor the pastors, as it were.

Looking to the interrogation of the bishops-to-be, we see this fleshed out a little more. Bishops are, on the one hand, actively to teach and preach the doctrine of Scripture. On the other hand, they must 'banish and drive away all erroneous and strange doctrine contrary to God's Word'. This involves not only teaching but also leading by example, through a holy life of righteousness and loving the lost or needy. They must also actively correct and punish those in their diocese who teach false doctrines or are disobedient to God. A key part of this ministry of preaching and discipline is, of course, the selecting, training, ordaining and deploying of the next generation of ministers to continue such a gospel-focused legacy.

In the rest of this chapter, we shall read the answers to questions posed to four current evangelical bishops – men and women who took the vows and heard the prayers in the Ordinal that outline their calling and ministry. Ministry today is both the same and yet very different from what it was at the time of the Reformation, when the guiding principles of the Ordinal were written. Let us now explore what evangelical episcopacy looks like today, as the bishops each respond to the same series of five questions in their own way.

Sophie Jelley – Suffragan Bishop, Doncaster

Do we need to reimagine the ancient office of bishop for the modern world?

I find the term 'faithful improvisation' helpful here. COVID-19 has forced us into uncertainty, but I believe that it has simply accelerated our need for innovation and will help us to recognize the heart of our identity as evangelical Anglicans, and to ask, 'Who is missing?' and, 'How can we help them join in fully?'

Areas for reimagination include the radical rejection of an unhealthy culture of deference; a tangible commitment to the most disadvantaged in society. Building a racially diverse church, both reflecting his kingdom and enabling full participation among the whole people of God in fulfilling his mission. A fully developed theology of lay ministry. Equipping the church to be a compassionate, prophetic voice leading the way in responding faithfully and hopefully to the issues of the day, including climate emergency, the inequalities in the society in which we live and serve, and the historic legacy of poor safeguarding of the most vulnerable – a source of serious lament.

What does it mean for you to be an 'evangelical' bishop?

I express this identity through a commitment to a *personal relationship with God*, who loves me as an individual and calls me to play my part corporately among the people of God, baptized into his church and called to his service. In this, we are called away from the radical individualism of our times into something far greater. I am motivated by this love to share his love with others through *personal evangelism*, I want every person to know that they are created, made and loved by him, and to have the opportunity to know Jesus personally. I trust in and teach the *forgiveness of God* through the death of Jesus as the uniquely perfect gift, given that we may know life in all its fullness. In my experience, people often carry wounds and burdens from the past, some deeply hidden. I want all to know the freedom and joy available in following Jesus, whatever their circumstance. I follow a daily rhythm of *reading and receiving from the Bible*, as the Word of God to his people; through careful and critical engagement of heart and mind, to read and *teach the faith* and apply it to daily life. *Intimacy in prayer*, living in the company of Jesus, is a lifeline. Openness to the *power of the Holy Spirit*, bringing gifts to God's people both at the Lord's table and in ways that reflect God's kindness in daily life. Belonging to a *global church* where we can both give and receive, as children of the same heavenly Father.

If evangelicals are 'good news' people, I seek to be a 'good news' bishop, bringing joy and confident faith to this role played out across church and society.

How do you navigate being an evangelical bishop, working in a broad church?

Building relationships is essential. I seek to listen well, recognize the image of God within, respect deeply held convictions, use language carefully, pray with and for those from whom I differ, while acknowledging my own flaws and frailty. Learning to disagree well and exercise a ministry of reconciliation lies at the heart of the gospel and it has not always been our strength. While working for the 'highest possible degree of communion', as expressed in the five guiding principles, we also must recognize that we are living in testing times. Our society is increasingly polarized and social media has a significant impact (not always for good) on the ways we communicate with one another. These challenges are real, but they are a key to our witness to the person and work of Jesus. I believe that the Holy Spirit of God is inviting us into a new era, as a church in which we are known for our listening and our loving before anything else. We still have deeply held convictions, but the way we live them is the first thing people see and it matters greatly.

What new opportunities does a move to episcopacy bring?

This role brings significant gospel opportunity, wide scope for pastoral encouragement, the chance to develop leaders for the future and the opportunity to offer specialisms locally and nationally. It is immensely complex and challenging but, equally, rewarding and stimulating. If you feel called to work on a wider canvas, play your part and are motivated by seeing others reach their potential under God, then it may be right to consider this call.

Do also wrestle with the question of personal ambition: it needs attention and no position will address the deeper need within, only God can do that. We need humble ministers who love God and people in every part of the church's life and leadership.

How can evangelicals in a diocese best support their bishops?

I am blessed to be in a supportive diocese with very able ministers, both lay and ordained. My top tips include these.

- **Encouragement** building one another up in love includes the bishops – we are human, too, and genuine encouragement enlarges the heart.
- **Pray for us** The work is complex and challenging, though rewarding, so prayer for wisdom is appreciated.
- **Play your part** Go to chapter meetings, study days and gathered worship opportunities. Attend the synod, get involved in committees, so you can help, by your presence, to influence for good, and keep mission at the heart of everything.
- **Promote the kingdom** Find ways to bless what is happening in the diocese and encourage others by being a positive influence. Think ecumenically; ask, 'Where are we better together?'
- **Preach the gospel** and help people come to know Jesus for themselves – nothing is more important than that.
- **Communicate** If you have questions or concerns, tell us. Don't huddle in groups behind the scenes, tell us what is on your hearts and minds so we can hear, weigh, test and pray with you. Do also meet with others to encourage and build up – that is part of being the church!
- **Provide** Encourage generosity, preach about giving and don't be afraid to talk finances. Seek help and challenge us about this where you have questions.
- **Whatever is good . . . think on these things** Commit to hope for the church, now and always.

Julian Henderson – Diocesan Bishop, Blackburn

Do we need to reimagine the ancient office of bishop for the modern world?

In any church, there has to be proper oversight to teach and protect sound doctrine, administer appropriate discipline and lead the people of God in prayer and mission.

I don't think we need to reimagine the role but, rather, ensure godly men and women are appointed.

What does it mean for you to be an 'evangelical' bishop?

My main focus in the past eight years has been to try to put the Bible back into a place of authority within the diocese and the Church of England. Tradition, reason and now 'lived experience' are all challenging the supreme authority of Scripture in determining what we believe about God, salvation and godly living. The 'Living in love and faith' process is not so much about relationships and marriage but how we determine these important matters and doctrines.

How do you navigate being an evangelical bishop, working in a broad church?

It is not easy to maintain a clear evangelical stance in the public arena of a diverse diocese, as that immediately sidelines those who hold a different view. My involvement in 'The beautiful story' (a video by the Church of England Evangelical Council) is a case in point. I have had to work hard at maintaining good relationships across the board in the diocese, when it is known that I hold a view which is deeply unpopular for some and contrary to the prevailing culture of the day. Being open about my convictions, rather than maintaining silence or offering a bland, watered-down set of views, is how I have navigated being part of a broad church and the House of Bishops. And I seem to be tolerated and accepted for holding my views. I have chaired the diverse North West Bishops group for eight years and am asked to chair meetings of the House of Bishops.

What new opportunities does a move to episcopacy bring?

It has been a huge privilege to serve as a diocesan bishop, guiding and steering a diocese into a more biblical pattern of being and doing, changing the culture. One of the key advantages is the opportunity to build a team and make appointments that will further the mission of the church.

But plenty of compromises have to be made, which some evangelicals might struggle with. My view is that if I am able to teach the Bible message and preach the gospel, then I will wear anything and so on. I have drawn the line at the Angelus!!

How can evangelicals in a diocese best support their bishops?

The best support is affirming notes, emails and prayer. I meet with the Diocesan Evangelical Fellowship (DEF) a couple of times a year, as well as the ReNew subset. Also willingness by evangelicals in the diocese to get involved in committees and meetings of Bishop's Council, Synod, etc, the stuff many try to avoid, is a huge blessing and means I can turn to others in those settings for a steer, rather than always having to give it myself.

Rod Thomas – Episcopal Visitor, Maidstone

Do we need to reimagine the ancient office of bishop for the modern world?

The practical outworking of the office of bishop is dependent, first and foremost, on an understanding of the Bible's teaching on oversight of the church. If we take Timothy and Titus as 'proto-bishops' in the early church (that is, ones sent by the apostles, with their authority, in order to address issues affecting a number of churches), then the question is, 'How do we best apply the role that we see there to our modern conditions?' In addition, we are not starting from a blank sheet, so we need to take into account our history and legal structure as well. This being so, I believe that the questions we need to ask are, 'How best can the office of bishop achieve the biblical ideals of teaching responsibility, safeguarding apostolic doctrine, accountability, proper management of the church's affairs, representation of the church to the wider world and the provision of appropriate pastoral guidance to those experiencing particular need?'

It may be that, as a result, the number of local churches a bishop should reasonably be expected to oversee should be limited. We might also want to suggest new ways in which the different roles of diocesan and suffragan bishops are carried out (for example, giving suffragan bishops particular national responsibilities so that diocesan bishops are better able to focus on dioceses), but it is important to start from the biblical criteria, rather than seek to arrange episcopal ministry purely from the standpoint of managerial efficiency.

What does it mean for you to be an 'evangelical' bishop?

One of the distinctive aspects of evangelical bishops is their theological perspective. My hope is that I will always ask the question, 'How can I best serve the gospel and prosper the ministry of the local church in relation to the issue I am facing?' I do not wish to suggest that this concern is exclusive to evangelical bishops but, rather, that it will predominate over other concerns.

How do you navigate being an evangelical bishop, working in a broad church?

The first thing to say is that there are important advantages to being in a broad church: it helps us to see issues from different standpoints and to stop us becoming too inward-looking. Playing a part in such a church requires an ability to listen and the humility to learn from those who have drawn their conclusions from other traditions. It requires mutual respect and, sometimes, hard work to ensure that we are finding the right language to enable us to communicate with understanding and appreciation. That said, we have important contributions to make, reminding the church of the primacy of Scripture in our understanding of doctrine; emphasizing the significance of local congregational life for evangelism and discipling; articulating the work of Christ on the cross and the need for salvation; and urging the church to commit herself to making new disciples by proclaiming and seeking to exemplify the gospel.

What new opportunities does a move to episcopacy bring?

Having oversight of a large number of parishes equips bishops with a pastoral perspective that can be very helpful in enabling individual parishes to address problems. There are particular services that need to be conducted by bishops (such as confirmations) that provide unique opportunities to promote the gospel, and there is a way in which episcopal messages gain wider traction than would have been the case through ministry in a purely local parish setting.

How can evangelicals in a diocese best support their bishops?

One of the things I have most valued is the consistent prayer support that has been offered to me throughout my time as a bishop. I have been very conscious of the Lord's hand on events as a result of other people's prayers. Apart from that, the most supportive thing that evangelicals can do is to have a balanced approach to episcopacy: respecting the roles bishops have, but not overemphasizing them. Evangelicals have fairly independent mindsets (which inevitably characterizes those who believe the Reformation principle of the right to private judgement), but they sometimes find it difficult to accept episcopal decisions that directly affect them. However, when problems arise with others, they sometimes immediately assume that the solution rests entirely with the bishop when, in fact, he or she may not have the legal power to act.

Keith Sinclair – retired, Birkenhead

Do we need to reimagine the ancient office of bishop for the modern world?

Episcopacy is always in danger of being mesmerized either by antiquity or modernity. We imagine either the 'ancient office' or the 'modern world' hold the key to its efficacy. From antiquity there is the danger of elevating episcopal jurisdiction so that the bishop's jurisdiction becomes the mark of the true church; from modernity, there is the felt need to embrace contemporary models of leadership, so the models, rather than apostolic direction, begin to shape the priorities of the episcopal diary. Instead, Acts 20:28 – 'Keep watch over yourselves' – is the recurring need, both in antiquity and in modernity (as reflected in the fact that this verse shaped much of the Ordinal). The primary calling remains keeping watch over self and the community ('the flock' is the community of believers and disciples), so that self and community are led by God as Shepherd, indwelt by the Holy Spirit (who is the source of episcopal authority), as self and community are shaped by the atoning death of the Lord Jesus (the community obtained through the blood of his own Son). The modern world has not graduated from the need for this ministry. Then there were 'savage wolves' (v. 29), who, according to Paul, 'distort the truth', scattering the flock (as Jesus himself had warned in John 10:12). There were wolves then, there are wolves now.

What does it mean for you to be an 'evangelical' bishop?

To be an evangelical bishop should mean no more and no less than to be a bishop in fulfilment of the commission given and promises made at ordination. In so far as any part of that calling is forgotten or over-whelmed by other responsibilities, it is the calling of an evangelical bishop to model that calling, as it is given in the gospel, for the advance of the gospel, to be shaped by the gospel. For example, the Ordinal after the reference to Acts 20:28 mentioned, says that a bishop is to proclaim the gospel of God's kingdom and lead the people in mission. For me, to be an evangelical bishop means taking this evangelistic responsibility seriously enough to prioritize evangelistic missions in the diocese. This calling also means being a 'guardian of the faith', shaped by the holy Scriptures (which bishops say that they accept); this means intentionally teaching the doctrine of Christ as the Church of England has received it and refuting error.

How do you navigate being an evangelical bishop, working in a broad church?

In the light of the above, I think evangelical bishops should be jealous for the whole of the episcopal calling set out in the Ordinal (because it takes its cue from the apostles and prophets) and pray for wisdom and courage when they think that one or more aspects of that calling are being mar-ginalized or denied. This has always been the case; it is more acute now because there are more avowedly evangelical bishops and there is a more explicit threat to the teaching of the church, as rooted in the Bible, in relation to human identity, marriage and gender. This means that evan-gelical bishops will need grace and courage when they believe parishes and clergy, as well as dioceses and fellow bishops, are neglecting or distorting the gospel to say so, and spell out the implications of persisting in this neglect or distortion.

What new opportunities does a move to episcopacy bring?

All the opportunities of the gospel. As an Anglo-Catholic bishop said to me among those newly arriving in his diocese for an evangelistic mission (sponsored by the then Archbishop of York), 'People of the Diocese of xxx are great at putting on social events; it is up to the bishops to turn them into gospel events.' Amen, and not only for missions but also for assemblies, countless services of confirmation and baptism. Turn them into gospel events – that is, events at which the gospel is explained and an invitation to respond is given. The opportunities for keeping Scripture and the gospel front and centre in all appointments are unparalleled in the many different kinds of services bishops may be called to be present at and contribute to.

I think a good age to consider episcopal ministry would be after gaining some significant parish experience, perhaps late forties to mid-fifties. The best place to test a calling, after Scripture, is the Ordinal.

How can evangelicals in a diocese best support their bishops?

Prayer is the obvious way; sometimes everyone else is prayed for in evangelical churches except the bishop! Keeping short accounts, so, if it is thought that a bishop is not guarding the faith or refuting error, a way of respectfully expressing this can be found. Concern, prayer and the willingness to be corrected if the bishop's preaching, reporting or blogging has been misunderstood.

At this critical moment in the life of the Church of England (June 2021), evangelicals may be able to offer more support than they know, because of their commitment to gospel outreach and giving. However, such support (and challenge) has got to pass the 1 Corinthians 13 test. One can have all the marks of evangelical orthodoxy in the world, but as St Paul himself reminds us, without love they are 'nothing'.

Part 2

GOD'S PEOPLE IN GOD'S CHURCH: STORIES AND PERSPECTIVES

Introduction

THE REVEREND ADAM YOUNG

I had been studying at Wycliffe Hall for more than three years by the time I came to identify myself willingly as an 'evangelical'. It was only following my mission trip to Uganda, as part of my ministry training, that I would adopt the label. For me, the trip was a turning point in my life, faith and ministry. The influence that the East African Revival's legacy – with its focus on the power of the blood of Jesus, walking in the light and sharing testimony – had on me at this formative time helped contribute to my sense of not quite fitting in with the usual church groupings in the Church of England. Since starting my curacy in 2012, I have found myself straddling two of these groupings, with a foot planted in each: one in the charismatic, generally egalitarian, New Wine group and the other in the complementarian, generally cessationist, Church Society group. Though not a unique position, it has certainly helped to give me a unique perspective on many of the debates among evangelicals in the past ten years.

Through being in the networks for both these groupings, I've had the privilege to hear the testimony of faithful servants of the Lord from across the spectrum of evangelicalism within the Church of England. I've heard and wept at the lows and rejoiced and sung (sometimes with hands raised high, depending on context!) at the highs. It really has been a privilege and I've felt very blessed by both networks. I've also felt blessed to see the wider spectrum of evangelicalism coming closer together in the past five years as unity in the gospel has become a more central value in the face of increasing opposition to the truth of God's word.

In the past ten years, I've seen the Junior Anglican Evangelical Conference (JAEC) run by the Church Society intentionally expanding its scope to try to involve and encourage the next generation of evangelicals of every stripe. Having to leave that conference and its online community due to no longer being 'junior' will be a real sadness for me. For the past three years, I've also witnessed the growth, passion and evangelical unity of the church-planting initiative, Hull 2030, which has brought together evangelical Anglicans and non-Anglicans across the city of Hull to pray and raise the profile of church planting – the hope being to see twenty churches planted by 2030.

At both JAEC and Hull 2030, the sharing of testimony, of struggles, of ministry, of vision, of life has been central to their success. That God's church is for God's world is an evangelical conviction – we all long to see the nation (indeed, all nations) come to Christ in worship and joy. That shared conviction has led to this book, in which evangelicals from across the Church of England and other Anglican Churches have said, 'I am excited about what God is doing through the church in the world; I want to share my story and my part in God's plan.'

The first part of this book looked in depth at some of what unites us: history, faith, conviction and ecclesiology. At the end of the book is a collection of doctrinal statements that unite us all theologically. Here in the middle, though, are the stories and perspectives of the individuals who are united on these core matters. These chapters are honest stories and reflections on where those children and ministers of God find and have found themselves. They are snippets of the wider tapestry of what God's church is doing in God's world.

The voices recorded here come from across the evangelical spectrum and have faced their own challenges and joys. They each minister in a unique context and bring to that context their own unique perspectives and understandings of life and ministry. They each focus on particular issues in contemporary evangelicalism and each hold a shared hope that things have been improving and are improving in terms of evangelical unity in England, which is why they are sharing their stories.

In each of the stories the hope is that readers will be both encouraged and challenged. We should be encouraged to see God at work across evangelicalism and across a wide variety of contexts. We should be encouraged by the overcoming of challenges and the desire for gospel-centred unity among Christians. Yet we should also be challenged by that which makes for uncomfortable reading, where things have not gone smoothly or easily and real pain has been experienced. We should be challenged to strive to do more, to plant more churches, turn more ministries around, serve more faithfully where God has placed us and be more loving and united around essential doctrines in a way that doesn't compromise our deeply held beliefs on other matters.

As with any collection of testimonies and stories, we won't necessarily agree with all that we read or like it. On the one hand we might think, 'I would have done that differently' or, on the other hand, 'I wish I had done things that way.' That's OK. The key thing about these chapters that is so exciting and new is these stories are being shared together, because of unity in the gospel, from across the evangelical spectrum of the Church of England, in one place. The accuser is overcome by the blood of the Lamb and the word of their testimony (Revelation 12:11). The sharing of testimony and stories, of our lives, was a key characteristic of the East African Revival and I find it exciting to see that happening here in this book.

5

Culture shocks

THE REVEREND SAM HAIGH

Coming to faith, following Jesus

I became a Christian in 2004, when I was eighteen years old and a friend of mine invited me along to church, at St Mark's in Utley,[1] near to where I was living in Keighley, West Yorkshire. Prior to that point I hadn't been a regular churchgoer. I would have called myself a Christian, but I certainly didn't know what it looked like to follow Jesus or know very much about the Christian faith at all.

Despite that, I was quite open spiritually, so I would do things like tarot cards and other darker spiritual things, and I was happy to explore different kinds of spirituality. When my friend invited me to go to church, I had no reason to refuse the invitation, so I went. I got more than I bargained for! I met some Christians who were very nice, met some Christians who were my own age, who lived a very different life from the way I was living at the time. I was going out and drinking heavily, had come from quite a chaotic background and dabbled in recreational drugs and things like that. These Christian friends, by contrast, lived in a totally different way and that was really attractive to me.

After a few weeks of being in church and beginning to understand some of the basics of the gospel, and to see what the Christian life looked like, lived out alongside these new-Christian friends, I went home one evening after a home group meeting and lay on my bed and prayed a very simple prayer. I remember calling out to God and, at that moment, had a very tangible experience of the Holy Spirit but, having absolutely no idea who God was then, very little understanding of what was happening. I was just aware of something that was very transformational, in terms of encounter.

I had a very physical feeling of being washed, being cleansed, a sort of weightlessness, which freaked me out as an eighteen-year-old, but was an undeniable experience of the Holy Spirit. This led to a radical life change, and things have not been the same since.

> I have been crucified with Christ and I no longer live, but Christ lives in me. The life I now live in the body, I live by faith in the Son of God, who loved me and gave himself for me.
> (Galatians 2:20)

Quite quickly after becoming a Christian, I felt a sense of call, a sense of excitement at the idea of serving God full time in some sort of capacity. At the time, I was working as a mechanic. I'd left school at sixteen, I had one GCSE and my job was nice, but it wasn't particularly fulfilling. My new-found faith was something that I was incredibly excited about. I wanted to share my faith with my friends, my work colleagues, the people around me, and I noticed that at a church we had a vicar who did just that, but in a full-time capacity.

About six months after becoming a Christian, I went to Soul Survivor, at Shepton Mallet, with Mike Pilavachi and all the rest. A group of us, from the church I was at then, went down there – maybe fifteen of us. I went to a seminar called 'Getting collared', by Frog Orr-Ewing,[2] and it was the first time I'd really heard what a vicar does outside Sundays. It was also the first time, I guess, that I was awakened to the incredible opportunities for the gospel within ordained ministry.

Having had a fantastic week and that seminar still on my mind, I came back from Soul Survivor and went to talk to my vicar. He was very gracious and gave me opportunities to serve, over the course of about a year, in youth groups and I went on to lead a group, a sort of young adults house group, which grew and flourished. I also had the opportunity to preach at a midweek service and at Sunday services. My vicar was very good at getting alongside me, giving me opportunities to explore my calling, pointing me to different avenues and the diocesan director of ordinands (DDO) in West Yorkshire.

It often surprises people that, as a bus mechanic with one GCSE, I ended up studying at the University of Cambridge. It had taken me two years to get to a Bishops' Advisory Panel (BAP), confirming the calling and just having more experience, time to develop and be discipled as a Christian, which was very valuable. I was accepted for a course of training for ministry and went off to Ridley Hall in Cambridge in 2008. It was quite a culture shock.

Personally, academic achievement wasn't something that I had ever sought before. I'd never excelled particularly in academic terms. I had just wanted to leave school and get myself a job. To find myself in Cambridge, then, where people were cycling around with top hats on and going off to balls and galas and so on, was quite alien to me.

The first year, particularly, was quite a difficult time, in terms of getting up to speed with things such as writing essays. I couldn't actually remember ever writing an essay at school! I ended up absolutely loving it, though and I got a 2.1 by the end of my time at Ridley, which was great. I had a great time at Cambridge, which I look back on as some of the golden years of my life.

At this point in my story my wife, Hannah, needs to be introduced! Hannah and I met when I first went to church, and we started dating a few weeks after I became a Christian. She was sixteen and I was eighteen. A year later, we got engaged and, a year after that, we got married, so we've kind of grown up together, in the sense that our young adult lives were quite intertwined. She comes from a believing family, a very different background from mine. My upbringing was quite chaotic. My dad was never on the scene, it was just me, my mum, my brother and my sister. We moved houses quite a lot and childhood was marked by a lot of other change, a lot of chaos, a lot of drinking, a lot of uncertainty.

To meet Hannah's family, who, by contrast, were committed Christians, well-heeled middle-class people, was another culture shock. Seeing these very stable, very loving, very hospitable, just all-round lovely people, a Christian family, all having this shared faith in Jesus that they took really seriously, had quite an impact on me as a person. To be welcomed into that was hugely beneficial, has shaped me and had a huge positive influence on the way that we do family now ourselves, many years later, with our five kids.

Discovering expository Bible teaching

When I was at Ridley, I went to what might be called a fairly conservative evangelical church – Christ Church Cambridge, where Steve Midgley is one of its senior ministers.[3] That was my placement while I was at college, for three years, and the thing that had the most impact on me at that time was being introduced to expository Bible teaching. I remember sitting down with Steve in his study when I was planning a sermon on Matthew 24:11–26, and him asking me which theological concept most related to Barabbas being released and Jesus being condemned. I didn't really have an answer and I didn't really know what he was trying to get at.

What Steve pointed out to me was that Matthew, in his Gospel, is attempting to show us how the guilty Barabbas goes free, while the innocent Jesus is condemned, which is a very clear picture of substitutionary atonement. It was as if a lightbulb went on and I understood that the Bible wasn't a set of stories put together in a random fashion. Here, Matthew was attempting to communicate something in the way that he wrote down his story, and I found that a really powerful experience.

My theology and my trust in the Bible as being authoritative really deepened at that time and was important for me at Ridley. After training, I went off to St Mary's, Wootton, where Peter Ackroyd is vicar, and continued to develop the practice I'd learnt of teaching the Bible in a systematic way, one that allows the Bible to speak for itself, week in week out. It was another very significant time and helped shape me in a way that valued and honoured the Bible and allowed it to speak for itself, which is something that's really precious to me.

These foundations have informed how I understand what it means to be an evangelical. If I was trying to define what an evangelical is, it would come down to something about the authority of Scripture and the underlying belief that the Bible is the primary way that God speaks to us, and its purpose is to point us to Jesus, the Jesus we read about in the Scriptures. So I think, for me, that is what being an evangelical is all about.

Across tribes – integrating the charismatic tradition

Hannah and I really valued our time at Christ Church Cambridge and St Mary's, Wooton, both in the more conservative evangelical tradition. Through reading the Bible and grappling with various texts, we couldn't escape the fact that, actually, often in the Bible there are miraculous encounters with Jesus, that healings take place and we are to be both hearers and doers of the Word of God (James 1:22–25).

Paul writes in 1 Corinthians 4:20 that, 'the kingdom of God is not a matter of talk but of power', which resonates with my experience of my conversion. This is also integral to Hannah's spirituality, as she comes from a much more charismatic, free evangelical independent church than me. This, in fact, was a cause of tension in our marriage – we argued a lot about theology and practice! I definitely went in a very non-charismatic direction, mainly because I'd had an encounter at a Soul Survivor event that had freaked me out a little bit, so I pushed back on the charismatic expressions of church and pursued a more conservative, more logical, theological approach.

As well as the encounter at my conversion, we'd received what I would describe as a prophetic word when we first got married. Someone we trusted had suggested that God would bring us to a place where we were singing off the same hymn-sheet and the story of our marriage has been one of God bringing us to a place where we've both learnt from our time in Cambridge and then in Bedfordshire. There is an emphasis on teaching the Bible, but also on ministry in the power of the Holy Spirit through the Holy Trinity Brompton (HTB) network and Soul Survivor, and via Hannah's background as well.

In reading the Scriptures, there developed this conviction that there was an absence, in our own ministry and spirituality, of the expectation that God could heal, God could speak, God could show up and do the unexpected. Hannah and I both began to feel strongly that, after curacy, we wanted to step out into a more charismatic context. That prompted us to apply for jobs in churches that were more charismatic than the ones we'd been part of so far, wanting to take the best of what we'd learnt and valued from the conservative evangelical world into a charismatic context to see how it would work.

I got a job as an associate vicar in north London, at a group of three churches in Tollington parish, in Holloway, near Islington. It was a great opportunity for Hannah and I to step out and exercise a ministry that was in both Word and Spirit. That translated into preaching books of the Bible all the way through, a topical series here and there, but intending to preach the whole counsel of God. We also pursued an emphasis on people responding to the Word in prayer ministry and prayer meetings and having more space, as it were, for the Holy Spirit to show up, to speak and do the unexpected.

We spent three-and-a-bit years in Tollington. Sandy Millar planted in Tollington after he left HTB and retired, and after our time there we spent nearly eighteen months at HTB. I went there with going to Preston in mind. When I got in touch with HTB during my time at Tollington, I said that we'd love to church plant. We didn't have a specific geographical area in mind – our families are spread all over – so we were happy to try anything. HTB are talking to dioceses all the time, so there were a couple of opportunities, one of which was Preston. Being from the North with a working-class background, Preston was a great fit.

We came up to Preston in 2017, walked around the church building, around the city, met some people from the diocese and prayed hard about it. We felt a real sense of call, a sense of excitement, at being in Preston, at the heart of Preston, knowing that it has some amazing churches, doing some fantastic work, but also that there was definitely a gap in the market, as it were, for a more charismatic Anglican church.

Lessons from HTB

Now to him who is able to do immeasurably more than all we ask or imagine, according to his power that is at work within us.
(Ephesians 3:20)

I think what I learnt was that a lot more is possible than we think. I guess I saw the outworking of that, I saw that in practice. I think hearing the story of HTB and how it has transformed from where it was in the 1980s to how it is today had a huge impact. It is a story of God's provision, but also of a church that grew and gave away its resources and people again and again, and how that led to more growth.

I would say my biggest takeaway was a sense of excitement and an expectation that more is possible. You see that in action at HTB. It's far from perfect, by its own admission, but at the heart of the leadership is a real desire to see as many people as possible connect with the message of Jesus, to see churches grow and flourish and be revitalized – and see a significant social impact as well.

A big part of this culture is audacious faith.

I remember, I had my first encounter with that sort of audacious faith when I took a little trip to Preston and a contingent from HTB came up. One of the problems we have with our building is that there's not a great deal of space, extra space to do kids' work, so we were thinking about how we could get around that. We looked at a warehouse at the back of the church, a stone's throw away, and one of the chaps from HTB said that we could buy the warehouse.

I literally laughed out loud, but he was being deadly serious, because they'd seen God do that kind of stuff over and over again, to provide where there is a gap. That audacious expectation – that God can and will provide – was something that I really soaked up at HTB. That's a real part of its DNA.

Another part of its DNA is a real heart for the gospel; the urgency of the gospel is apparent. Nicky Gumbel, the vicar, and the rest of the leadership team do a great job of keeping the emphasis on the newcomer, on the non-Christian, and making sure that, in terms of financial and time resources, the general focus, everything is weighted towards them. All is subordinated to the goal of introducing people to the person of Jesus. The way you see that is through the Alpha course, and I think, having led groups on the course there, you get to understand that this is a primary thing for them.

The urgency of the gospel – the Alpha course today

Going to HTB I had my questions as to whether or not the Alpha course was still effective – particularly the way it was in the 1990s and the early

2000s. In my experience in north London, we ran it once a year and maybe twenty or thirty would come, which made for a good course, but we never really broke through that to increase the numbers. During my time at HTB, however, seeing how the course works when it's done well was something that changed my mind about that.

There's a sense in which Alpha is doing several things at once. It recognizes that, for many people, evangelism is not just a one-off event. Alpha creates a process in which a seeker is able to link to a process of being introduced to the person of Jesus, step by step, over a long time period. Leadership development is also built into it, so, theoretically, someone who joins Alpha as a seeker or non-Christian and comes to faith, or really enjoys it, would be invited to come back on the next course as a helper. Then, they are introduced to leadership responsibility from the beginning of their faith journey, but also their time in an evangelistic setting is prolonged as they are invited back.

I think that understanding the approach taken with Alpha has helped me to see its effectiveness. Indeed, during my time there, the course would have had more than 1,000 people attend, and a reasonable number of those were Christians being introduced to the core culture of the church. It certainly wasn't a waste of time them being on the course, being introduced to the idea that evangelism is of primary importance in the life of a church, and seeing the way in which people came to faith, then have a zeal to invite friends along. Seeing the way in which the Alpha course grew and then snowballed was really inspiring.

HTB and the evangelical tribes

The HTB network is essentially an evangelical and evangelistic movement, so I think there is crossover between what it is doing and any church or movement that prioritizes teaching the Bible, holds the Bible as the authoritative word of God, sees the need for conversion, the urgency of the gospel and the sufficiency of Jesus. In theology, it has a lot in common with any other evangelical movement, though its practice is quite distinct from them, more akin to that of the New Wine movement.

HTB is quite clearly influenced by John Wimber and his ministry in the early 1990s and, therefore, takes on that character in terms of its prayer ministry and charismatic experiences.[4] Potentially, the thing that distinguishes it from New Wine is the evangelistic emphasis, because that becomes the primary driver. I think there are three primary emphases in any Sunday service: first, it's formational, the emphasis being on teaching the saints, equipping them for works of ministry, and the church is very much geared towards equipping Christians to live out their Christian life; second, it's potentially experiential, so you are wanting to invite people to a Sunday service so that they can encounter the person of the Holy Spirit and have a personal experience that spurs them on so that they can live their lives more faithfully; potentially third, it's evangelism that is the primary driver in your Sunday service. The last of these is what HTB does. Its primary driver, I'd say, is evangelism.

I see the HTB model fitting in among other churches easily and not competitively (New Wine as broadly more experiential, Con-Evo as more formational). I can only speak from our experience of this in Preston, but we've been very keen to emphasize that we are a church for people who don't go to church. At the core of this church is a group of very focused Jesus followers involved in their own discipleship but that group is not interested in recruiting other Christians with discipleship or courses or meaty teaching per se. Although we would hope that the teaching has meaty substance, we are essentially a church for those who don't go to church.

Church planting and mission

HTB started planting churches in London in the 1980s, and was very successful at doing so into either closed or very small churches within London, to revitalize them, give them a new lease of life.[5] Then, in 2009, Archie Coates (now the Vicar Designate, HTB)[6] left and took a team of about thirty-five to St Peter's Brighton. There is now a Sunday attendance there of around 800, with probably about 1,400 who would call St Peter's their church. In many ways, that was a barrier-breaking moment. HTB had been planting in London, it had been relatively successful at revitalizing churches, making them more missional, which was great, but for the first time this had been tried outside London, and it had worked.

Preston is the twentieth plant outside London by HTB and it is being deliberately planted as a 'resource church'. The vision is that a resource church resources the wider deanery and the wider diocese, and the primary way we do that is through church planting. The diocese has designated funding for a pipeline of curates, who will spend two or three years with us. The idea is that they will, like we did, soak up some of the missionary zeal, then, in three years' time, rather than doing a traditional curacy, where they learn all the ropes, they will go off with a group of people and plant a church, in a new housing estate, in the same city or beyond, another part of the diocese or region. That's the primary way in which we are a resource church.

The second way in which we resource is through expertise. The team we have and the teams that go out have lots to offer in terms of training around the Alpha course. We have a couple of youth work experts, who will be a real asset to this diocese in terms of training and sharing wisdom and upskilling people.

A common question is, where do the resources come from? Is it just a clever managerial strategy cooked up in the higher echelons of the Church of England? No, I think it's biblical – a biblical strategy. I see Paul in his missionary journeys going to very strategic cities to plant a church that goes on to plant other churches and be very influential in that city. So I see what HTB is doing in partnership with many dioceses as a model that has been replicated all over the world. It's not a new idea. I see it as a biblical idea, following the example of Paul.

The story of Preston Minster

For HTB to plant into any area, they need to be invited to do so by a bishop. That invitation came, in around 2016, from Bishop Philip North, at which time they began to look for a leader to head it up. Bishop Philip, the then Archdeacon Michael Everitt and the previous incumbent met and discussed the idea of Preston receiving this church plant, to prepare and smooth the way. They consulted extensively with the existing congregation, the diocese, other churches, local stakeholders and the free churches that might be particularly affected by the arrival of an HTB church plant.

In this way, the diocese did a fantastic job of preparing. People felt that they understood what was happening. Preston Minster was already a united parish, with St Georges, prior to us arriving, and both churches were run by one incumbent who was Anglo-Catholic, so the tradition of both churches was Anglo-Catholic. Instead of dividing the parish to form two, Bishop Philip hoped that this would still be somewhere where the Anglo-Catholic presence has a place in the city. It can go on to learn from the missionary zeal of HTB and become, in a sense, a centre of catholic evangelism, not just for the diocese but also for the region as well. It's an important aspect of the project.

We can work together because we have a shared high Christology – a high view of Jesus and his death on the cross, and the need to invite others to respond to that. We see these described and enshrined in the Thirty-nine Articles of Religion, which is part of the reason I am proud to identify as an Anglican (see Appendix 1).

The essence of Anglicanism

The essence of Anglicanism is given in the Thirty-nine Articles of Religion. Article 19 says that the church is a place where the pure word of God is preached and the sacraments are celebrated. For me, that is at the core of what being an Anglican is all about. It's a place where the Bible is taught and the sacraments are celebrated.

While an increasing number of evangelicals are looking with concern and scepticism at the Church of England, I still believe that there is tons of potential here. My reasons for that go to the heart of Anglican history and theology.

First, we have the heritage assets. While, in many ways, it is very frustrating to have these ancient buildings in great locations that cost thousands to keep each year, nonetheless, non-Christians still walk into many of them off the street, cold, without any faith, simply because of the buildings and their locations. I also believe that there is a sense of safety that the established church engenders. In many ways, what we are trying to do in the Minster is breathe life into something very old – that is, the physical space is ancient. It's been a Christian site for well over a thousand years, and that is grounding and brings with it a sense of our heritage. In a world of constant change and instant gratification, there is something incredibly appealing about these buildings. They've stood the test of time and are a sort of prophetic symbol of God's presence in our towns, cities and villages throughout the generations. There is something powerful about the space.

We are in a privileged position, in the Church of England, particularly in Lancashire, where Christendom clings on. People who are not familiar with the church feel comfortable enough to regularly walk into its buildings. They don't go to church, but it's their parish church that they don't go to.

Second, there is the fact that it is established. Because it is the Church of England, people can feel reassured that it's not a cult! There's a certain legitimacy that comes with it, even today. I became a Christian at eighteen with no church background and a massive part of it for me was that it was Church of England, so it wasn't too weird. There's something about the buildings and the institution that almost function as handlebars for non-Christians taking steps towards faith in Jesus.

I think it's really important that the Church of England holds on to its orthodoxy and the trappings of the Thirty-Nine Articles of Religion, the Book of Common Prayer, *Common Worship*, the structure of bishops, priests and deacons. It all gives, from a leadership and from an ordained perspective, a sense of connectedness to the wider church, which I personally really value. Our doctrine is articulated in these liturgies. It all provides a framework within which we can flourish. In our parish, we represent both evangelical and Anglo-Catholic spiritualities and we try to represent the phrase 'generous orthodoxy'. I don't mean that in the way Brian McLaren meant it but, rather, as orthodoxy with a very clear boundary of believing that the Bible is the primary authority, there are a number of primary issues around the cross and the necessity of people hearing and responding to the gospel, and a number of primary issues around who the person of Jesus is – they're absolute red lines. Within that, however, there are several secondary issues we can agree to disagree on, in order to focus on the primary goal of introducing people to Jesus.

The future of Anglicanism

I'm really excited about the potential of the institution of the church, which could be quite stale, to have new life breathed into it. I believe that there is a move of God across England, for the many churches that have dwindled, the many that have died, closed, the many that have become ineffective. I'm very excited about those churches and the institution they represent coming back to life with a fresh move of the Holy Spirit and evangelistic zeal.

I would advise people in my youthful situation to explore ordination in the Church of England at the earliest possible opportunity. I think the position of the Church of England in the nation and society is unmatched by any other denomination, as it is uniquely positioned to reach a much bigger number of people for the gospel.

I say this with full awareness of some of the storm clouds coming our way. There are challenges to our orthodoxy, which I think is probably the biggest concern for evangelical ministers – the sense that the church could potentially drift into heresy or error or compromise. Personally, at the moment, I feel very confident that the church is a broad church: it's very clear on what it does and doesn't believe when it comes to the major issues.

Another of my concerns is that the Church of England moves into areas of moral and theological compromise, such as adopting forms of blessing for same sex-marriages and so on. Bearing in mind the fate of other mainstream denominations, the Episcopal Church in the USA and the church in Canada, I think that would be to its detriment. For me, it's quite clear to see that the progressive agenda does not in any way tally with church growth.[7]

We do the gospel a disservice when we adapt what God has clearly said in Scripture by adopting an agenda that is not God's agenda but the world's agenda. I'd be very concerned if I saw the Church of England move in a direction that would attempt to overturn a strongly held belief in what marriage is and has been, what's good for human flourishing. For me, that's another one of the storm clouds on the horizon.

In the middle of that storm, though, I see incredible opportunities emerging all over England for churches to unite in the gospel, new churches to spring up and new life. At HTB, we'd often talk about closed churches being monuments to a long-forgotten king. We would imagine people walking past, saying that the king is dead. As we reopen these church buildings, they become not symbols of decline or death but, instead, symbols of the resurrection.

Hannah and I represent two different spiritualities – she is much more charismatic in her faith and I am more conservative in mine – but we really value both. I think that what's really sad, as we look across England at both our networks, HTB, New Wine and other more conservative churches and networks (such as St Helen's Bishopsgate and the Church Society), we see almost what R. T. Kendall calls 'a great divorce' of word and spirit:

Readers of *Holy Fire* will recall my view that there has been a silent divorce in the church, generally speaking, between the Word and the Spirit. When there is a divorce, sometimes the children stay with the mother, sometimes with the father. In the divorce between the Word and the Spirit you have those on the Word side and those on the Spirit side.

Those on the Word side emphasize earnestly contending for the faith once delivered to the saints, sound teaching, expository preaching, and a return to rediscovery of justification by faith and the sovereignty of God (as taught by Martin Luther, John Calvin, and Jonathan Edwards). What is wrong with that emphasis? Nothing. It is exactly right.

Those on the Spirit side believe that the honour of God's name will not be restored until we get back to the Book of Acts where there were signs, wonders, and miracles – gifts of the Spirit in operation – and where prayer meetings resulted in places being shaken. If you got into Peter's shadow, you were healed; if you lied to the Holy Spirit, you were struck dead. What is wrong with this emphasis? Nothing. It is exactly right. The problem is, it seems to be one or the other – throughout much of the world.

When the Word and Spirit come together at an optimum level – as in Acts 2 – the simultaneous combination will result in spontaneous combustion.[8]

Of course, none of us intentionally seeks to emphasize this divide, but I think there's an incredible amount of missional energy that the church could tap in to by working together with evangelicals of different flavours. Imagine a church unleashed!

I also think that conservatives have loads to learn from charismatics and charismatics have loads to learn from conservatives – the language doesn't matter. Evangelical Anglicanism, for me, is Word, Spirit and sacrament. One thing that I'm super-excited about, therefore, is seeing tribal lines being broken down, so I've been excited by a number of things that have been happening, such as the Junior Anglican Evangelical Conferences (JAEC) that have happened through the Church Society, churches outside and within the Church of England that hold the tension between different groups, such as Newfrontiers. I'm really excited about evangelicals of all flavours working together for increased evangelistic effectiveness.

Notes

1 St Mark's is now a part of Keighley Shared Church (see: <https://keighleyparish.org/our-churches>, accessed December 2021).

2 F. Orr-Ewing is now Rector of Latimer Church (see: <https://latimerchurch.org>, accessed December 2021).

3 For more about Christ Church Cambridge, see its excellent website (at: <www.christchurchcambridge.org.uk/whos-who>, accessed December 2021).

4 S. Millar has reflected on this at length. (An adapted, shortened piece on this subject is S. Millar, 'Remembering John Wimber', Vineyard Churches, 10 August 2012, available online at: <www.vineyardchurches.org.uk/articles/remembering-john-wimber>, accessed December 2021.)

5 For more, see 'London churches', under 'Our church network' on HTB's website (at: <www.htb.org/network>, accessed December 2021).

6 Diocese of London, 'New vicar chosen for Holy Trinity Brompton', Diocese of London, 5 December 2021 (available online at: <www.london.anglican.org/articles/new-vicar-chosen-for-holy-trinity-brompton>, accessed January 2022).

7 Further exploration of this subject is beyond the scope of this chapter, but one example of a discussion of this topic can be found in an article by H. Sherwood, 'Literal interpretation of Bible "helps increase church attendance"', The Guardian, 17 November 2016 (available online at:

<www.theguardian.com/world/2016/nov/17/literal-interpretation-of-bible-helps-increase-church-attendance>, accessed December 2021).

8 R. T. Kendall, *Prepare Your Heart for the Midnight Cry* (London: SPCK, 2016) pp. 7–8.

6

Faithful from the fringe

THE REVEREND CHARLES LAMONT

I was brought up in one of those fringe families that the Church of England so happily attracts – we went to church when it worked for us on a weekend and not when it didn't. It was like a second or third option throughout my childhood, until we moved to Norwich. We hadn't found a church, because that's what fringe families do – they move and don't find a church and fall away – but I had a saxophone teacher at school who was a Christian. I told him that I was a Christian (I was fourteen) and he said, 'Oh, what church?' I said, 'Um, I'm not going to one at the moment', and he said, 'Why don't you try out the one I go to, Holy Trinity Norwich?' Naturally, I took the whole family there on Sunday, but I got the church wrong, so we went to a Quaker Friends meeting house, which didn't do my family any favours in terms of trying to get them to go to church! Then, the week after, we found the right church and we went there . . . and we stayed.

I was taught the Bible there, and part of that was an ongoing robust discussion with the youth worker there at the time, David Thornton. I was deeply entrenched in progressive liberalism and socialism from my family's background, so didn't understand why the Bible wouldn't allow people to be people. That is, until I worked out that we weren't called to be people, we are called to be Godly, and that is a different type of person.

The then vicar there read the Bible with me weekly – and I gave my life to Jesus when I worked out that I had to make a choice: I couldn't just live the life I wanted to live with the ideas that I thought were great; I had to direct myself to the Lord. So that was my journey to faith.

The Bible had not been important in my earlier churchgoing years, because the church we went to then did not put one in front of me. In our life as a fringe family, it wasn't a thing. When we moved to Holy Trinity

Norwich, though, it was *the* way to see who God is. As I was presented with the gospel, presented with the Scriptures, I came to an understanding that this is how God has communicated with humanity all this time. It is his Word so, in it is everything . . . along with prayer. That is, prayer and worship – and by 'worship' I mean in the form of the lifestyle of a Christian, as opposed to the music of a Christian. I am, though, deeply interested in music, because of my generation.

The fundamental thing I learnt from these experiences was that, along with prayer, the Bible is *the* way to understand who God is, so it is deeply important. Growing through getting to know it, I decided to go and read theology at university to increase my understanding.

I wanted to see what academia said about the Bible. I wanted to see what the world thought of it as an historical book. Alongside it, I purposely read and purposely sought out discipleship books and ones on psychology. I was mentored all the way through the secular reading required on a Theology degree course, and read discipleship books all the way through as well, to counterbalance anything that wasn't claiming to be the divinely inspired Word of God. That both helped and worked. I decided to do this because people were looking at the Bible with all sorts of views. At the time, I wanted to pick – I did pick – a university that had a Christian faculty or, at least, a predominantly Christian faculty, which is why I ended up at Nottingham.

That was a great time. I learnt to look at the Bible from a wider viewpoint and then home in on what it is if it isn't the Word of God, and how he's done that, how he's used humanity to create this piece of communication. As a result, now the Bible is central in my ministry.

I am an evangelical, I believe that there is good news and it has been presented through the written Word of God. I believe that it is there to train humans in godliness and holiness, and we then take the good news out to the world. It's central to everything we do. We will not gather without opening the Bible, to read or be taught from, and it is our lifeblood. Every time we do it, we find something it has to teach us, challenge us and train us. That word, 'training', is a biblical word, isn't it? It is one that we often dismiss and replace with 'discipleship', which is a fine word, but it doesn't, I think, speak to us in the same way as the word 'training'. There is an expectation that we, as Christians, are trained in the way of the Lord, which means, bit by bit, getting better; bit by bit, lifting heavier weights; bit by bit dedicating ourselves to a life of holiness so we see the kingdom clearly. Still dimly, in a glass darkly, but we see it more clearly.

One of the things that I'm quite interested in is the calling to the priest-hood. I don't know whether it is the charismatic tradition or the catholic tradition within the Church of England that loves the idea of it, but I wonder if it's possibly both: the accidental mediation the catholics like to bring into the Church of England or the charismatic 'the holy spirit has a special anointing on your life for the priesthood' idea. They end up quite similar in standing, I find, even though the language used by them is very different. I wanted to go into church ministry, but I didn't want to be the incumbent of a church. I didn't want eldership. I wanted to do youth work or missionary work and, as I put it, do the fun side of Christianity before I settled down to do the boring church side.

My vicar at Norwich, Alan Strange, said, 'Well, why don't you get ordained first and *then* do all the fun stuff.' He challenged me to get ordained, prove my worth and be trained for ministry. So I said, 'All right, then, why do you think I should do that?' He told me what characteristics a leader should have, according to the Bible, and said, 'I think you are nowhere near there, but you can move there and you have the desire to be there, so let's work on that. I'll send off a letter to the bishop and we'll see what happens.'

He duly sent a letter at Christmas, the first year I was at university (2009), and by April in my third year (2012), I was through. I went to lots of interviews and said that I could see myself doing this at some point, I could see myself doing all sorts of things – school chaplaincy, missionary work or youth work. I also told them the truth – about my growing love for Christ and my growing love for serving his church – and I got through. There were no scary bits for me, although there was some preparation involved, but, standard for me, not a lot, and that's how I got through.

Formal training begins – on the fringes of a broad college

I wanted to train at Oak Hill, as I count it as *the* place to be trained in the ministry of the Word, which I think is the most important thing in church leadership – and that also means pastoral care, by the way, compared to all other church colleges out there. However, I was told by my diocesan director of ordinands (DDO) that I would struggle to get a job in the Diocese of Norwich if I went to Oak Hill, which was quite well known.

This brings us full circle to my eighteen-year-old self saying, 'I don't want to be a vicar, I want to do the fun stuff in church, I want to do missionary work, I want to do youth work, I want to do whatever.' This translated into not being willing to be bracketed as being from a particular wing of the church, so my heart started to grow for churches that aren't preaching the gospel, churches that have a great missionary position, geographically, socially or institutionally, ones we could preach the gospel in and see lives saved for Christ. Also, churches that could be turned around to be gospel ministries. With this in mind, I discerned that the best route was to go to a broad college.

From my perspective, at the time, this meant that I considered Ridley Hall in Cambridge, St John's College in Nottingham and Wycliffe Hall in Oxford. As I was already serving in a ministry in Nottingham, I had friends there and was very involved with St Nic's Church, I stayed there. I might not trust the training, so I might as well carry on with the ministry – and that's what I did. I carried on with ministry all the way through St John's, at times struggling with that, because certain staff at St John's wanted to stop me doing that all the time. My experience at St John's was challenging, as, on the one hand, I perceived that I was being asked to stop doing ministry, and, on the other hand, because of the type and quality of training I was receiving. I sought a different level of mentorship and a different life outside. A lot of that was provided by St Nic's, a lot by other church leaders, and books. So I carried on, got through my course at St John's and then looked for a curacy.

A curacy – on the fringes of the M25

During my diaconate year and my priestly year, my wife Hannah was working in London, so we looked around London for a broad church for a curacy, because defining myself as conservative that early on would define my future ministry. As I didn't go to Oak Hill and I didn't have any particular network background, I wasn't known, so I couldn't get a curacy via those routes. I was, for a time, exploring a curacy just outside Nottingham, but the reality was, all looked good until they said, 'Hang on a minute, there's no paper trail.' That's dangerous because my CV, as far as that point in my life was concerned, was that I'd trained at St John's College and had no particular history before that, so it is difficult for many churches to take a punt on a person with that sort of background. I ended up in a broad curacy, which was great because there was absolutely no training there, so I was let loose on quite a large parish, with quite a large number of worshippers (460 on the roll) and could carve out my own ministry. Essentially, I focused on one-to-one Bible reading and gospel preaching. We saw lots of people renew or come to a real faith in that situation, not supported by the incumbent but not challenged either, so we could just get through. I say 'we', as it was now me and Hannah.

We were sure that we wanted to give the younger years of our lives to revitalization at that point – the sheer need for the gospel in the UK had convinced us of that. Having then been in a curacy church with a deanery with other churches, I was on the deanery exec., the standing committee and getting involved in cathedral stuff and other churches, so I was even more convinced of this deep gospel need. I felt that this was a need in those churches that called themselves evangelical, too, because I sensed that, often, the charismatic renewal had affected these churches in such a way that their focus was on emotion and not the gospel. So that's where my heart started to go – to enable the pursuit of charismatic renewal and discipleship not as a distraction but as a good addition to the life of the church and the life of the Christian. So I started to look for that. I looked beyond the relatively comfortable broad church of my curacy and into a different kind of fringe.

Really, I wanted to be bold and take on a wider or even liberal church, so that's what I started to apply for in my third year of curacy, when I was allowed to do so. I applied for around fifteen and got interviews for eight, maybe nine or ten, and I worked out that, every single time, I was the wildcard. I was the young, fiery, unknown, completely different from the other four people picked. There were often four liberal catholics and me. It was very clear in the process that I was everybody's 'Oh, that might be a fun interview' and the bishop, or whoever the patron was, had pushed them to consider somebody who was not the norm. Obviously, being somebody who was not the norm, I didn't get any of the jobs. The response, from the patrons, normally, or else the bishops and the archdeacons, was 'You're great and, actually, you were our choice, but the parish said no.' I don't know if they say that to everybody, but they said it to me. 'You were our choice, but the parish reps said no because you are too dangerous to be in charge.'

Becoming an incumbent –
fringe to everyone, perfect for God's call

Before I'd started applying for jobs, I accidentally clicked on a Facebook link one day, for something called the Antioch Plan.[1] I didn't know what it was – there was simply a picture of the River Thames. I clicked on the picture and the wording mentioned church planting and revitalization in London. There was a bit of information, but I didn't read that, and a phone number at the bottom, so I rang the number. A man named Richard Perkins answered and I said, 'Look, I'm interested in revitalization. I'm an ordained Church of England minister, what have you got?' At the time, he was running the Co-Mission church-planting stream, but they called it revitalization as well because they were Anglican and they liked the idea of it. They hadn't had many opportunities more recently. They'd had a few opportunities about ten years ago, but none of their recent plants were Church of England at all.

In this task of revitalization, I am inspired by the words of Isaiah 61:4:

They will rebuild the ancient ruins
    and restore the places long devastated;
they will renew the ruined cities
    that have been devastated for generations.

This didn't entirely mesh with my experience. At this point, I was carrying on with making lots of job applications and we were in the three months that I was allowed to be employed by the Diocese of Guildford as a curate. I was not having success in getting a job, they didn't really know how many places I was applying for and so they started to push me. I said, 'The right thing will come up' and they said, 'We're worried about this, it won't', so we prayed.

Then I got a phone call out of the blue from a guy called Richard Coekin. He said, 'You're ordained and on the church-planting stream. I think there's a church nearby here, Raynes Park, that we might have an inroad with. I'd be really interested in talking to you.' So I went up and met Richard and, to cut a long story short, he said, 'I'm going to put your name forward for this job because there's no-one else and I don't want to lose this opportunity for the gospel.' I left and, ten minutes later, I got a phone call from the local archdeacon. He didn't tell me the name of the church, but said that there was a church looking for a candidate, how they'd tried to do other things, but they hadn't worked, and did I want to come to meet him. I said, 'Yes, fine' and met with him the next day. The previous vicar had died,[2] there were twenty-two people worshipping on a Sunday, no money and no living. They'd suspended the living of the church because there was no money and no future.

This liberal catholic parish had asked for three things in their next vicar, if they were to get one. That the vicar would:

- provide same-sex marriages;
- hold services jointly with their Muslim friends;
- not believe in the Holy Spirit.

At which point, the archdeacon said that they'd pretty much asked for three illegal things in their vicar, but they weren't going to get anything like that; they needed to change.

Then he told me the background. He and some others had gone to see people at one large London church and they'd said no because they were no longer planting in London. They'd gone to another, and they were open to it. That was given to the church as an option and they said, 'Absolutely not, we're not having evangelicals here.' They went back and the diocese, being a liberal diocese, were nice to the church and didn't force anything on them. So they'd said no twice, at which point they went to Dundonald Church and said, 'Well, what are your thoughts?' and Dundonald said, 'We'll plant, we'll take it. We'll give them a curate, we'll pay for everything, we'll put them in.' They went to the church and said, 'Look this is our option now', and they said, 'No, we'll literally chain ourselves to the building. That church is coming nowhere near here.'

That's where my ordination came in handy and so my name was put forward. I met with the diocese and they liked me, because I wasn't a typical conservative evangelical in attitude, even though I was in theology. I could get on with both Richard Coekin and with the wider church, because I am someone who can relate to people.

I had two interviews with the archdeacon, then I met with two reps of the church and, at the end of the meeting, although it was difficult, and the reps did what they weren't allowed to do and asked me particular questions about sexuality and other things, they all agreed to appoint me. The church had no choice: they were given me or nobody. I was in the room when that was said – 'This is Charlie, or no vicar.' I got the job! I was in my final month of curacy and that was how I got this place.

The reality is, I wanted to work on revitalization, but there was no church that would accept change, and no church that would accept an evangelical, and many prejudices against it. The process insisted on a diocese saying, 'We need an evangelical in this area, geographically.' It was only a liberal diocese that was bold enough to say we need balance in a deanery, so, we need an evangelical. They were also bold enough to appoint a conservative, not a broad person. That was all down to the archdeacon, who is an open charismatic evangelical. He got the trust of the bishop, and he has slowly been putting evangelicals into churches in Southwark. That's the reality.

Funded from the fringe – for mission and ministry

This post was, or used to be, a half-time post. It's all that could be afforded for the church to revitalize itself. Nobody asked me if we would be willing to take half a stipend and a house, which we would have been, as a couple, but nobody asked me that – they just tried to find the rest of the stipend, so I allowed them to go with that! They did. They went to the Good Stewards Trust, which holds a fund of money to enable richer churches to support poorer churches by giving grants and plants in the region. It was the first time the Diocese of Southwark, which is a liberal diocese, had been to the evangelical Anglican diocese and asked for funding to cover half the ministry. The trust, involving fourteen local churches, chatted and agreed to provide half the funds, with the diocese funding the rest.

This was an absolute triumph of peacemaking. An absolute triumph in terms of the diocese realizing that these guys were serious, not just taking money from us, but helping us when we are in line with their theology. That is triumphant. It is triumphant for our archdeacon, who pushed for that and came up with the idea. It is triumphant for our bishop, who humbly asked for the money. In and around that, Co-Mission is the other friend of ours, as it has supported me, continues to support me, has financed a ministry trainee, is willing to say that it wants this church to succeed and its ecumenical focus on planting is powerful for my situation here. People from the free Church of England, Baptist, Anglican and others have come together and said, 'We want you to win because you are gospel-focused.' That is extraordinary, and has given me a lot of strength to bring this into being. Otherwise, on my own, it would have been deeply, deeply lonely and I don't think that we would have got as far as we can do now.

There are a couple of things that show a church is a living church. One is its finances; the other is the people count. No-one really knows how many people that is, but more than fifty is a living church, I would say. Financially, we are nowhere near. The diocese says about £75,000 is needed to be able to afford our own vicar. We're not there yet.

It's almost three years since we started and what it looks like, what it looked like from the beginning, is that the key thing is being genuine with the church. Being open and honest. Loving its people as Christ loved everyone. Teaching the gospel fervently without bending it for them. The biggest issue that comes up between some of the legacy members of the congregation and me is that they hate the fact that I refuse to preach anything other than the Scriptures; they're not used to that, there were no Bibles in the church when I arrived, there was only the Lectionary on the lectern, which obviously includes bits of the Bible, but no Bibles. So I preached and still preach the Bible, exegetically – we go through passages and so on – and the members of the original congregation hate that. I also do it for twenty minutes, I don't do it for eight, which is what they'd like. That is non-negotiable.

Another bone of contention has been what I wear. I stepped out on my first week without robes on. No-one had formally told me that I needed to wear robes, so I took that liberty. It was a decision made in the vestry before the service: 'Am I going to put these robes on or not?' I walked out without them. If the congregation had asked me to put them on, I would have, but nobody did, and they didn't for four weeks. At four weeks I said, 'Well, nobody has said it, to me; when one person asks, "Are you going to wear robes?" I will reply, "Yes, I will, when it's appropriate – and do you want me to wear them every Sunday?"' 'Well, yes,' they said, 'we're used to that.' I said, 'Well, look, let's talk about that', so we talked about it at the PCC and found that most people were OK with it and some of them quite liked it, so we decided on no robes. It was a really easy win, playing an 'I'm new here' card. There have been a few of these kinds of things. I 'casualized' the formality they were used to by being a human with them all in the service. The person at the front of them during the service was no different from the person they saw at coffee after.

I have taken a lot of gambles and let a lot of things go, relying on my character and personality, but I love them. I met with them and spoke with them openly. Some of them left almost immediately but, overall, we've lost about six people of the twenty-two who were here at the beginning. We will probably lose a few more, because, over time, some will learn that my theology is nothing like theirs. Some have softened to the gospel, but the six who left have also responded to the gospel. They said, 'I don't want to believe in that.' The first person who left said to me, 'I have never met a Church of England vicar in my forty-four years here who has stated that Jesus is the only way to salvation.' I said, 'Unfortunately, you have met one now, and that is the belief of the church.' She said, 'I will go but, Charlie, the difficult thing about all of this is that you are b***** lovely!'

I think what has happened in this process is what I need to pin my ministry on. We cannot bend the gospel, for those who want to have their sexuality games, their hierarchy games, their power games. The gospel needs to be held strong. The church preaches a completely different life, a life in all its fullness, but we're going to preach that by being boldly lovely rather than brutally horrible. The issue is that a lot of us are brutally horrible at times, because we don't like 'them', but we are called to love 'them'.

This love is quite distinct from the loveliness and niceness that has infected many churches. The original congregation didn't particularly like the loss of the 'lovely' sermons they had listened to before – they didn't challenge their lives. One person said, 'There are so many nice things in the world, Charlie, like butterflies and flowers, can't you talk about them as well in your sermons?' There is this extraordinary expectation that they are simply going to come to church and be cosy and, somehow, grow, when, in fact, they need to come to church to be *challenged* and, as a result of that, grow.

The process of revitalization has been helped by the fact that the diocese has given me a five-year contract that I can pin everything on: I can say that we've got five years to grow or die. We will shut this church in five years if we do not grow. Having that is great because I have something to work to and people underestimate what they can do in five years. They overestimate what they can do in one, but they underestimate what they can do in five, and we're not going to do either.

After two months, two PCC meetings and lots of talk, we decided to have two separate services. They wanted an evening. I said no, as, otherwise we'd have two churches. We can't have a morning church of liberalism and an evening church of Christianity – we are one church. So I said that there can be two *new* services, not one new one and one old one. Robed in the Anglican style (rather than the illegal vestments they were used to), we have moved to Order 2 for Holy Communion in *Common Worship*, in contemporary language. We also started a new service, which is liturgically light, a service of the Word, that has every element you have to have but nothing else. We have also gone completely 'charismatic-esque contemporary', as far as we can, with our people. By the time these changes had been made, we had about seven people join us who were looking to do something new.

With those seven, we started a new service, and we quickly gathered about five more people. Since then, we've been growing and the most people we've had so far has been thirty-eight, on a Sunday. Every week, we are averaging about thirty in our new service. These are people who have not been converted but have moved to the area and see us as a viable option.

After twelve months of being here, we started a small group at the same time as we split the services. That group has grown – there are about eighteen people who have come to that – and it has become our core group, a group that enables us to plant a church. We're now training its members up, including me, to be part of a church-planting group, where we own what we are doing and will be moving into mission. I would say that, in this way, church planting is pretty similar to what we are now doing, we just had to start a year back, to break the inertia that had built up in the church.

The other thing to add, regarding the process of revitalization, is that it involves taking the power off everyone and not allowing people to continue doing their jobs as they have been, but making little changes. This is done simply to show that the parish is not running the church, the vicar runs the church, and the parish enables that and, together, we become a team. A little bit of the power is taken off to enable it to be given to all the people, because, previously, individuals held power. When people say that the parish runs the church and the vicar serves it, normally it is, in fact, three or four powerful laypeople who run the church and do so in the name of not letting the vicar become the powerful one, but these laity become powerful. The vicar has to become the powerful one, but so as to hand the power back to the collective priesthood of all believers. We also have to take it off non-believers!

I don't want to talk about what I can see happening now because I can see something pretty average growing and pretty sustainable growing, but only just, and I don't want that. I think one of the things we have needed to learn from Holy Trinity Brompton (HTB)[3] is the deep need to pray big, to allow the Holy Spirit to do some much bigger things than we can do on our own. I don't know, but I hope that what will happen here is we'll become the first of many sustainable and exciting revitalizations that are outside the HTB movement that have had money planted through it, and people. I think it is doable to revitalize a church under gospel principles and have that as your centre. You can move a section of a church into another building and do a graft – that's fine, it's not bad – but I do think we can do grass-roots stuff and it can be successful within the Church of England if we preach the gospel and if we are bold and brave with our love and our community work.

I want, then, in five years to see 180 weekly worshippers, and giving to be well above what we need to be sustainable. That's our audacious five-year plan that we have now drawn up. It can only work in the power of the Spirit; it's impossible on our own, so we'll see. We're also willing, though, for that *not* to be what God's will is. He wants the gospel to be preached, so he will call whoever he calls – it's not our doing. Equally, if he doesn't want this church to succeed, then it won't. All we can do is run into the harvest fields and try our best, but we've got to do that with the gospel, otherwise we are tool-less. My hopes are that the church can loosen itself from the god of tradition, loosen itself from the god of the mind and cling, instead, to the god of the universe, who has good news, and that's what a gospel-less church hates. God has revealed himself. If it's not mysterious, it's not God, which is what the tradition allows for, the unknown. Liberalism hates it, because God seems to have said things that don't meet the current cultural view. Liberalism goes with the cultural view, because the mind is the most important thing, which is what culture speaks through. Christ breaks both those things – mystery and the mind – and goes straight for the heart. That's what we'll see build this church.

Red lines on the road to growth

I have red lines, but I don't know where those red lines are right now, because it all depends on the options that are given. There are red lines concerning the sexuality debate. The clear issue is that, if it is decided to enforce the marriage of same-sex couples on all priests/presbyters in the Church of England and on every parish, then that's a clear red line. I'd need to go. I believe that that can't happen. The church won't be that foolish, because it would lose half the clergy.

My sense is that evangelicals are very scared because they think that Justin Welby has turned down all the options given by the Church of England Evangelical Council (CEEC), so they see the situation as giving them no option but to leave. Many from the Renewal and Reform constituencies are planning to go because they don't think that Justin Welby will stand up for the gospel, but I know for a fact that many liberals are frightened of Justin Welby *because* he's an evangelical, so they're running around saying, 'What are we going to do?' The issue with the liberals is that they're never going to go, because there are no red lines for them –

they are happy to live in a world where they can protest. Us evangelicals, however, can't be in a world where we are forced to do something unholy.

The question of sexuality doesn't feature in day-to-day life, it's more like a background noise. It's not a distraction at all for mission; it's a distraction for discipleship. People can come to Christ and it becomes an issue when you read the Bible with them and the question comes up, but most of the time it doesn't, in my experience. People aren't as aware of the church's anti-gay stance as those within the church think they are, so the fear of having to discuss it is not that great. When it does come up, though, many people hate the stance and they don't understand it, so it is easier to avoid it. In avoiding it, though, we cause ourselves real issues because then we have to avoid other bits of Scripture as well, but it's easy to. So far, I've had this conversation with three or four people but none of them is a convert yet, so it's not an issue. They know the subject is there and want to understand it, but do not pursue it.

As I say, for mission, it's not an issue, but it is for doctrine, and the church has to stand on solid doctrine. That is because, in our training and our discipleship, we have to have a firm foundation in Scripture. The minute that's lost, which it is in practice, we have an issue. The wider church as it is, four churches in my locality have same-sex couples leading them – ordained people who are living with people of the same sex and they are in civil partnerships. That's a disgrace. That's a disgrace from a church discipline point of view, it's a disgrace to the gospel, because what it is saying is that we are not holding up holiness; but it's also saying that we are not holding up church doctrine. So, as I say, in practice, we've lost something. They'll tell you off if you don't wear robes at Communion, though recently that's changed; they'll tell you off if you don't wear robes at the Communion rail, but they won't tell you off if you are living with a same-sex partner or in a civil partnership that looks like a marriage. So in our hierarchy, we are completely hypocritical, and that means we've lost trust in all oversight.

I believe that Justin Welby's silence is another reason for our loss of trust in oversight. He focuses so much on prayer and unity that no-one can disagree, but what that does is enforce that prayer happens between people who cannot unite regarding the resurrection of Christ. So my prayer for the wider situation is that the Church of England would hold the line on sexuality and the liberal parts of the church would wither and fade. I would love, and my prayer is this, for the Church of England to go back to Canterbury, close half its buildings and start a new mission on gospel principles. I would love that. We're so obsessed with being powerful, though, and the state church – 'a Christian presence in every community', which is the largest lie, one that we've been saying for years – and we're so obsessed with being the chaplain to the town, the chaplain to the hospitals, that we have lost so much of Christ. The sexuality debate is a result of that.

Will we have to leave? I think so. Do I want to? Absolutely not. Do I think that God can transform the hearts of those who will be voting and those making these decisions? Absolutely, so that's my prayer.

I've shared my story to give a sense of what can happen when a heart is captured from the fringe by the gospel. It is one that, at least in part, is only possible within the structures and with the resources of the Church of England. What is happening at St Andrew's Wimbledon[4] is the kind of revitalization and gospel growth that I pray will be multiplied all over the country and beyond. The creative coming together of the Commission, the diocese, and my own availability is something that I thank God for, even as I pray for the renewal and sanctification of the wider Church of England.

Notes

1 As of December 2021 the Antioch Plan website is not live, but it was reported on by *Evangelicals Now* (see The Co-Mission, 'Second crack at London', *Evangelicals Now*, November 2016, available online at: <www.e-n.org.uk/2016/11/uk-news/second-crack-at-london/e3f3c>, accessed December 2021). It is an initiative of Co-Mission (see: <https://co-mission.org/planting>, accessed December 2020).

2 See: <https://standrewswimbledon.com/st-andrews-history> (accessed December 2021).

3 For an example of this, see Chapter 5, Culture shocks, by Sam Haigh in this volume.

4 For information on St Andrew's Wimbledon, visit its website at: <https://standrewswimbledon.com> (accessed December 2021).

7

Blissful ignorance, mutual flourishing: an evangelical woman in the church

THE REVEREND ESTHER PRIOR

I went to the University of Zimbabwe full of ambition about a future that I was going to carve out for myself through hard work, networking and determination; but I left with a sense of excitement about the future that I discovered God wanted to give me.

I had a dramatic conversion during the final year of my degree. After a couple of years saying 'No' to invitations to join my Christian friends, I finally said 'Yes', to accompany them on a young adults' Easter camp. We arrived on Maundy Thursday, and it was during the very first session that I came to Christ. That evening, I sat down as one person and stood up as another. I was immediately aware, as I gave my life to Jesus, that I had been transformed. I understood from my experience that Jesus had changed me long before I knew anything about the promise that, in Christ, we become a new creation. Never one to do anything by half measures, I immediately became involved in a large, thriving evangelical charismatic church in Harare where my passion for the local church as an agent of hope and transformation was birthed and nurtured.

There were a few things that were to have an impact on my call to ministry that I was unaware of at the time as my new life of faith began to unfold. They were that:

- nineteen days before I met Jesus, women were being ordained in Bristol for the first time;[1]

- the Anglican church in Zimbabwe didn't ordain women (and still doesn't);
- my vicar was complementarian (I hadn't even come across this term before);
- women leading in church was a divisive issue.

Ignorance, as they say, is bliss! I was able to immerse myself in my new life with innocent abandon. Several formative things happened very soon after my conversion, however, that were to change the course of my life. The first was learning about the ripple effects of a transformed life. People commented on the change in me and I was able to give a reason for the hope that I had found: God graciously and wonderfully used my testimony to help lead several others to Christ. As a young Christian, not only did I learn that God could transform lives but I also learnt that he could use me in the process.

I was in my final year at university, reading Politics, with the rather modest ambition to become the Secretary-General of the United Nations one day. One of the first things I noticed about the 'new me' was that my vision for the future seemed to have changed. I wanted to 'work for God' – whatever that meant. At first, I thought it was the flush of my new-found love for Jesus. I fully expected normal service to resume after the initial excitement died down, but there seemed to be two tracks running concurrently – the 'God track', leading to something . . . *unknown*, and my own track, carrying on with the plans I had devised for my life.

I completed my undergraduate degree and began a Master's in International Relations. I knew I had a problem when I sat in lectures and knew that the track I was on was no longer the one that excited me and I could not see myself fitting into the picture I had painted for myself. So it was that, during this time, my mum lost her 'little go-getter', as I laid down my ambition to head up the UN and allowed *my* track to merge into God's. I found a new purpose that surpassed all my former dreams. I have, since then, had the joy of living with the unshakeable sense of being in the place that I believe God wants me to be, and the harvest has been a life founded on peace. No – a better word would be shalom. What I have gained is a life of wholeness and completeness. My mum still talks about 'her loss', but admits that she gained a daughter whose sense of walking into God's future has been a blessing to behold.

Merging into 'God's track' involved having a conversation with my vicar about my sense that I wanted to 'work for God'. He advised caution: 'If God is calling you, he won't change his mind. Go and do a "normal job" and, if you still feel the same way, come back in two years.' He told me later that he never expected to hear from me again! I got a job that I enjoyed, but those two years became centred on my church community and a growing ministry. I became a worship leader and youth leader, essentially putting my hand to the plough wherever needed. Those two years were also marked by persistent nudging, with Romans 10:14b–15a pursuing me like the hound of heaven:

And how can they hear without someone preaching to them? And how can anyone preach unless they are sent?

I became more and more convinced that this 'call' was something that I should pursue, but I didn't know how to go about it or what it meant – beyond serving in my home church.

As my vicar's recommended two-year pause was coming to an end, God opened doors, paving the way for me to become the parish worker at my home church, St Luke's, Greendale. Our parish worker at the time made a spontaneous home visit to me. He said that he wasn't entirely sure why he had come, but he felt that he should tell me he was leaving for Youth with a Mission (YWAM) and felt strongly that he should ask me to apply for his job. He had no idea about the sense of urgency that was building up in me. God's timing and purpose seemed to kiss each other. I applied and was shortlisted. At my interview, I told the panel that I wanted to serve, that I would do anything – as long as they understood that I would never, under any circumstances, preach. Eleven months and what seemed to me to be an irresistible, even dramatic, call later, I preached for the first time, in December 1997.

Another two years passed and God opened more doors, leading me into his future. Under the patronage of the then Bishop of Rochester Michael Nazir Ali, I found myself at Trinity College in Bristol as an independent student reading Theology. As mentioned above, in Bristol, just nineteen days before I became a Christian, there were women being ordained for the first time. I have always found it quite remarkable that this happened just as the Spirit was drawing me to Jesus and, a decade later, I was in Bristol again, caught up in their story.

My time at theological college marked the end of my 'blissfully unaware' era! I discovered that the label 'Christian' was not necessarily enough. Up until then, I had thought it was a given that the Scriptures were the undisputed authority in the life of people of faith. I assumed that a Christian's life is one in which God's presence and power are at work in and through us and, sometimes (in fact, in those early days of my walk with Jesus, *often*), working in miraculous ways. I learnt that such convictions made me a 'charismatic evangelical'.

It was at theological college that, for the first time, I was properly confronted with opposing views, and I found that I had to examine my faith and decide what was important to me. I realized that, for me, if Christian faith wasn't defined by the uniqueness of Christ and his perfect atoning sacrifice in my place, and if it wasn't defined by Scripture, I would have to call it something else. This time of reflection took me back to the insight about faith in Christ that I had had at my conversion. I remember taking on board the uncomfortable, maybe even painful, implications of the uniqueness of Christ. I remember thinking that if I believed, as indeed I do, that Jesus is 'the way, the truth and the life', this inconvenient and objective truth would not and could not change if it became personal – that is, I couldn't change what I believed if the person not following Jesus was someone I loved, such as my mum, sister or a beloved friend. This poignant moment was very formative and has since informed my wrestling with Scripture. Things were about to become very personal indeed!

When I was trying to understand if my changed ambitions were a 'normal' part of new-found faith, I spoke to my friends to ask if that had been their experience, too, but none of my peers had felt the same kind of dramatic change in life ambitions. Eventually, someone asked me if I thought God might be calling me. I remember asking what that meant – having very little knowledge of churchy jargon at the time. From then on, I followed what I believed to be the promptings of the Spirit, only to realize later that these promptings were leading me into a theological landmine.

I was soon confronted by 1 Timothy 2:9–12, and had to wrestle with what it meant for me to hold to the authority of Scripture in the face of the apostle Paul's words to his mentee, Timothy:

I also want the women to dress modestly, with decency and propriety, adorning themselves, not with elaborate hairstyles or gold or pearls or expensive clothes, but with good deeds, appropriate for women who profess to worship God.

A woman should learn in quietness and full submission. I do not permit a woman to teach or to assume authority over a man; she must be silent.

Although I hadn't really encountered this passage before, it became increasingly clear (sometimes in very painful ways) that, on the basis of these verses, some people took real offence at my emerging leadership because I was a woman. In the midst of being called 'Satan's bride' and 'Jezebel', I sought God's will and I remember asking him to give me a story to tell that would vindicate my sense of call. That story includes the profound change in my complementarian vicar, who said at our wedding, 'What do you do, as an evangelical minister who for years has taught against the ordination of women and led Bible studies to support one's position, when into your life comes a female parish worker who has a clear calling to ordained ministry?!'

One of the things that he *didn't* do, and that I knew I also *mustn't* do, as I sought to come to an understanding of God's will about the role of women in the church, was simply to go by personal experience. If we did that, our conclusions would be very subjective and we could all come up with our own understandings based on our experiences. My position was – and still is! – that the Bible must remain the norm of truth and the ultimate authority from which all my thoughts and actions should flow. I realized, therefore, that I couldn't talk about the Bible being normative for my life without confronting head on the difficult texts – texts like this in 1 Timothy 2.

My rule of thumb is this: when making decisions about controversial subjects, one shouldn't just go to difficult passages in isolation and come up with normative binding statements in relation to them. What needs to happen, I believe, is, first, that we need to ask questions about the whole biblical witness on the theme. In this case, that means asking the question, 'What does the whole Bible say about the role of women?' For example, as Linda L. Belleville writes in 'Teaching and usurping authority':

The relationship between the sexes was not intended to involve female domination and male subordination. But neither was it intended to involve male domination and female subordination. Such thinking is native to a fallen creation order (Gen. 3:16).[2]

We need to understand a lot more about the context that shaped that understanding. When we do this, the circumstances of the place may then be distinguished from what is meant to be a permanently binding instruction. The driving force has to be a 'big picture' understanding of God's dealings with his people, as revealed in the biblical story and, in this case, the radically new model of ministry that is ushered in by the death and resurrection of Jesus and the giving of the Holy Spirit.

When I did this, I realized quite quickly that the passages which restrict women's roles do not reconcile with the actual practices of Jesus or even Paul himself, nor do they reconcile with other Old and New Testament texts where women were clearly exercising the roles that seem to be prohibited in 1 Timothy 2:9–15.

So what is the wider biblical context? How does the Bible answer the question, 'What is ministry, how is it to be done and by whom?'

Let's look first at the creation/fall narratives, which show that, historically, ministry began with the stewardship responsibility that God first assigned to Adam (Genesis 2:15), then, equally, to Eve (1:28). The fall brought about a structure of hierarchy, with Adam ruling over Eve (3:16). It was only then that 'ministry' became separated into predetermined roles for the woman and the man, coinciding (in our fallen humanity) with the cultural suppression of women.

The creation story suggests that the responsibility for ministry was given to both men *and* women, as people who shared God's image. As the story moves on beyond the fall, with God's covenant with Abraham (and, subsequently, Israel), ministry evolved as the privilege of a few 'ruler'-type individuals, with the majority of people remaining on the outside looking in. Gradually, three categories of people emerged as what we might call today 'ministry specialists' on behalf of the people: priests, prophets and kings.

- **Priests** Male recruits from one of the twelve Hebrew tribes. Their function was to minister in worship before God and to offer sacrifices on behalf of the people.
- **Prophets** A group comprising men and women who were called from all walks of life to speak God's word to the people in times of need and situations of crisis.[3]
- **Kings** Before Israel demanded a king, God sent judges to bring some order to their recurring anarchy. The judges were men and women called from all walks of life. When the monarchy was established, a third category of ministry specialists was established: the kings. From the time of David, legitimate kings were males from the tribe of Judah. With time, the idea of kingship developed to anticipate the coming King, the Messiah God would send into the world.

By the time of Jesus, although women had a big place in the home and family, their social position was very low. A woman was a 'thing', entirely at the disposal of her father or her husband. She was forbidden to handle or read the Torah and deemed not worthy of being instructed in it. Women ranked with slaves and children in Jewish public life. In the Jewish morning prayer, a man thanked God that he was not 'a Gentile, a slave or a woman'. Gentiles were generally held apart, if not in contempt. A strict rabbi would not greet a woman in the street, even if she was a relative. This background sheds light on the truly radical nature of Jesus' dealings with women. Jesus planted seeds for change. He had many followers who were involved in ministry with and around him, including a group of women who travelled with him and the Twelve (Luke 8:1–3).

With the unfolding ministry of Christ and the giving of the Holy Spirit, there was a shift in understanding that had profound implications for ministry. The Body of Christ, the church, was now God's temple and all believers together his priesthood. The New Testament teaches that individual members, along with their gifts and talents – given as the Spirit wills – are God's gift to the church. In this respect, no limitation of gender is indicated. Obviously, local congregations need leadership, but leaders are no more than stewards for Jesus, who remains the head of the church, his Body. This stewardship is about *servanthood*, not competition to be a ruler or have a position of authority.

Furthermore, at Pentecost, Peter announced that, as a result of the new availability of the Holy Spirit to all believers, everyone would have access to the ministry of prophecy. This ministry of the Word, alongside teaching and preaching, had a place of primacy in the early church. As the church grew, so did the number of prophets, teachers and preachers. The apostles' message was entrusted to faithful people, who were able to teach others.

Women were among those faithful teachers. Women taught and exercised leadership in the early church – several with Paul's knowledge and approval. It was Mary Magdalene who was the first to see and testify to the risen Lord (John 20:11–18). Priscilla, with her husband Aquila, was a valued teacher who led Apollos to the knowledge of truth (Acts 18:2, 18, 26; Romans 16:3; 1 Corinthians 16:19; 2 Timothy 4:19; Apollos was ranked with Paul in the leadership of the early church). Euodia and Syntyche, despite their quarrel, were women who laboured for the gospel (Philippians 4:2–3). Philip the evangelist had four daughters who were prophetesses (Acts 21:9). There were many women who were honoured for their labour for the gospel in Romans 16 – including one female apostle called Junia (v. 7).[4] The existence of these authorized female teachers and leaders should be brought to bear on the interpretation of the controversial passage in Timothy.

With this biblical background – of ministry being open to all as the Spirit enables – Paul's scattered restrictions, including those in 1 Timothy 2:9–15, came as a shock to me. Moreover, in light of his own track record with female co-workers and his declaration of the mutuality in equality that Christ ushers in, this prohibition sounded oddly discordant when considered together with the rest of his teaching and practice.

That begs the question: what was going on in Ephesus (where Timothy was stationed)? What was Paul addressing there?

There is overwhelming evidence in the New Testament that the church in Ephesus was the site of an acute crisis, created by a massive influx of false teaching and cultic intrusions.[5] Ephesus was the economic, political and religious centre of Asia Minor. The temple to the goddess Artemis was a central feature and female leadership dominated that religious scene. The cultic intrusions had a lot to do with this. Such circumstances demanded extraordinary measures and, undoubtedly, the restrictive measures prescribed by Paul in Timothy played a decisive part in the doctrinal survival and health of the Ephesian church.

Paul's teaching in 1 Timothy 2:9–15 cannot simply be dismissed as culturally conditioned and, therefore, irrelevant to church today, however, as many are tempted to say. Nor should it be seen as a decree of timeless and universal restriction and punishment. Rather, it was and is a corrective. While the norm is the unrestricted priesthood of all believers, there were (and are) certain local situations, such as the one in Ephesus, that have called for particular restrictions. Paul chose to deal with this specific threat to the integrity of the gospel by refusing to give women permission to teach. His words to Timothy laid down a principle that protected the teaching ministry and the exercising of authority by incompetent persons – and this is a principle that is valid for all time.

The church where I served as a leader in my own right for the first time was not in danger of heresy, but we were in danger of becoming a female-dominated church. The imbalance in the ratio of male to female that I found was of great concern to me and I made it a priority in my leadership objectives to restore balance. We became intentional about ensuring male presence at the front. For instance, when I was leading and preaching, I wouldn't want other women on the rota to read, pray and assist at Communion. We launched an all-male worship band to lead worship once a month, we planned special services with men in mind and I benched women (myself included) for a time when it came to preaching at our family service. All this was not a move against women, nor was it set as a law to be followed for ever. We had a *particular problem* at the time and we were trying to address it. When the tide turned, which, by God's grace, it did, this intentional preferential bias towards male participation passed. I found this experience enlightening.

The main point to make, though, is that I believe it is good to interpret Scripture in the light of Scripture and to interpret the more obscure, difficult texts in a way that reveals the clearer and simpler messages that are within. In the face of a challenging text such as 1 Timothy 2, then, it is important to seek to discover what the Bible *as a whole* says about women.

To do this, instead of reading Scripture through the lens of the passage from Timothy, a thorough attempt must be made to explore the thematic horizon of the whole of Scripture in order to provide the starting point for interpretation. Women are called to give of themselves to Christ's service, which makes it of critical importance that we wrestle with and appropriate *apparently* contradicting texts.[6]

Having come to what I believe is a faithful biblical understanding that the Christian faith is good news for women and the Spirit of God chooses to empower both men and women for leadership, I went through the process that led to my ordination in 2003.

Having said all that, this wrestling left me certain about yet another uncomfortable truth. I can see how my fellow brothers and sisters, also seeking to honour and empower women, can reach a very different conclusion from mine. I always say, when asked about my attitude to complementarians, 'I think they have a leg to stand on!' Although I disagree with them, I can see how faithful reading of Scripture *can* lead to people thinking very personally about me: 'I wish I could endorse her leadership, but my reading of Scripture restrains me.' My hope is that people who think this can listen to my story, see my desire to be formed by Scripture and say, 'Even though I disagree, I can see why she might read Scripture and think God might be calling her.' I believe this is what can form the heart of our desire for mutual flourishing. That is why we (evangelicals with differing convictions about women's role in ministry) wrestled together and agreed that this was not a first-order issue. Sadly, this grace-and-truth tightrope isn't always easy to walk, as the rather bruising encounter that I had with a conservative evangelical institution proved over a decade later.

One of the ways that God shows his kindness to me is that he seems to turn up the volume to prepare me for things that otherwise would be impossible to attain or endure. For about two years before a vacancy came up at the church where I currently serve, there was a series of events that seemed to be pulling me towards my current post. The first was my brother-in-law saying, 'This is strange, I know, but I think this church will become vacant and I think that's where God wants you next.' I tried to go my own way but, eventually, it seemed impossible for me to deny that God was indeed calling me here.

As soon as I reached the place of surrender, I found out that the sole patrons don't normally permit women to apply. This was followed by several months of bruising encounters that, thankfully, at that stage didn't involve me directly, although I was aware of them. I felt solidly at peace through it all. The many 'coincidences' that had occurred around that time seemed to be linking my future to this church and the obstacle that arose made me feel the whole thing was set up perfectly for God's grace.

After what was a painful time for the patrons and all concerned, the vacancy was advertised (in 2018). I applied and was appointed, with the patrons involved in both the shortlisting of candidates and interviews. I cannot begin to describe the sense of being in the centre of God's will that I felt, nor the vindication and joy when I was told that I had got it but, alas, it was to be short-lived! A message came through that the patrons felt they couldn't, in good conscience, present me. This ushered in an excruciatingly painful time that, thankfully, lasted only a few weeks, but at the time, we had no idea how long it would last. Their decision not to present me meant that an announcement couldn't be made, which, in turn, meant that our family could not move forward at a critical time. This was very difficult because it felt to me like we were being held to ransom. A loophole was found, however, and an announcement was made that I was to be the new Interim Priest-in-Charge, Vicar Designate. An interim licence is within a bishop's gift and I was also made the Vicar Designate because, after nine months, the patrons' right to present would lapse and my appointment could go ahead without their involvement.

A couple of months after my appointment, I found myself in a Jerusalem hotel with about 160 delegates from the UK. I was the only female incumbent from England. The great and the good of the UK conservative evangelical movement were there – among them, of course, my new patrons. Both I and they felt that we were the wounded party in the appointment process, with those wounds still very raw. Never one to tolerate the elephant in the room, I decided to approach them for a personal conversation. I talked about how difficult and painful the process had been for my family. I guess I went in hoping for an apology or understanding at least. Instead, what I got was, 'It's not that simple, this is a first-order issue and we felt bullied!' If ever there was a defining moment that summed up what mutual flourishing is not, this was it. Both sides were hurt and wounded by what had happened, as we acted on our deeply held convictions about what Scripture teaches.

Many tears later, and with an increasing sense that my name was coming into play – that maybe I was in Jerusalem 'for such a time as this' – I went to a Global Anglican Future Conference (GAFCON) in response to a generous invitation. I went, mainly, because I was curious and because of my affection for one of the founders, Bishop Nazir Ali, but I began to see that maybe I was there for another purpose. My presence enabled a healing conversation between our patrons and myself and I was able to confront another elephant: me. My very presence was an elephant in the room. At a UK meeting to talk about the future of GAFCON UK, therefore, I said something like this: 'I feel like I have gatecrashed your party. Some of you have been very gracious and made me feel welcome, but many of you have not. I am a friendly evangelical woman who would sign the Jerusalem Declaration in indelible ink, but if you can't make *me* feel welcome, then we are a long way away from mutual flourishing.' I think God used that moment to help us heal and to enable a conversation about what mutual flourishing might really look like in practice.

Though our patrons were not a formal part of my licensing service that followed shortly afterwards, they came. Their presence, for me, was a grace-filled demonstration of mutual flourishing.

I think mutual flourishing has to begin with genuine agreement that this is not a first-order issue. I would love it if it ended with my complementarian brothers and sisters listening to the stories of evangelical women like me, who believe that they have had a compelling sense of a call from God to lead, women who have wrestled with the Scriptures and are not 'on a journey' away from evangelical convictions, but genuinely hold that everything the Bible says regarding matters of faith and Christian practice is wholly useful and true, incapable of leading us into error. I would like them to listen, not so that they change their minds (because, although I disagree, I can see why they hold their position), but to allow us to flourish. To do so because, although they disagree, they can see how, through serious engagement with the Scriptures, we also might have a leg to stand on in our conviction that God has called us to be leaders in his church under the headship of Christ and empowered by the Holy Spirit. Maybe, too, they could even own to the fact that at times complementarians have used hurtful and unhelpful language and at times they have failed to heed Paul's exhortation to 'Let your gentleness be evident to all. The Lord is near' (Philippians 4:5).

I had a conversation with a complementarian in Jerusalem and I found myself having to assure him that 'love' is not a liberal or unbiblical word! It would be good to hear more complementarian leaders acknowledging that sometimes they have overstated what complementarianism entails, which has led to the tragic lack of flourishing of the gifts and contributions women bring in the church.

To my fellow leading evangelical women, I would say that I am not unfamiliar with the pain that conversations and actions around our leadership has caused. Maybe for some of us forgiveness and healing need to be sought first. Maybe we can only go on by acknowledging that listening will be accompanied by further pain, but can we also say, 'I disagree, but I don't think your desire is to oppress me. I can see why you would look at passages such as Timothy and reach the conclusion not to affirm my leadership in Christ's church. I disagree, but can we agree to love one another and work out in our relationships how we can stand together for the gospel?'

Are there ways of disagreeing about leadership roles without wounding one another? Is there room for disagreement about leadership roles that still enables us to create space for mutual flourishing as a reconciled community?

I don't know if I am asking the right questions or making an appeal that can be heard and acted on. What I do know is this: I see my brothers on the 'other side'. I see among them people with whom I have known love and fellowship – despite our differences. I see others who have hurt me profoundly and still do – as if they can't help themselves! In both friend and 'foe' (too strong a word?), though, I see people passionate about the gospel, people who are courageously holding on to biblical truth when it is increasingly difficult to do so and I see people whose gospel partnership I would miss if we fail to find ways to flourish together.

As you can see, I am intimately acquainted with the pain that the outworking of mutual flourishing can cause. However, I remain absolutely committed to it and it can be a beautiful thing. If I may, I'd like to illustrate this through a friendship that has developed between myself and a leading complementarian evangelical, who has become one of my greatest gospel partners. He knows that I disagree with him profoundly on women's leadership in the church, but he also definitely knows that I respect and accept that he reads 2 Timothy, for example, differently from me and concludes that, though we love each other, he can't in good conscience agree with me on the question of female oversight. That conclusion didn't stop him from coming to my licensing service into a church with complementarian patronage. Our differences on this have not hindered our gospel partnership as we have worked together in various ways. There have been times when, in complementarian circles, my friend has jumped to my defence and times in my own egalitarian circles when I have done the same for him. I offer this friendship as a picture of mutual flourishing. A life-giving and beautiful picture.

I want to serve in a church in which complementarian evangelicals can flourish, even as I follow the call of Christ on my life as faithfully as I know how. Together, we can proclaim good news to the poor, bind up the broken-hearted and proclaim freedom for the captives.

Notes

1 See article: 'Celebrations mark 25 years of women's ordination to the priesthood' Church of England, 11 March 2019 (available online at: <www.churchofengland.org/more/media-centre/news/celebrations-mark-25-years-womens-ordination-priesthood>, accessed December 2021).

2 L. L. Belleville, 'Teaching and usurping authority', in R. W. Pierce and R. M. Groothius (Eds), *Discovering Biblical Equality* (Leicester: Apollos, 2004), p. 222.

3 For readers surprised to see the claim that men *and* women fulfilled this role, see: <www.cbeinternational.org/resources/article/priscilla-papers/women-prophets-old-testament> (accessed December 2021).

4 One evangelical defence of this is S. McKnight's book, *Junia Is Not Alone* (Englewood, CO: Patheos Press, 2011). A. Bartlett's treatment of this issue in *Men and Women in Christ* (London: IVP, 2019) is also robust and fair.

5 For a good summary of this, see B. Witherington III's *Letters and Homilies for Hellenized Christians: Vol. 1: A Socio-Rhetorical Commentary on Titus, 1 – 2 Timothy and 1 – 3 John* (Nottingham: Apollos, 2006), pp. 218–219.

6 D. and D. Tidball's *The Message of Women* (Nottingham: IVP, 2012) does a good job of this, and at an accessible level.

8

Women and the Junia Network

THE REVEREND SOPHIE BANNISTER

My aim in this chapter is to do two things: first, to explore something of the opportunities and challenges facing evangelical, ordained women in the Church of England; and, second, to tell you about the work of the Junia Network, which exists to support and advocate for this specific group of women. I've tried to do this by sharing with you some of the stories of a few women I've got to know through the network in my time on the committee. You'll be hearing not just my voice but also the voices of women who are single, married, older and younger, and at different stages and in different types of ministry. I hope you'll enjoy finding out how a shared passion for the gospel and a willingness to respond obediently to God's call have sustained and shaped these women through their ministries so far.

My story

On the day of my deaconing, the buttons wouldn't do up on my cassock. In the crypt of St Paul's Cathedral, between button six and button eleven, my six-month-baby-sized stomach presented itself. For once, I was grateful for the billowing folds of my surplice. As I manoeuvred my way, and my tummy, through the service, praying that I would (a) not faint and (b) be able to get up again after kneeling before the bishop, I was aware of both the privilege and awkwardness of my position. Privilege, because ordination as a minister in the Church of England came, for me, loaded with a sense of joyful honour; and awkwardness, because the route to and through ordination had not been all that straightforward, doctrinally or practically. Having to explain where I stand and why I often need to move forwards in a slightly different way from my evangelical male compatriots has regularly been a part of my experience as an ordained, evangelical Anglican woman.

It all started when I fell in love. No, actually, that bit came later; it started when the vicar of what became my sending church suggested that I might like to think seriously about full-time ministry. That's when I first really became aware of the need to carefully examine my convictions regarding women and leadership (specifically, to what extent those convictions were truly biblical), and of the consequences of those convictions for my future life within a divided church. What happened when I fell in love at theological college, with a fellow ordinand, is that life got a lot more complicated – especially because he was a year ahead of me in his training. By God's grace, we ended up married and living in north London, undertaking a conservative evangelical curacy (him) and finishing off theological training at Oak Hill College (me). Also by God's grace, we managed to fit in my pregnancy in between training and curacy, plus a move to my curacy, which was split between two charismatic churches with links to the Holy Trinity Brompton (HTB) network. Our current challenge is juggling a new incumbency (him) and maternity leave (me) in a parish where we hope to worship and minister and share childcare together for many years to come.

Perhaps you are now wondering quite where my husband and I stand on the evangelical spectrum. I say this to illustrate what I mean by often being required to explain myself (or, strictly speaking, *ourselves*). Probably the easiest way to describe my/our theology is to say that we are Reformed charismatic, which means that we find ourselves in agreement with the core convictions of both conservative and charismatic sub-cultures, but not in a way that means, in agreeing with one, we have to reject the other. It's fair to say, too, that he is a bit more conservative and I'm a bit more charismatic. This is complicated further, of course, by my being a woman, which means that we belong to each group in some ways but not in others.

It turns out that other ordained women relate to this. The majority of those I spoke to in preparation for writing this chapter gave voice to similar feelings of awkwardness. Feelings of finding great joy in being ministers of the gospel, while at the same time not quite fitting fully into any evangelical tribe, of having constantly to deal with assumptions (your own and those of others), needing to be wise and gracious when others are not always or when the system is not accommodating in the way you need it to be. These are common to many ordained evangelical women in the Church of England.

That is why, as well as sharing some of their stories, I also want to bring to your attention the work of the Junia Network. Originally called AWESOME, this network was started eighteen years ago to support evangelical ordained women who were finding themselves isolated and under-represented at both a diocesan level and within the wider evangelical constituency. The first goal of the network simply is to provide support. One of the ways we do this is to organize an annual retreat, which includes solid biblical teaching, time to rest and reflect, and an opportunity to encourage one another in ministry. Another way is by linking up evangelical women in a diocese so that they can meet to pray. A significant part of my role has involved facilitating mentoring relationships for ordinands and curates with women who have experience in ministry. The network is now large enough that normally we have someone in the network with the kind of life and ministry experience an ordinand or curate would love to learn from.

The second key goal of the network is to advocate for evangelical ordained women, at a national and diocesan level, and within the wider evangelical constituency. Since 2011, two members of the Junia Network committee have sat on the Transformations Steering Group, which was set up by the then Archbishop, Rowan Williams, to explore ways to enable the ordained ministry of women to flourish. It regularly reports to the College of Bishops. That has given our network the opportunity to advocate on behalf of evangelical women on various topics, including: increasing the number of younger women coming forward for ministry, introducing more flexible and family-friendly working policies, and encouraging more women into the leadership of larger churches.

As to the wider evangelical constituency, the Junia Network has a seat on the Church of England Evangelical Council (CEEC)[1] and has always tried to build relationships with conservative evangelical groups. To this end, from 2010 until 2011, the Junia Network's committee and Reform held a series of consultation meetings to discuss topics such as the exegetical and hermeneutical differences regarding gender hierarchy (the papers produced are available on our website[2]).

Ever since it started, the Junia Network has been keen to support and represent evangelical Anglican women in all three orders (deacon (permanent or otherwise), priest and bishop), of all 'flavours' of evangelicalism (wherever they stand on the complementarian–egalitarian spectrum and/or the charismatic–non-charismatic spectrum), and at whatever stage they are in their journey towards and in ordained ministry.

I first came across the network via the book *The Gender Agenda*,[3] which was co-written by Lis Goddard (chair of the Junia Network until 2021) and Clare Hendry (previously Conservative Networks Liaison rep on the committee). The book examines each of the key Scriptural texts relating to women and leadership, from contrasting complementarian (Clare) and egalitarian (Lis) positions. Their shared commitment to the authority of Scripture and the grace with which they agreed and disagreed was a great encouragement to me as I began to enter a conversation in which the stakes for myself and others felt remarkably high.

Making family life and ordination work: Philippa's story

It was at a young women's vocations day that Philippa found her assumptions about ministry challenged. She attended the sessions caught between a sense of calling to ordination and an inability to see how she could make ordained ministry and her desire for a family work together. So far in life she had only seen ministry modelled by people who were single or who had older children, and from her own experience of friends who were children of clergy, she felt that ministry required too great a sacrifice by families. She remembers sitting in a lecture room, crowded with other women, listening to someone ask a question about ministry as a parent of young children. How could their education be combined with the demands of ministry, including having to move house at inconvenient times? One of the members of the panel responded, 'If God has called you to this, he's called your family, too, and he will take care of you all.' On hearing this and from women who had been ministering with young families for some time, Philippa found her objections disappearing, as she realized what ministry could be for a family: not a burden but a mutual calling.

While at theological college with two small children, Philippa found that her college and sending diocese were willing to be flexible and creative in accommodating her as a parent as well as an ordinand. Her grant funding for study has been continued during a period of maternity leave. The diocese ensured that she was kept in touch. Her experience accords with mine and that of others – that, increasingly, dioceses and colleges are starting to regard ministry and parenthood as mutually enhancing. Women are now encouraged to have their babies at a time that works for their families, rather than delaying pregnancy until after training or curacy. More women have role models to learn from, as they see other women who are managing to make it work.

All of which brings great encouragement to the Junia Network committee, because helping to make the way into ministry easier for young evangelical women sensing a call to Anglican ordination has been a priority for the network. The vocation days for young women that Philippa found so transforming were initially set up and run by AWESOME, in partnership with Ministry Division. Wonderfully, these have now been taken over by dioceses, as they recognize their effectiveness in helping women to find their way through perceived barriers that otherwise make it easy for them to delay or even rule themselves out of entering the discernment process. Slowly, we are seeing more young women joining men in ordained gospel ministry. Also, we have always been conscious, particularly, of the need to reform maternity and paternity policies, which to date have varied wildly across dioceses. Our hope is that the new Church of England-wide family-friendly policies that came out in 2020, after several years' work by the Transformations Steering Group and TRIG,[4] will mean that more parents will be able to navigate their training and ministry with increasing ease.

AWESOME's original strapline was, 'God's strength made perfect in weakness.' This is a paraphrase of the apostle Paul's conviction that, in Christ, the challenges (internal and external) we encounter in life can serve as an opportunity for God to be glorified, so long as we allow ourselves to be driven to him rather than to self-reliance (2 Corinthians 12:1–10). It is intended to serve as a reminder to the committee always to look to Jesus Christ for the power to serve in the face of difficulties. As I reflect on the stories that I've been told as I've been preparing to write this chapter, I am amazed and encouraged by the way in which Philippa and the other women we are still to meet have allowed the sanctifying power of God to shape the way they relate to and minister within the Church of England and the wider evangelical constituency.

Staying faithful if misunderstood: Hilda's story

Take Hilda, for example, who finds herself in a multi-parish benefice where she finds that, too quickly, she is labelled 'happy clappy' by some and 'liberal' by others (and 'too traditional' by yet others!) Despite the emotional stress of juggling her incumbency while also taking care of vulnerable parents and making sure that she spends enough time with her children and grandchildren, she is determined to do what she can to resist evangelical tribalism in her area, and to be open to collaboration in the gospel wherever possible. For her, attending the annual Network retreat has been essential. She attended first after her ordination, and has attended pretty much every year since, simply because she finds it the one place where she can be understood. A place where she can discuss the joys and challenges of her ministry across different parishes confidentially with peers.

Building bridges between evangelical tribes: Kate and Fiona's stories

One of the main ways in which I see ordained evangelical women allowing God to be powerfully at work through weakness is in their willingness to turn being misunderstood into an opportunity for bridge-building, especially across the breadth of the evangelical constituency.

Kate remembers chatting with another ordinand about the challenges they both faced – as conservative evangelicals wanting to be ordained – in finding a curacy. The other commented that, in order to find one, she had decided that she would have to become charismatic. She was joking, of course, but making a serious point at the same time. For some women, not fitting fully into an evangelical camp can make going all out for Jesus in ordained ministry a lonely task. They find that they must let go of dreams of curacies at a church they'd really like to be a part of (including flagship conservative churches). The temptation to become something you are not or to diminish your sense of calling in order to increase your options is strong.

Yet, while Kate is open about how hard she has found putting herself forward for ordination, she is also clear about her desire still to have a foot firmly in conservative evangelicalism – something that, historically, has not always felt possible for women. Kate strongly feels the benefits of having been 'brought up' in her church: she loves, in particular, the church's passion for evangelism. She finds her community and support there and that, doctrinally, she still resonates most strongly with other conservative evangelicals, even when they do not believe that she should be ordained. At the same time, with the other women at college, she finds that they have a mutual recognition of one another's calling, though they do not always agree on everything.

In this disjointedness, Kate has started to glimpse an opportunity for bridge-building, using her relationships within both groups to help overcome false assumptions. One of the things that she appreciates about the Junia Network is that we are open to all evangelicals, and that the committee has always tried to foster relationships across the evangelical spectrum. This means that we have members who are conservative evangelical and feel at home with us, and they can act as mentors to women like Kate who are just at the start of their ordained ministry.

Now let's meet Fiona. Throughout her time as a parish incumbent, Fiona has also actively embraced the role of a bridge-builder, as she, too, comes from a conservative evangelical background. Whereas, before, she felt the awkwardness of not knowing quite where she belonged, now she feels that she belongs in several groups and, having built up trust and friendship, is in a position to forge links between them. She cites the example of the ordination of women bishops. At the time, she found that, because she understood opposing views of the argument (and also the language in which the different groups spoke), and was willing to act in a spirit of generosity, she was able to articulate both views faithfully. This enabled her to help people to examine their false assumptions about those holding opposing views. Consequently, she has found herself acting as a visual aid for others, who, because of their friendship with her, are then less likely to make unhelpfully sweeping statements about '*all* women' or '*all* evangelicals'. Recently, Fiona began a new ministry as an archdeacon and is excited to see how her 'bridge-building' experience will help her to support and encourage male and female clergy from across all church traditions.

Initially, Fiona was wary of the Network – not generally being keen on women-only groups – but she has found it, like Hilda, to be the one place where she doesn't have to explain herself. As she points out, if you are evangelical, female, ordained and Anglican, in most circles, usually you will have to explain at least one of those aspects of yourself. In the Junia Network, all four of these aspects are taken for granted, which is partly why we can provide such a unique space in which to equip and encourage evangelical women for their ministry.

Breaking the moulds and being yourself: Ruth

For Ruth, holding deep convictions has gone hand in hand with self-acceptance.

Until recently one of the few evangelical Anglican women leading a large church, she was blessed in her curacy with a training incumbent who helped her to understand and nurture her own unique gifting and calling. At one point in her curacy, he noticed that she was starting to preach like him. 'Don't you dare become a carbon copy of me!' was his considerate comment – feedback that has stood her in excellent stead.

Now Ruth is adamant that every emerging leader needs at least one person like that, someone who is secure enough to provide a space for them to develop their own style of ministry, without requiring them to conform to his or her way of doing things. In Ruth's experience, part of her journey into greater security has also meant becoming comfortable with not finding an exact fit inside any one particular evangelical group.

Training the next generation of clergy: Liz's story

The last woman I want to tell you a bit about is Liz. She has much wisdom to share on the landscape, past and present, for women in ordained ministry and theological education.

Liz worked in a theological college following a PhD and a curacy before becoming an incumbent. She returned to work in theological education after that and has been there, in total, for eighteen years now.

Liz's journey into theological education was not straightforward, in that she never imagined holding the role that she does now. She was deaconed in 1989, before women were able to enter the priesthood, and while she dreamed of teaching in a theological college, she did not expect there to be many openings in her subject – Church History.

When reading the church newspaper one morning some years later (having, in the meanwhile, married late and had a son, then aged six), she saw a job advertisement for a tutor in spirituality at a theological college and, without thinking, said out loud, 'That's my job!' Her husband encouraged her to go to interview, she got the job and has worked there ever since.

In the relatively short time since the ordination of women, there has been a rise in the numbers of women teachers in theological education, though, Liz observes, overall, they are small, especially in Biblical Studies. She knows that, because there are not that many such teachers, it is still novel for some students to be taught by a woman, so she feels the responsibility of the opportunity she has to make a good impression as a female tutor.

Liz has not had the bruising experience that many women of her generation had on entering ordained life, but she has had her share of challenges, including a parish that (back in 1992) decided it didn't want a female deacon in charge. What impresses me about Liz, however, is her emphasis on the need for a gracious confidence. She observes the effect of our increasingly narcissistic culture on students, noting with concern a lack of robustness, which tends manifest in a sense of affront that anyone should disagree with their sense of vocation.

Continuing the story: what next for evangelical women?

This small collection of stories sharpens a question for me: how will we respond to the 'thorns' we experience during our ministries? How can evangelical women in particular respond to a sense of vocation, to the assumptions they come up against and the normal stresses of life (whether single or married, with or without children) in a way that will demonstrate the power of Jesus Christ?

Clearly, it is easier now to be evangelical, female and ordained in the Church of England than it was even five years ago, but many of the after-effects of damaged relationships between different evangelical groups linger on. There remain practical challenges that are yet to be worked on: how to make it easier for clergy couples to minister, for example, which will be a key issue on the Transformations Steering Group's agenda in the months and years ahead. There are still very few evangelical women leading larger churches, taking on senior roles and entering theological education.

Having said all this, clearly evangelical women are not the only people to feel, at times, that they are 'isolated and under-represented' within the Church of England or that they don't fit very neatly within any particular evangelical tribe. Many people, for reasons of cultural or educational background, class, ethnicity and so on, have responded with obedience to God's call and rejoiced in the privilege of proclaiming the gospel as ministers – only to find their way complicated by misunderstanding, assumptions and practical difficulties. Even if, for some, the way has been relatively smooth within the wider evangelical Anglican constituency, all of us face the challenge of witnessing Christ winsomely and wisely wherever God has placed us in this confused and complex world, in our parishes, schools, workplaces and so on.

The work of the Junia Network and the lives of the women I've been privileged to chat with and who have shared their stories with us offer us some ways forward, primarily in terms of mutual support and advocacy. It's not only women who can advocate for and support women: women can advocate for men, and vice versa; and men can advocate for men. Once we recognize in one another a passion for the gospel, the chances of us revisiting and correcting false assumptions increase, making it more likely that we will be able to build mutually supportive relationships that will enrich and strengthen our ministries. It's much easier to allow the power of God to work through our various weaknesses if we know that we have the support and friendship of our evangelical brothers and sisters around us.

How can you help to improve relationships between other gospel ministers in your area – and, in particular, those you may have been tempted to avoid or misrepresent because they don't quite fit into your tribe? How might a shared passion for the gospel enable you to work towards greater understanding and mutual support?

Who could you be mentoring in their discipleship, evangelism and preaching? Is there anyone you see in your church with a calling to ministry and/or to theological training (especially those of a different gender, and/or from a different background or ethnicity to you) who would benefit from you investing time in their development? Even if (in the case of a woman) you end up drawing the lines differently in terms of what you think she can (under God) end up doing ministry-wise, wouldn't it be better if she had the benefit of your experience in handling Scripture well and learnt how to develop deep, strong biblical convictions on the things that matter most?

My hope is that, in generations to come, our evangelical constituency will be able increasingly to unite around a shared passion for the gospel and a love for Jesus Christ, forgiving and forgetting what lies behind (and the wounds we have inflicted on one another historically) and pressing on together. If we can find more ways to collaborate with, support and advocate for one another while also honouring our consciences, the opportunities for the gospel in this land could be considerable.

Notes

1 The CEEC is 'a network of networks, bringing evangelicals in the Church of England together for the sake of the gospel'. See its website for further information (at: <www.ceec.info>).

2 The papers can be found via links on the Junia Network's website (at: <www.thejunianetwork.org.uk/reform>).

3 L. Goddard and C. Hendry, *The Gender Agenda* (London: IVP, 2010).

4 TRIG is the Transformations Research and Implementation Group, which works with the Ministry Division to take forward key areas of concern. In this instance, TRIG linked with the Remuneration and Conditions of Service Committee (RACSC), which reviewed this key suite of policies.

Note

The Junia Network exists to support and advocate for ordained, evangelical Anglican women. How can we help you?

You can find out more about us via our website (at: <www.thejunianetwork.org.uk>) and our Instagram and Twitter feeds (at: <@thejunianetwork>).

If you are female and considering ordination, we would be happy to chat with you, especially regarding any concerns you might have. We can also put you in touch with other evangelical women who are just that little bit further down the road, as a way of helping you to navigate any 'roadblocks' you perceive at the moment. Please get in touch with us (at: <hello@thejunianetwork.org.uk>).

If you are female and ordained (or an ordinand) and want to add your voice to ours, please do join our membership (at: <www.thejunianetwork.org.uk/join-us>).

If you know someone who doesn't yet know about the Junia Network but you think that she would value getting in touch with us, please point her our way (at: <hello@thejunianetwork.org.uk>).

9

Turn-around ministry in the Spirit

THE REVEREND RACHEL MARSZALEK

I turn around (facing conflict)

I am fourteen years old and have been excused from Chemistry to fetch my exercise book from my locker. My timing is bad: there is a line of Year 11s waiting to go into *their* classroom. Their teacher is late, so this affords them two minutes to assess me, as I stand in the otherwise empty corridor. Height, face and deportment. The opinions are sharp and hurtful. God seems to say, 'Turn around'. So I do. 'Face them and smile'. So I do. I sense the peace and presence of God and must have entered the classroom with such an expression on my face, as the teacher asks if I am OK. 'Yep!' I reply, thinking, 'What was that?'

Three years before the incident in the corridor, I wake in the night to hear conversation downstairs. I know instinctively that my grandfather has died. I pray a prayer and it is followed by feeling that same sense of peace.

I am an overly analytical and slightly anxious child who has a reputa-tion for doing brave things. I have always felt led by a presence of some kind, which I associate with something going on in the vicar I watch kneeling behind the table one Sunday a month. As he says, 'We are not worthy so much as to gather up the crumbs under your table.' The church is All Saints' Church, Cheadle Hulme. As these words are spoken, I kneel. I am wearing my brown bobble hat, with not nearly as many Brownie badges of virtue as I would like, and push my fingernails into my tightly clasped hands until I can see the marks, which assure me of my piety because I do not understand grace. When the vicar also says that this God is 'the same Lord, whose *property* is always to have mercy', I think only of the *property* we are about to leave, together with friends, school and everything I call home, and at such a time as this, in the middle of our grief!

Returning to three years later, I am at my locker in the hallway again, still teased for the Mancunian accent that flattens my vowels when my new West Midlands buddies seem to express theirs like antipodeans, accentuating my feeling that not theirs, but my world, has turned upside down. I fumble through the teenage years, anxious to win better assessments from teachers and boys, against whose judgements I measure myself.

Fast forward and, at twenty-one, I'm coming to the end of an English degree, ready to teach texts in which I am discovering much about the human condition, I turn around again. This time it is away from another student in a nightclub, who's asking me if I will dance. I keep turning and get right on out of there. I feel liberated to see a choice so clearly before me: one day, I will marry my boyfriend from home, whom I have known since the age of sixteen.

I have felt what I now know is called spiritual consolation in corridors and in the middle of the night . . . and on that dance floor, where I also experienced the Spirit of wisdom – and, perhaps, a divine outpouring of the fruit of self-control. I am yet to grasp quite what it is Jesus has done for me, even though I have been brought up, somewhat sporadically, in various churches, all my life.

We turn around – we are born and born again!

Now I am teaching English at a secondary school in Derbyshire and, at the age of twenty-eight, happily married to that boyfriend from home, and our first child has burst on to the scene. I had a rare thing called a euphoric birth experience. Perhaps it also had something to do with the gas and air! For a year I don't have the blues but the pinks. I thank God for new life. I don't appreciate that this is also a prelude to my own rebirth in faith.

A short while later, I am sitting in a garden centre cafe with our first child on my lap, musing with my husband about the community with whom we have just worshipped. We have moved into a house three doors down from St Nicholas. We decide to break from our parents' churches to go there. It is time to grow up spiritually.

Neither of us has ever encountered anything quite like what we have just experienced before and such love between the church's members, who did everything possible to welcome us. We each have testimonies from our childhoods of what we know now was the work of the Spirit. We are each familiar with the customs of the traditional Anglican and, for my husband, Catholic Church. Here, though, there was more . . . and this sense of a living relationship. The evangelical gospel was preached.

On weekends at Chester with the grandparents, whom Lee Abbey converted, I would enquire about a piece of furniture in an alcove, asking why it was shaped like that. My mother informed me with the same tone you might remark on the weather, that at six o'clock each morning, kneeling there, my grandpa talked to God! Church, until St Nicholas, had not been teaching me how to do that, so I didn't know what I didn't know and, in defiance, shook my head at the curate, who kept insisting that we attend their Alpha course. When we finally gave in, it changed our lives.

Gospel turn-around – amazing grace

When my sin was transferred from one flattened-out and extended palm to another by the man whose plummy accent I rather liked, I suddenly saw . . . and I went free! Like a shake of an Etch A Sketch, it seemed that God had erased the image I had always drawn of myself. 'His property is always to have mercy!' I couldn't 'right' myself with fingernails dug deep. To understand what I was experiencing, I began to devour the Scriptures.

I turned to the leader of my Alpha table, saying, 'I have to know my Bible like that man' (of course, that man was Nicky Gumbel) and I spluttered, 'Everything is going to change.' I turned up at my vicar's door, apologizing, explaining how I appreciated that this deluge must be tiring, for I was surely one of many to whom this thing was happening and was there anything at all I could do to serve the church? He invited me in. Over the next three years, I gave up teaching English at my secondary school and watched my local Anglican church walk into renewal. I did any kind of ministry thing there that they would let me.

Turn our lives around (testing)

We then sold up to test our 'call'. If it was less easy to access church (it was a few feet away), would we really cut the mustard?

We moved to a new church that would seriously challenge us. We had been introduced to life in the power of the Spirit and now could immerse ourselves in the Word, for theirs was expositional preaching. Only thing was, the vicar there was complementarian. I remembered myself as a teen, one time transfixed near the door on which hung my grandfather's cassock, aware that, because of my gender, there would never be a cassock for me. Dropped off at Bible study, by my husband, I was about to invite him in when I realized that we were all women, taught by the vicar's wife, whose notes were drawn up by her husband. This could never be.

Thereafter, I became a thorn in their side. At times I was gallant, exegeticing '*kephale*' with whoever would listen. At other times I was less agile, stuck between a rock and a hard place. I discerned a call to ministries that my worldly friends gave me every encouragement to get into, for theirs was a woman's world! At church, there was a headship ceiling. I decided that I needed to stop blogging my way through 1 Timothy 2:11–15, isolated in my front room, while two children of mine were in part-time daycare – and get some help with the Greek.

Time passes. Now, Christina Baxter is addressing the General Synod in the podcast I am listening to. I Google her name and see that she is the principal of a theological college[1] half an hour down the road from me.

A year as an independent student at theological college settles me into the open evangelical tradition. One particularly significant Communion service confirms that, finally, I am to present for a Bishops' Advisory Panel (BAP) – I have kept a vocations officer on hold while I searched for a scriptural warrant. I then begin college again, but this time for residential training as an ordinand. My first essay is 'Reasons for and against women bishops' and, at last, two years' worth of studying various sentences from the apostle Paul comes tumbling out for more than a few module credits. I feel released!

Academically, this culminated in a Master's thesis on those thorny sentences that I would spend ten years reading and writing about. At college, I could also explore the atonement theology debate that I had been blogging about[2] and carry Fulcrum's *Canal, River, Rapids*[3] in my handbag, to understand that the 'evangelical' stream has various rivulets, each with a current.

At this point, the Anglican blogosphere continues to obsess me and I stare at the faces on the header of the Church of England Evangelical Council website and imagine the conversations they have. New Wine summer conferences have become our annual pilgrimage and I imagine how different my teenage years might have been, if only I had known God in the power of his Spirit better then. I have fallen completely in love with Jesus. I am born again, but still toddling about.

Turned in the least likely direction

Curacy sees us moving again and, at New Wine, just ordained, I receive a prophetic word. I have gathered with new curates who are also mothers. We discuss the juggle it is in a church that's still getting to grips with the practicalities of us. I stand to leave and someone waves at me. He has a keen sense that God has a word, speaks about an oak tree and I am overcome by the Spirit.

My husband leaves to collect the children from their groups. He has been very patient with me, as I have rather inelegantly experienced my own charismatic renewal. When he returns with children in tow, 'It's our future incumbency', I say. Further words that week confirm it. So, in 2014, I am appointed to a church with a famous oak tree on its neighbouring common. I do not even visit the church to see it worship before starting.

This flag-flyer for all things New Wine, Fulcrum and the CEEC is, in fact, called to a parish more 'Modern Church',[4] yet with traditional fixtures and fittings! Pews are in dark wood. Organ, liturgy, robes, sacristans, servers, the Eucharist and the *New English Hymnal* are its characteristics. I can see why this seemed surprising to some, if not me. I was turned around to face my beginnings – in a traditional, liberal Anglican church.

Minister and writer John Richardson encouraged us to listen for our call outside our tradition. I am at a Junior Anglican Evangelical Conference (JAEC), full of junior Anglican evangelicals with more Jakes than Jackies, for sure, but I have written to John to ask if my very female presence is OK. He leads from the front and seems to tell me that I won't be heading to an incumbency like the ones that renewed me any time soon. I'll be turned around in another direction.

At interview, I spoke about presence, participation and prayer in the power of the Spirit. I took Street Pastor flip-flops out of my backpack and reflected on being real and connected. For participation, I took out the space blanket and threw it around my shoulders to illustrate the imputed righteousness of Christ to suggest how the evangelical gospel is at the heart of my message. For prayer in the power of the Spirit, I shook up a water bottle, but thought it best not to sprinkle the panel. Then questions came thick and fast – where did I stand on issues concerning human sexuality? I chose quickly between two 'o' words - 'orthodoxy' or 'obedience' – and expressed how I am *obedient* to the church's teaching that marriage is between one woman and one man. Before I knew it, Bishop Pete Broadbent was stretching out his hand to me in the local pub, to which he had sent me, while the panel cogitated. Life turned around again in just three hours.

Several weeks later, I am robed and declaring that, 'We are not worthy so much as to gather up the crumbs under your table; but you are the same Lord whose character is always to have mercy', the church this time is All Saints, *Ealing*.

It is just over seven years since I first sat in my car to the side of a famous Jubilee oak tree before interview. I have taken my story to diocesan evangelical fellowships and involved myself in the CEEC's strategy for the new General Synod. I have prayed about how we respond to the 'Living in love and faith' process and what kind of church might emerge post-COVID. Each time I tell my story, I spend less time afterwards picking over every word I have said. I love that I am serving and have gained perspective on the adventures I have had. I have seen how my experiences are micro within the larger macro conversations that the Church of England is having.

A turn-around ministry

These first seven years of my turn-around ministry have seen me observe the culture, plant in a warden and the church community buy its first

Bibles. I began an intentional form of discipling. I renewed the PCC and began equipping a lay team. Currently, I am building a leadership team and looking for signs of change and renewal in our worship. These seven years of ploughing are often less necessary when appointed to an evangelical church, but there are, I think, quite a few 'church revitalizers' like me. Many of us are women in 'middle-of-the-road' parishes and under the soil digging upwards to come to the surface before we see the fruit of any solid Word and Spirit ministry. Evangelical women are breaking new ground, bringing a gospel that is crucicentric, conversionist, activist and biblicist,[5] motivated, to spin a phrase from a seminal narrative for me, by 'the re-conversion of the Church of England'.[6]

My first year began with 'conflict transformation' – an approach that does not seek to manage or end conflict, but to wait and see it transformed. I was confronted with this image on arriving, of an old wine bottle that, on opening, releases dregs as well as sweeter stuff. For twenty-five years of a plurality with another church, my church's PCC had wandered around in circles, as though in the wilderness. There was a feeling of fatigue and a need for direction. In a heart-felt attempt to re-energize the church from a very challenging time through the 1980s, my predecessor had sought to maximize a feeling of 'belonging' again, after many had left. He did this by introducing social events and an annual pantomime. Associate ministers were put in charge of All Saints under his rectorship and served between four and seven years, each, with interregnums in between. The living would come under sole tenure again, with me. With plurality dissolved, the church was needing to rediscover its identity. The intention to foster community had been an honourable one, but remembering my 'not knowing what I cannot know until it has been revealed', I knew parties and pantomimes to be fantastic fun but the magnetism of the gospel, once it grips a person or a community, has God's word not return to him empty (Isaiah 55:11). To borrow a somewhat unsubtle aphorism, some on the PCC had not progressed beyond belonging and on to believing and behaving.

On arrival, I shared with the PCC that I would be observing governance and church life for a year. I was arrested by a framed montage of photos of the church community propped up on a radiator, with the glass hanging in there, in huge shards. Like those separate shards, trying to keep the whole picture together but fracturing, the church was run by groups and subgroups. To borrow a phrase that I associate with my Area Bishop, it needed simplification.

At my first annual church parochial meeting (APCM), I used the Churchwarden's Measure to plant in a warden to assist me who had both an evangelical heritage and leadership experience. This wasn't such a leap because his family lived so locally that they could see my church from their bathroom window. They were considering joining us anyway. They had been discipled in church contexts committed to Word and Spirit ministry and so could shore up the direction I would be taking us in.

Soon after, this family helped me persuade members of the church to donate ten pounds each for Bibles. Pews were soon dotted with the distinctive blue Anglicized NRSV. I could begin asking that they turn to a certain passage as I preached on it. The junior church received a visit from a New Wine practitioner who encouraged a curriculum of Bible stories rather than a thematic approach, which had not served the church well. The importance of the Scriptures was emphasized by a leader I invested a huge amount of time in. She has now completed training as a lay minister with St Mellitus and has a renewed vision of faith for herself and her church family.

A Friday toddler church was launched to serve the community and attract people into the future of our church, as those children grow and sense a call to the wider fellowship. We have also had little children who have brought their parents to church and we have made room for them in the heart of our worship by removing some pews from the nave and providing a sofa and floor cushions. More recently, we have brought the table into the nave, so that, as they break pitta and eat grapes, bread and wine can be offered to the adults and they and the children can all participate. There is now this splendid cacophony of chatter and tumbling from young ones who also join in with 'trespasses' forgiven and from 'temptation' deliver us. All of this has helped warm up our worship so that we are now less mini and monochrome cathedral-style and more joy-filled parish church for the everyday.

While this was my daily experience – in the thick of everyday ministry, spotting servants for Christ in the flock and investing in the spiritually hungry – in my first year, bi-monthly, I was in mediation with the PCC.

Many there were infrequent at worship and fatigued from nearly two decades of governance. Every little detail was contested. There was never a honeymoon for me. That first year was very difficult – they thought I was planning a takeover. Had I also planted the youth worker? Perhaps, with hindsight, the fact that he turned up such a short time after I did, and then I planted the warden before him, means that I need to forgive those who rewrote the youth worker's narrative. Instead of hearing his nudge from God, which was his testimony, however, they decided that I must have head-hunted him. I hadn't.

His background was New Wine, like mine, and his testimony told of a sudden conversion – Jesus meeting powerfully with him, aged nineteen, and his friends having to explain to him that he was speaking in tongues, because he hadn't understood what his own mouth was saying! His youth work has been high energy and engaging. Among other things, he teaches memory verses for prizes each week. Children have joined from my youngest daughter's school.

On their learning John 3:16, however, an allegation came from some members of the PCC that, 'as vicar', I had 'told a child they would go to hell'. Three months later, the PCC decided that, even if I *had* said such a thing, it was below the threshold for spiritual abuse. That was in 2015.

I realized then that what I was facing was playing itself out large in public life. I became a reader of Jordan Peterson, whose support for a young teacher launched him into the public domain. In a university in Toronto, faculty members interrogated a teaching assistant who had deconstructed the gravitas of a particular unit of grammatical speech. This caught my attention and I realized that I could easily have faced similar scrutiny as a teacher of English. The pronoun is a contested marker in identity politics. She was accused of being transphobic for bringing to students' attention the political power of language.

Evangelical understandings of the Scriptures were under just as much scrutiny, micro and macro, for me. Blogging my way through atonement theology, I had been shocked by Steve Chalke's use of the description of Jesus as a victim of cosmic child abuse.[7] I thought about how my profession of a creedal faith incubated in the Book of Common Prayer, Alternative Service Book and *Common Worship*, and brought to such life through renewal, was considered almost unusual. I began to realize how countercultural our Anglican evangelical narrative is – not just to the wider world but also, now, to some parts of the church. I was supported through these early days by my bishop as I explored the call on our lives with the PCC. I wanted the accountability and to manifest undefended leadership; help people to explore the fears that they were projecting on to me.

My aim – to communicate joyfully our distinctive identity and beliefs – was met with what Yeago describes as a 'tarring of any attempt to commend a posture of deference to the texts, with the dreaded fundamentalist brush'.[8] Before too long, a group from the PCC left. I was saddened that we had not been able to reconcile; that my yearnings for the renewal of the Anglican Church were thought incompatible with the lectionary and the liturgy, in which my own call had been birthed, and through which our church worshipped. It was good to teach the Anglican Church in North America's *To Be a Christian*[9] as part of my attempt to clarify our shared identity around the creed that we all similarly confessed.

Reframing (to turn around and redeem) the narrative

I sought to reframe the recent history of the church for the sake of my healing and the church community. Some of those who left returned to vicars who were there before me but had moved locally so I spoke of their loyalty to those two ministers and God being at work to reconcile them, perhaps. As I noted earlier, the church's development had been, in part, arrested at 'belonging', with no long-term investment in the next steps because so many former associate ministers had joined and then left. I was hearing a call to push through this and 'stay'. In Lederach's *Little Book of Conflict Transformation*, he describes how identity is under 'constant definition and redefinition'[10] and so we are to create processes that help people to respond to the identity claims of others healthily rather than merely react to them.

In my first eighteen months, a small group of people were vying for their 'liberal', 'democratic' and 'naughty' self-given-identity – adjectives that they had chosen when asked to describe themselves by an area dean who attended a PCC meeting. He wrote their words up on a flip chart for all of us to see. I was ethically conservative, theocratic and perhaps also 'naughty', in that I am *not* conflict averse but will seek to bring stuff into the light, imputing resilience to those who claim faith with the expectation that we can do business as salty ones, seasoned with grace.

The Church of England is facing similar tussles over identity and our behaviour is not always the best. Take the Archbishop's statement after the General Synod failed to take note: 'We need a radical new Christian inclusion.' This phrase has been seized on by advocates for change to traditional teaching about what it means to reflect the Godhead through our human unions. Though we are encouraged by writer/psychiatrist Glynn Harrison to tell 'the better story', as we teach theological anthropology, human flourishing and Scripture's unchanging ethic for marriage and singleness, we are still not doing too well, as evangelicals, at being heard. I lament, as I did in the early days with my PCC, that what we are saying somehow can't be heard as good news.

As I write this, last Sunday's readings have included the apostle Paul's: 'My message and my preaching were not with wise and persuasive words, but with a demonstration of the Spirit's power, so that your faith might not rest on human wisdom, but on God's power' (1 Corinthians 2:4–5). Yeago's words resonate as he says, 'the future . . . may depend on those who quietly go about learning how to do theological exegesis from the tradition . . . and then actually let the voice of the texts be heard in their preaching and theologizing'.[11]

Seven years in, I have been joined by two evangelical colleagues: a curate and a New Testament scholar. I thank God for his provision. I did not head-hunt them! I am guilty only of saying some prayers. It has been about remedying the idol of ecclesiological obsession so that God, in his good timing, suddenly could give us, all in the space of six months, new leadership for our movement forwards, with a church that now knows its direction depends on Christ.

Vicars can't make things happen, the Spirit will blow where he wills. When I first arrived, it was all about *the vicar* and *the physical church building*, not so much about *the gospel* and *mission*. I first had to take myself out of the pulpit-turned-stocks and prattle on about how we are all in it together (I began to preach from the floor). As Mike Bird explains, 'evangelicals believe in the church and are genuinely committed to it'.[12]

As I move up and down the nave, I want to convey a church that we take with us because *we are church* and this commits us to Scripture and ethics. Only then are we going to be able to offer anything countercultural and life-giving to the world.

Fundamentally, my evangelical Anglican temperament is shaped by the Bebbington quadrilateral, but 'biblicism is not bibliolatry, and crucicentrism does not mean ignoring the resurrection . . . [and I have] respect for *historic* Christian orthodoxy . . . the "catholic" dimension of evangelicalism'.[13] I lost part of the first PCC before I could really impress this on them.

Turn around to arrive back where we started but with fresh understanding

In some ways, though inevitably costly, turning around in the Spirit ministry in churches like mine is not so hard after all. All the fundamentals are there: Old Testament, Psalm, New Testament and Gospel, every Sunday. The Creed is confessed. The liturgy professes 'historic Christian orthodoxy'. In fact, it is a wonder that such churches ever drifted away from extolling the unique authority of the Bible, the sufficiency of the atoning work of Christ, conversion and evangelism. If, somehow, the liturgy's emphases on these distinctives is professed with the mouth but not believed with the heart, the first strategy in turning around such a church is for the sermon to put these distinctives back, being careful not to present some kind of dichotomy between orthodoxy (truth) and orthopraxy (love), which appears to do us such damage these days.

The church needs to proclaim confidently and teach the biblical definitions of love, the good news and repentance in a culture that seeks therapeutic salve and the securing of self-given identity markers. I was experiencing in micro what the church is going through at the macro level. It is the *euangelion* (good news) we are announcing; it is not good news that only suits the agenda of one group of people. 'When Jesus began his public ministry by announcing, "Time's up! God is taking over!"', explains Allan Chapple, 'it is wonderful news if you trust God's promises and love God's purposes – but very threatening and unsettling news if you do not.'[14]

What I have learnt is that a distinctively evangelical Anglican gospel calls its people to repentance and joyful transformation. Herein lies stability, renewal and confidence. I began by returning to first principals, teaching what is happening in the sacraments. I am encouraging belief in the creeds professed and confidence in a distinctive Christian presence. J. I. Packer describes how 'all forms of liberalism are unstable. Being developed in each case by taking secular fashion of thought as the fixed point . . . and remodelling the Christian tradition to fit it, they are all doomed to die as soon as the fashion changes'.[15]

My prayers for the Church of England, in such a defining time, post-COVID, is that we would hang in there as evangelicals; discern the fashions of our times; confidently extol and teach the gospel; and pray for the local Anglican church in whatever ways we are serving it. This season ahead will be significant and I believe that it can be turned around in the Spirit.

Notes

1 Dr C. Baxter was principal of St John's College, Nottingham, from 1997 to 2012.

2 For background, see D. Tidball, D. Hilborn and J. Thacker (Eds), *The Atonement Debate* (Grand Rapids, MI: Zondervan, 2008).

3 See G. Kings' seminal analysis of evangelicalism's three streams, 'Canal, river and rapids: Contemporary evangelicalism in the Church of England', *Anvil*, 20(3): 167–184, September 2003 (available online at: <www.fulcrum-anglican.org.uk/articles/canal-river-and-rapids-contemporary-evangelicalism-in-the-church-of-england>, accessed December 2021).

4 See <https://modernchurch.org.uk/aboutmc>. It is interesting that this organization associates evangelicalism with fundamentalism.

5 D. W. Bebbington, *Evangelicalism in Modern Britain* (London: Routledge, 1989).

6 Commission on Evangelism, 'Towards the conversion of England', paper, The Press and Publications Board of the Church Assembly, January 1945, which J. Richardson borrowed from as he spoke about the reconversion of the Church of England at the Junior Anglican Evangelical Conference in July 2011.

7 See Tidball, Hilborn and Thacker, *The Atonement Debate*, Chapter 1.

8 D. S. Yeago, 'The New Testament and the Nicene dogma: A contribution to the recovery of theological exegesis', *Pro Ecclesia*, 3(2): 164, 1 May 1994.

9 The Anglican Church in North America, *To Be a Christian* (Wheaton, IL: Crossway, 2020); also available online at: <https://anglicanchurch. net/wp-content/uploads/2020/06/To-Be-a-Christian.pdf> (accessed December 2021). This is a resource that I highly recommend.

10 J. P. Lederach, *The Little Book of Conflict Transformation* (New York: Good Books, 2014), Chapter 8, Practice 5.

11 Yeago, 'The New Testament and the Nicene dogma'.

12 M. F. Bird, *Evangelical Theology* (Grand Rapids, MI: Zondervan, 2020). Kindle location 15879

13 Bird, *Evangelical Theology*, Kindle location 281.

14 A. Chapple, *True* (London: The Latimer Trust, 2014), Kindle location 422.

15 J. I. Packer, *A Kind of Noah's Ark?* (London: The Latimer Trust, 1981), p. 158.

Part 3

GOD'S CHURCH IN GOD'S WORLD: TRAJECTORIES AND FUNDAMENTALS

10

The hills and valleys:
the ebb and flow of evangelicalism
in the church in Wales

THE REVEREND DEAN AARON ROBERTS

Introduction

I was ordained in 2016 into the Church in Wales at twenty-five years of age. At the time of my ordination, and for two years after, I was the youngest serving cleric in the province. Before considering ordination, in that time where one tests and discerns a vocation, I was repeatedly told by a varied cross-section of society that if I really *was* called to ministry, I would be better off looking to serve in the Church of England or even in a free, independent evangelical church somewhere. It did cross my mind, especially during those times prior to my selection when all it felt I was doing was jumping through an endless run of hoops. I persevered with Wales, however, and was eventually recommended for training. I went to Trinity College, Bristol (under the sterling leadership and oversight of the now Right Reverend Dr Emma Ineson), which was very uncommon, as the province of Wales doesn't like its ordinands leaving the province for training. The rest is history.

Wales is an interesting province. It is fair to say that there is a stigma attached to Wales, that it is a place no Anglican ministers want to stay in or move to if they want to grow and flourish in ministry. I have no hard evidence for this, only a number of anecdotal conversations that go something like, 'So, where are you ministering?' 'In Wales, just outside Cardiff.' 'Oh. I'm sorry. I'll pray for you.' I did think at first that the offer of sympathetic prayers was something to do with being Welsh, but on more thorough investigation, I found that the prayers offered on my behalf were so that I could cope with the perplexing beast that is the Church in Wales.

Fast forward to 2019 and, praise the Lord, I'm still in Wales! I have just finished my curacy and am moving into my first post of responsibility. There is no doubt that ministry in general is hard work when done properly, but I think that the Church in Wales adds a few more complications into the mix, especially if you're an evangelical. What follows is my exploration of why this is the case.

Few in number?

Unlike in other parts of the Anglican Church, those who are card-carrying evangelicals in the Church in Wales are few in number, proportionally speaking. Indeed, evangelicals have never been in the majority and, at their peak, they were 'an influential minority of the clergy during the mid-nineteenth century.'[1] In the twentieth century, the attention of John Stott was drawn to the Welsh situation, where he saw a need for evangelical ministers within the Church in Wales to be encouraged, mentored and given practical support in their ministries.

Out of his holiday home, 'The Hookses' in Dale, Pembrokeshire (now in the care of the Langham Partnership), Stott started gatherings for evangelical ministers and young people in order that they could receive spiritual input and formation, as well as opportunities for networking and fellowship.[2] The evolution of these gatherings culminated in the formation of the Evangelical Fellowship in the Church in Wales (EFCW), which began officially in 1967.[3]

The EFCW still exists today, and I sit on the Executive Committee as the clerical representative for the Diocese of Monmouth. We continue to share many of the same priorities and the vision that John Stott had: to be a vehicle for encouraging and supporting clergy and laity who are evangelicals within the Church in Wales. We aim to organize various events and conferences for people to come and learn, grow in their discipleship and, of course, meet others. We are also making an effort to strengthen our links outside Wales, by looking to the Evangelical Fellowship of the Anglican Communion (EFAC) and the Church of England Evangelical Council (CEEC), where I sit as an observer, representing the Church in Wales, at its annual meetings. Personally, I have found the fellowship and robustness of the CEEC to be very encouraging, and I do hope that, in the challenging days ahead, the EFCW and CEEC will continue to move closer together to work to safeguard the gospel in the Anglican Church in the United Kingdom.

In 1985, there were 52 clergy serving in the parochial ministry of the Church in Wales.[4] As of September 2019, approximately 110 clerics are members of the EFCW. Given that there are 478 parishes and a total of 411 stipendiary and 154 non-stipendiary clergy currently serving in Wales, the statistics seem to suggest that, numerically, evangelicals are in a stronger position than they ever have been previously in Wales – 19.5 per cent, in fact![5] Why, then, is there a continuing suggestion that the evangelical voice in Wales is small?

From the perspective of numbers and statistics, one must be cautious. The EFCW membership register details all clerics who are members, but it doesn't detail whether they are in stipendiary posts, retired, active in ministry or, indeed, currently ministering in Wales. Some addresses on our books seem to suggest that a number of members of the clergy have retired and moved to England, but still want to support, through prayer and financial support, the work of the EFCW.

Added to that, the general 'church scene' in Wales has been one of fragmentation and disunity until very recent times. If you travel through any town or village in Wales, you will see the historical evidence of this. There are numerous chapels and churches built side by side on the same street to accommodate the different emphases of Christian discipleship and living. Sadly, the same is true, in part, of the evangelical wing of the Church in Wales.

Two historical, but second-order issues (in my opinion), and a misunderstanding of the broadness of the EFCW, have caused some evangelicals to refrain from joining. These issues are, namely, the ordination of women and the continuing provision and use of the gifts of the Holy Spirit. Despite the fact that ordained women have served on our Executive Committee and the EFCW has worked with New Wine Cymru, as well as having charismatic members on the Executive Committee (like myself), there is still a persevering opinion among some evangelicals within the Church in Wales that the EFCW is only interested in headship, cessasionist evangelicals. That is not the case, and there is still an enormous amount of work to do to change that perception.

Given the overall picture of the Church in Wales, and the predictions concerning its demise by 2043, there is a higher calling for evangelicals to wake up, smell the coffee and join forces to unite as one voice and proclaim the core truths of the gospel to the people of Wales in word and deed.[6] How wonderful it is to do this, to work together in a team, especially when there are other factors that contribute to the suppression of the evangelical voice within the Church.

The Welsh Church Act

Originally, the Church in Wales was part of the established Church of England. In 1920, it became the Church of England in Wales, when the province of Wales became autonomous and so was affiliated primarily with the Anglican Communion rather than the Church of England.[7] Carved out of the province of Canterbury, the Church in Wales became a province in its own right, eventually comprising six dioceses.

Many are ignorant of the fact that, while the Church in Wales puts on a good show of being the state church in Wales, it is not. It is a disestablished church. Not only is it disestablished but it is also disendowed. The Church in Wales has never been financially affluent, but disestablishment brought a poverty to the Church in Wales that it had never known before.[8] In addition to the financial consequences of disestablishment, other powers and privileges were removed from the Anglican Church in Wales, such as the patronage system, representation in the House of Lords and the entwining of canon law with state law.[9] What does that mean in practice for evangelicals?

Money and people

There is no doubt that some will see disestablishment as a positive step. In terms of finance and the size of the province, however, the Church in Wales invariably has found it difficult to consolidate itself as a robust, totally self-sufficient institution. In practice, this means that it runs on a budget. It is true that there are investments, but most of the revenue from those investments goes to an increasingly bigger pension bill; there isn't even a separate pension pot. The financial struggles trickle from the top downwards. There is precious little finance to resource bread-and-butter ministry, and even provincial initiatives are achieved on limited budgets compared to those of similar organizations.

The size of the province also affects how the Church in Wales is run and governed. Many like the small size of the Church in Wales and its close-knit feel, including myself. Yet, when you scratch beneath the surface, what you find is that there is a very small number of people with the power to set the agenda for the whole Province, and even to make decisions without consulting the wider church. Take me as an example. Despite the fact that I am a junior cleric, currently I am on the Governing Body of the Church in Wales (that is the Welsh Synod), the Diocesan Advisory Committee and the Diocesan Evangelism Committee, as well as having been on working groups discussing the remuneration of the clergy, the ICT provisions of the Church in Wales and other similar groups since being ordained. I have also delivered training on parish nurture groups and contributed to teaching on growing healthy churches. There are others who are on many more committees than me, some with huge leverage in shaping the Church in Wales, for good or ill.

While the Church in Wales tries to take pride in its autonomy, it still looks over its borders to see what the Church of England is doing, and cherry picks elements of its findings to implement within the life of our own province. We have our own liturgical committee, but a good percentage of the material it produces is *Common Worship* with some tweaks to make it look authentically Welsh. There is a self-perpetuating myth that anything which works in the Church of England wouldn't work in Wales 'because it's different here.' Yet, so often, we find ourselves looking to the Church of England for guidance and direction due to our limited pool of resources, resulting in attempts to implement good practice on a tight budget and with small numbers of people.

Autonomy, autocracy and patronage

As I have suggested, the Church in Wales takes pride in the autonomy that was given to it in 1920 and guards that autonomy ferociously. Like all Anglicans, we claim to be part of the one, holy, catholic and apostolic church, yet when Wales wants to do something that falls outside the norms of Anglicanism, it will tend to do it. Coupled with this strong sense of independence comes the potential to operate in an autocratic way, which starts at the top with the Bench of Bishops – the six diocesan bishops of the Church in Wales.

The Welsh bishops have immense power in their province. As one bishop from another province commented to me, referring to the Welsh bishops, 'Don't you mean the six Welsh popes?' In a small province with fewer ecclesiastical bodies to go through, and a select pool of people able to sit on the decision-making bodies of the Church, it is much easier for bishops to steer the Church in Wales to where they want it to be than it is in England. This is especially so when they are given the right to co-opt members on to the various bodies in the church.

They would probably disagree, of course, but if one looks at the provisions for bishops to make decisions in the church structures, the influential power they possess can be seen. One example of this would be the election of a bishop. If, during an election, the Electoral College (the body that elects a new bishop to a diocese) fails to reach a decision after three days, the current bishops have the power to choose a bishop themselves.[10]

With the autonomy of the province weighing in their favour (as they do not have to answer to the state legal system as an English bishop would), they can also subvert the structures of the Church in Wales, because, in effect, the structures have the same legal clout as a private members' club or sports society. Despite us looking similar to the Church of England in how we operate, there is no legal weight behind the structures outside the province itself. One particular example of this is the way in which, since 2015, the Bench has used two straw polls to subvert the motion/bill procedure at the Governing Body of the Church in Wales to progress a revisionist agenda on same-sex marriage. The straw polls were within the *letter* of the law (in that they are not barred from taking place at the Governing Body meetings), but they went against its *spirit* in that, ultimately, they were used to shape the agenda to move closer to legalizing same-sex marriage in the Church in Wales.[11]

The way in which the Church in Wales is set up has profound implications for the evangelical legacy within a parish ministry context.

Evangelical clerics encounter problems when it comes to finding parishes to work in, finding a team in parishes in which to flourish in their ministry and to plan for succession after an evangelical leaves the parish. Why is this? The answer is because there is no patronage in Wales – at least, not like the patronage that exists in the Church of England. Whereas England enjoys lots of different sources of patronage from all stables in the Church, Wales has, in reality, one patron. That patron is the bishop. There are different ways in which clerics are appointed in Wales but, ultimately, the decision comes down to them in the end.[12]

In practice, this means that there is no such thing as an 'evangelical parish' or, indeed, an 'Anglo-Catholic parish'. They are only evangelical or Anglo-Catholic in so much as the current incumbent is such. When that person leaves, the jury is out as to what the parish will be next! Having said that, some parishes have remained a particular flavour for a very long time. When this happens, it is to be credited to a good incumbent (evangelical or otherwise) who has built up that parish's identity and strong lay leadership, when the parish has had to navigate an interregnum, as well as the bishop making a sensible decision. Of course, sensible decisions are not always made, and some decisions are made with particular motives behind them.

It seems, therefore, that if evangelical ministry is to thrive in Wales, what we really need is an influx of lay and ordained people who feel called by God to offer themselves in service and ministry to the Land of Revival, co-working with us who are ministering in the days of small things.

A liberal agenda

The subjects of the ordination/consecration of women and same-sex marriage are dominating conversations in the Anglican Communion, and Wales is no exception. Wales ordains and consecrates women now, and a code of practice was devised for those who couldn't accept the ordination of a woman – in particular, to the office of bishop. Many of those who were of a traditional Anglo-Catholic mind felt that the provisions were not robust enough and so left the Church in Wales. Most evangelicals stayed, and now the issue affecting us is that of same-sex marriage. One traditional Anglo-Catholic lamented to me that if evangelicals (whether headship or egalitarian) had made more of a fuss over the consecration of women to ensure provision for those who had conscientious objections, there might have been Anglo-Catholics left in Wales today to support them in the debate over human sexuality. I fear he may have been right.

Discussion and debate on same-sex marriage started to take off in April 2014. This took the form of a discussion and feedback session at the Governing Body. In an agendum item at the September 2015 Governing Body meeting, it was noted:

> Although these were informal discussions, notes from the groups suggested that in general Governing Body members were keen that the Church should be able to respond to same sex couples with more pastoral sensitivity than might have been the case in the past when dealing with remarried divorcees. Some members were clearly uncomfortable with the concept of same sex marriage, but others appeared to be open to the possibility of blessing such unions.[13]

A series of diocesan consultations then took place between the 2014 and 2015 Governing Body meetings. The same report issued by the Governing Body in September 2015 said that the diocesan consultations varied in their form and shape, so it was difficult to make definite statements. However, while there is undeniably a desire to introduce same-sex marriage in some quarters, it certainly wasn't a mandate as the percentage figures appended to the report show. Indeed, most of the dioceses, generally speaking, did not appear to be in favour of changing the doctrine at all.[14]

With that report as a background paper, the Archbishop at the time, Dr Barry Morgan, introduced the concept of a 'straw poll' to the Governing Body. It was made clear that the straw poll wasn't binding but would give the Bench of Bishops an idea as to how to move forwards in the area of same-sex relationships and marriage. The vote was held with three options to vote on.

The results were interesting (see Table 10.1 on page 167).

What the votes revealed was that the bishops were out of step with the clergy and laity of the province in their thinking on this area and,

Table 10.1 The results of a straw poll held at a Governing Body meeting on same-sex relationships

	Option 1: no change to doctrine	Option 2: blessing of same-sex partnerships	Option 3: introduction of same-sex marriage
Bishops	1	2	3
Clergy	21	1	26
Laity	28	6	32

moreover, the overall feeling of those on the Governing Body was different from the overall feeling of the province, as reported in the various diocesan consultations.

While the vote at that 2015 Governing Body meeting was declared a straw poll, nevertheless it gave the media an opportunity to declare that the Church in Wales was voting in the affirmative regarding same-sex marriages, even though the vote would have failed if it had been a formal motion or bill.[15] As a result, the issue was taken off the agenda, and I remember it being said by the Archbishop at the time that the Bench of Bishops would do further work before consulting the Governing Body again.

That work was to instigate LGBTQ+ chaplaincies, orchestrate a media push to advance a revisionist agenda, appoint LGBTQ+ clerics and LGBTQ+ allies to senior positions in the province, introduce private prayers for same-sex couples without any consultation with the Governing Body, as well as ensure a very active presence at Pride Cymru.[16] What we have seen in Wales, then, is a move to change the facts on the ground, which I believe to be a deliberate attempt to influence and manipulate the Governing Body and its composition.

In 2018, the Bench of Bishops revisited same-sex marriage, this time by inviting the Primus of the Scottish Episcopal Church to give a presentation on how his province had changed its view on sexuality and introduced same-sex marriage. The Governing Body was then asked to participate not in a motion or bill procedure, but another straw poll. They were asked to vote on the statement: 'Do you agree with the following statement: "It is pastorally unsustainable for the Church to make no formal provision for those in same-gender relationships."' The results revealed that seventy-six members voted 'Yes' and twenty-one voted 'No'.[17]

The result was hailed as a green light to explore the formal introduction of same-sex marriage. It isn't as cut and dried as that, however. A number of conservatively minded Governing Body members voted in favour of the statement because 'formal provision' was an abstract term, and felt that the meaning of 'formal provision' should be explored. In my opinion, they fell straight into the trap that the statement was intended to set. It has paved the way for the Bench of Bishops to set the agenda of the Church in Wales once again. Despite my attempts to highlight this undermining of the due processes of the Governing Body, it has fallen on deaf ears, and it seems that it is hard for bishops to be held to account.[18]

A lot of water has passed under the bridge since 2018. The Church in Wales has appointed its first female bishop in a civil partnership to be the Bishop of Monmouth. News reports said that Cherry Vann hoped to bring unity to the church and would not push or campaign for same-sex marriage in the Church in Wales.[19] However, while the world continued to navigate the complexities of the global COVID-19 pandemic, the Church in Wales proposed, debated and passed a bill to legislate a service of blessing for same-sex couples after a civil partnership or marriage in the latter part of 2021. The vote was passed by a two-thirds majority, one vote away from being blocked in the House of Clergy. It is a five-year experimental bill, but there is evidence to show that the direction of travel is uncompromising. Unsurprisingly, all bishops voted in favour of the bill in another demonstration of how the Bench is not representative of the whole of the Church in Wales.

For evangelicals, the decision to bless same-sex relationships has become a watershed moment for considering our short- and long-term future within the Canterbury-aligned structures of Anglicanism. Some have already resigned their licences, if they are ordained, or have left congregations, if they are laity. Others are actively looking to leave. Talks with the Global Anglican Future Conference (GAFCON) are already underway and it is probable that an alternative Anglican structure will take root in Wales in the next few years. Some are staying within the Church in Wales with varying degrees of uncertainty as to how permanent that decision will be.[20]

It is simply too early to tell what impact the direction of travel will have on the grass roots parish life of the Church in Wales and how the Bench of Bishops will handle the discontent among clergy and laity alike whose consciences cannot support a de facto change in the doctrine of marriage. There is a difference of opinion among evangelical clergy as to where the 'red line' is – is it blessing or marriage? Either way, all are agreed that, colour aside, a line has been crossed. Further provision will, without a doubt, have a more hard-hitting effect on the evangelical constituency. Additionally, anecdotal evidence seems to suggest that, while the Governing Body is being shaped and moulded into a more liberal synod, the rest of the Church in Wales is still largely *culturally* conservative if not *theologically*.

More briefly, a second issue that has highlighted an illiberal liberalism in the Church in Wales is the attempt to bar those who cannot accept the ordination of women from being ordained. The Venerable Peggy Jackson tabled a private members' motion at the Governing Body in May 2019 that would have seen 'traditionalists' being denied recommendations to train for ordained ministry.[21] Thankfully, the motion was heavily defeated by the Governing Body, yet, in a strange comparison to the same-sex marriage straw poll at the September 2015 meeting, the Bench of Bishops once again revealed how out of step they were with the rest of the Governing Body when some of them voted in favour of the motion.

Hope for Welsh Anglican evangelicalism?

With such serious issues for evangelicals in the Church in Wales to contend with, many ask, 'Can anything good come out of Wales?!' The answer is, 'Yes'. While there are serious issues that are in need of a lot of prayer and action from the evangelical wing of the Church, there are also signs of hope and growth.

In terms of organization, 2019 saw evangelicals and Anglo-Catholics come together to hold an 'Anglican Essentials Wales' conference, which aimed to draw orthodox Anglicans together for study, prayer and fellowship. More than 150 people gathered in Cardiff for the event – the first of its kind in Wales. The Evangelical Fellowship of the Church in Wales has also seen an increase in regular participation, particularly among younger clergy, and a special residential event was held for younger clerics.

The Church in Wales has also taken some positive steps to address its decline, with the introduction of a £10 million 'Evangelism Fund', aimed at getting dioceses and parishes to think more seriously about evangelism by using grants for new initiatives to be implemented across the province. It was a little worrying when I asked at the Governing Body meeting whether the grant-making body had a working definition of what 'evangelism' means and one was not given. However, it should be a point of prayer for all evangelicals that this money is used wisely and appropriately for true kingdom purposes.

It has also been announced that the Church Revitalisation Trust (born out of the Holy Trinity Brompton (HTB) network) is to partner with two Welsh dioceses to facilitate HTB church plants – one in Cardiff and another in Wrexham. This should be welcomed by evangelicals, but some have complained about HTB coming to Wales, mainly those who are liberals.[22] It should be a priority for evangelicals to encourage the bishops of the Church in Wales in their endeavours to see a growing church model being adopted in Wales, while cautiously bearing in mind that the Welsh bishops might want to meddle with it in the future. It remains to be seen whether HTB will be allowed to get on with the work they do so well without interference from the hierarchy.

Aside from these national developments, there are lots of stories at grass roots level of deepening Christian discipleship. There are reports of people coming to faith and asking to be baptized, a good number of evangelicals exploring ordination and church growth being seen, especially in rural contexts.[23] God has not abandoned the people of Wales, and it seems that God may still be willing to use the Anglican Church in Wales for his purposes.

As in many parts of our country, the ground in Wales is tough. We are living in the days of smaller things and unfavourable seasons, yet my firm belief is that, especially in desperate and unfavourable times, God may move in mighty power once again in the place that has been nicknamed the 'Land of Revival'. What we really need, apart from God's presence among us, is a tangible encouragement from outside Wales by way of investment; the investment of laity and clergy moving to Wales to join

God's work in waking the nation to the light of the gospel. We are a small province with many clergy vacancies available. We are depleted in spirituality, number, resources and money . . . but isn't it in our desperation that God can work through passionate individuals in unimaginable ways, even if they are the minority, if they are reliant on him? May I invite you to come and join us! Come and be desperate in a desperate province that we may once again see the conversion of a nation to faith in Christ.

Deled dy deyrnas; gwneler dy ewyllys, ar y ddaear fel yn y nef.
(Your kingdom come, your will be done, on earth as it is in heaven.)

Notes

1 R. L. Brown, *The Welsh Evangelicals* (Tongwynlais, Cardiff: Tair Eglwys Press, 1986), p. 3.

2 J. Bailey, 'Evangelicalism in Wales, 1967–2017', *Evangelical Times*, September 2017 (available online at: <www.evangelical-times. org/31705/evangelicalism-in-wales-1967-2017>, accessed December 2021).

3 For more on the history of the EFCW, see D. C. Jones's contribution in A. Atherstone and J. G. Maiden (Eds), *Evangelicalism and the Church of England in the Twentieth Century*, Studies in Modern British Religious History, Volume 31 (Woodbridge, Suffolk: Boydell Press, 2014), Chapter 10.

4 Brown, *The Welsh Evangelicals*, p. 170.

5 The number of parishes in the Church in Wales is reported in various sources to be more than 900 in number. This low number, reported by the provincial offices, includes parishes that are now 'ministry areas' or 'mission areas', which are parishes grouped together. Indeed, there are well above 478 church buildings with congregations worshipping in them each Sunday in the Church in Wales!

6 J. Hayward, 'Anglican Church decline in the West – the data', *Church Growth Modelling*, 8 July 2015 (available online at: <https:// churchmodel.org.uk/2015/07/08/anglican-church-decline-in-the-west-the-data>, accessed December 2021).

7 Even though the Act was passed in 1914, the First World War delayed its implementation until 1920.

8 Brown, *The Welsh Evangelicals*, p. 7.

9 N. Doe, *The Law of the Church in Wales* (Cardiff: University of Wales Press, 2002), pp. 5–7.

10 Doe, *The Law of the Church in Wales*, p. 132.

11 D. A. Roberts, 'Reflections after Governing Body: What's next for the uncertain province?', DeanRoberts.Net, 18 September 2019 (available online at: <http://deanroberts.net/2018/09/18/reflections-after-governing-body-whats-next-for-the-uncertain-province>, accessed December 2020).

12 N. Doe suggests that individual patronage still exists in the Constitution of the Church in Wales, though neither I, nor any of my colleagues, know of a Church in Wales parish that has private patronage. See Doe, *The Law of the Church in Wales*, p. 162.

13 Governing Body of the Church in Wales, 'Same sex partnerships', 16–17 September 2015, p. 2 (available online at: <http://cinw.s3.amazonaws.com/wp-content/uploads/2015/09/13_02_SameSexPartnershipNote.pdf>).

14 Governing Body of the Church in Wales, 'Same sex partnerships', pp. 4–6.

15 A. Wightwick, 'Church in Wales votes YES for gay marriage but we're still a long way from real change', *WalesOnline*, 17 September 2015 (available online at: <www.walesonline.co.uk/news/wales-news/church-wales-votes-yes-gay-10078543>, accessed December 2021).

16 BBC News, 'Bishop's Pride Cymru involvement "fantastic"', 26 August 2017 (available online at: <www.bbc.co.uk/news/av/uk-wales-41062386/bishop-s-pride-cymru-involvement-fantastic>, accessed December 2021).

17 T. Wyatt, 'Welsh Governing Body: No provision for same-sex couples is "pastorally unsustainable and unjust"', *Church Times*, 21 September 2018 (available online at: <www.churchtimes.co.uk/articles/2018/21-september/news/uk/welsh-governing-body-no-provision-for-same-sex-couples-is-pastorally-unsustainable-and-unjust>, accessed December 2021).

18 Roberts, 'Reflections after Governing Body'.

19 BBC News, 'Gay bishop will not push for same-sex marriage', 28 January 2020 (available online at: <www.bbc.co.uk/news/uk-wales-51274677>, accessed December 2021).

20 EFCW, 'GB meeting 6th Sept – full response', EFCW, 12 October 2021 (available online at: <https://eng.efcw.org.uk/2021/09/27/gb-meeting-6th-sept-full-response>, accessed December 2021).

21 T. Wyatt, 'Welsh archdeacon seeks to end conscience provision for traditionalists', *Church Times*, 1 May 2019 (available online at: <www.churchtimes.co.uk/articles/2019/3-may/news/uk/welsh-archdeacon-seeks-to-end-conscience-provision-for-traditionalists>, accessed December 2021).

22 J. Martin, 'Church plant draws resistance', *Living Church*, 8 April 2019 (available online at: <https://livingchurch.org/2019/04/08/church-plant-draws-resistance>, accessed December 2021).

23 D. A. Roberts, 'Reflections on rural church growth', DeanRoberts.Net, 7 February 2017 (available online at: <http://deanroberts.net/2017/02/07/reflections-on-rural-church-growth>, accessed December 2021).

11

The pain and joy of standing firm in faith in Scotland

THE REVEREND DAVID McCARTHY

On 4 March 2005, in a response to the Windsor report/Primates' Communiqué on sexuality, the College of Bishops of the Scottish Episcopal Church (SEC) said that it had 'never regarded the fact that someone was in a close relationship with a member of the same sex as in itself constituting a bar to the exercise of an ordained ministry'. This was a clear indication of the direction of travel the province would take. There had been no consultation and no discussion at synodical level. The significant number of same-sex partnered clergy and laypeople in the SEC almost certainly contributed to the pressure for radical change.

The SEC's statement was picked up by the press, including the BBC, which ran it as the lead item on Radio 4's *Today* programme. I remember it vividly because I wake up to the programme most days. I leapt out of bed that morning. Our phone rang not long afterwards, as a colleague from England with media connections was fielding calls from people at the BBC, who were looking for someone in Scotland who would speak for another position from that which the bishops were taking. I rang round my senior church leader friends, asking them if they would talk with the BBC. They all felt that I should do it so, reluctantly, I found myself speaking on *Today* and *Newsnight*, trying to put the case for upholding the teaching of the Bible and the traditions of the church. My aim was to do so with grace and compassion, and I was thanked by the then primus for doing so.

A website was set up to serve as an umbrella for the little group of churches concerned by the bishops' statement. The press needed a name for us, so we quickly adopted 'Scottish Anglican Network'. We were mostly evangelical or charismatic, but more catholic, orthodox and traditional clergy and laypeople expressed support of our stance.

We found that those who were unhappy with us could be quite dismissive. The Thinking Anglicans website suggested that I was, 'indefatigable in his efforts to make a big issue of all this'. Another group offered, 'Members of Changing Attitude Scotland are surprised that the small new grouping calling itself the "Scottish Anglican Network" has spent so much time on Easter Day debating homosexuality. Most of the Scottish Episcopal Church spent the day rejoicing in the news of Christ's Resurrection.'

We suggested that it was the bishops and Changing Attitude who were making 'a big issue of all this' in seeking to change the teaching of the Bible and what the church has taught since its inception.

We sought and were granted three meetings with the bishops – on 7 April, 22 April and 4 May 2005 – when six representatives from the Scottish Anglican Network listened to the bishops' reasons for their statement and they were able to hear our concerns. At one of these meetings at the General Synod office in Edinburgh, one of the sash windows blew in. The bishops were a little flustered by this. We, however, put it down to the wind of the Holy Spirit blowing into the room!

On 7 June, the bishops released a second statement to the whole church. Sadly, this failed to answer many of our questions and we were unconvinced that the stance the SEC had adopted was not against orthodox biblical teaching, the tradition of the 'one holy and catholic church', as well as the majority of the Anglican Communion.

At that point, however, the doctrine of the SEC (as defined in canon law) maintained the teaching that marriage was between a man and a woman. Some of us believed that a red line would be crossed if the canon on marriage was ever changed. If that happened, we would need to take action. The six leaders recognized however, that we would not all be able to take significant action. As in North America, the property of most congregations is owned by the SEC. The congregation I served, St Silas Church in Glasgow and the congregation I went on to serve in 2014, St Thomas' Church, Edinburgh still had trustees who had responsibility for the property. This meant that these two congregations had some measure of protection.

What action might be taken was not clear, but some of us knew that we would be unable to serve under the authority of a bishop who had led a diocese and province in a direction that was opposite to that of the majority of the Anglican Communion. There were other clergy who were not far off retirement who were desperately unhappy about it but who felt that they could do little to prepare their congregations for what was coming.

There followed a long process of discussion, campaigning by those in support of same-sex marriage and endless 'cascade conversations' (which often assumed that orthodox leaders had no experience of caring for same-sex-attracted family members or friends).

Over the next ten years we prepared for possible canonical change by building links with the wider Anglican Communion. I attended the first Global Anglican Future Conference (GAFCON) in Jerusalem in 2008 and was impressed by the breadth of the infant movement and the godly clarity of the leadership. I did not attend GAFCON 2013 in Nairobi, because we felt that the Scottish bishops were listening to us and by not attending, we were being gracious and not overly strident. In retrospect, it was a mistake. The bishops had launched a major campaign to make the evangelicals feel wanted. They sought to involve us in provincial leadership, a few people were made canons and I was invited to head up mission for the diocese in which I served. The new primus declared, 'The evangelicals are the new establishment.' Their campaign had worked. They were being inclusive of us, yet our friends around the world were concerned that our resolve had failed us.

In June 2015, the General Synod decided to begin the process of removing any reference to marriage being between a man and a woman from the canon, thus paving the way for same-sex marriage. It would take two years for the change to work its way through the synodical process.

Finally, in June 2017, the change to the canon for marriage was agreed after its second reading.

I had withdrawn from involvement in the General Synod, following the initial decision to proceed with canonical revision. I believed that the change was then inevitable and so any political effort to avert change was doomed, simply because those who should have prevented it, the bishops, were now actively supporting it. Only two bishops consistently voted to maintain orthodoxy. One of them, who we had much respect for, Bob Gillies, then Bishop of Aberdeen and Orkney, retired before the process was completed.

Some were critical of my withdrawal from the synod, arguing that my vote might have held back the change. This perhaps failed to recognize the facts on the ground. Members of the pressure group Changing Attitude, however, were vocal, influential and relentless. Even if the vote was lost, they said that they would not give up until they achieved what they described as 'equal marriage'. The number of same-sex partnered clergy and allied clergy was on the rise, partly because of ordinands being accepted for training and also clergy from England and Ireland moving into the much more gay-friendly Scottish province.

In the face of these changed facts, a few of us knew that we must still do something. On the day of the final vote, we arranged a press conference to make it clear that not everyone would go along with the new economy. Archbishop Foley Beach of the Anglican Church in North America joined us for that, as did Andy Lines who, later that month in Wheaton, Illinois, would be consecrated as a GAFCON missionary bishop by many Anglican Communion bishops to offer care in Europe for those such as ourselves who found themselves unable to serve in a province that had placed itself in error.

The canonical change meant that we now had to decide how to proceed.

By November 2017, a congregation of the SEC, Christ Church, on the Isle of Harris, had chosen to leave. This faithful little orthodox congregation gave up the building that they had built and a not inconsiderable sum of money. Instead, they began meeting in the home of a member of the congregation. Their courage and sacrifice served as an inspiration for others to consider following their path.

In September 2014, I had moved from St Silas Church, Glasgow, to serve as Rector of St Thomas' Church, Edinburgh. The former was founded in 1864. The latter church founded in 1844. Both had been independent evangelical Anglican congregations. As part of a wider grouping of churches known as the Association of English Episcopal Churches, they had sought official recognition from the Church of England for much of the nineteenth century but failed, though the first bishop of Liverpool, J. C. Ryle, had offered much support.

By the late twentieth century, the relationship of these churches with the SEC was much warmer, so much so that St Thomas' transplanted seventy members into a city-centre Scottish Episcopalian congregation and planted a new Scottish Episcopal Church in a neighbouring community. Strangely, therefore, those congregations were both in the SEC while the parent church was not. The leadership at St Thomas' took the decision to join the SEC, too, although it seems that the congregation was not widely consulted about this. By 1990, both St Thomas' and St Silas had joined the SEC, though St Silas joined as a private chapel and paid only the diocesan and not the provincial quota (during the nineteen years of my service there, the different bishops came to me every couple of years to ask if it was time that St Silas should pay full quota. I always invited them to come and persuade the vestry why doubling the amount given to the SEC was a good thing).

When I was interviewed for the rector role at St Thomas', I was asked specifically what my views were on same-sex marriage. I made it clear that I could not serve in a church that adopted such a doctrine and would seek to remove myself from its authority. When the canonical change came, the trustees and vestry were well-prepared for what was to come. We had prayed, discussed and planned. We were in solid agreement. What we did not know was how the congregation would respond.

As matters unfolded, I had many protracted and difficult conversations with members of the church. Some left before we got to the point of voting to leave. Others stayed, hoping to influence the decision. Letters and emails were received criticizing my leadership, sometimes in very aggressive ways. The stress was enormous. Sleepless nights and constant anxiety played havoc with our health. We did not know whether or not the diocese would fight the trustees for the property and, ultimately, we would lose our home. Yet we took heart from the encouragements we received from friends in North America who had faced this process ten years earlier and, with God's help, survived and prospered. We also had massive support in prayer from close friends both in Scotland and around the world. This helped us to know that the Lord was watching over us (Psalm 121:5).

We knew that some people had changed their views on marriage. Some tried to argue using science, others psychology. Some had family or friends who were same-sex attracted. That, perhaps, provides the maximum pressure on once-orthodox people to accept same-sex marriage. 'Love is love' trumped any previous biblical understanding of marriage. One person declared, 'I am a liberal'.

What all this told us was that, no matter how long a congregation's evangelical heritage is, one cannot assume all your people will be on the same page when it comes to sexuality. The zeitgeist is pervasive and resisting it can lead to one becoming a social pariah. Some church members are just not up for that.

We had several meetings with the congregation and the Bishop of Edinburgh was present. The Bishop sought to persuade us that we held a valued place in the diocese and we would not be forced to do anything. Yet, he failed to recognize the problem of the clergy and people being unable to submit to the authority of a bishop who was teaching error. It is also a strategy that affects the long term. New ordinands will tend to fall in line with whatever the central authority presents or risk not being ordained. As members of the clergy move on and retire, new rectors are more likely to have been formed by the current teaching of the bishops. We hear that the bishops now ensure that new clergy in the province are only welcomed if they can assure the bishops of their acceptance of the revised marriage canon, albeit with the proviso that they will not have to perform same-sex marriages. How long will it be before it becomes the expected norm?

After much prayerful deliberation, the congregation of St Thomas' finally voted to disaffiliate from the SEC. Some 72 per cent of members voted to leave. Around 15 per cent chose not to stay with the new congregation that would be formed. For some this was because they had become convinced that same-sex marriage could be blessed by the Lord. Others felt that separation was always wrong (I often found myself wondering when this was said, 'Why are we still Protestant, then?') A few wanted to remain in the SEC. Others joined local Presbyterian congregations.

No departure is easy for a pastor to bear. I was disappointed and hurt that so many chose to leave. Some left quietly. Some sought to influence and persuade others to join them. The pain of separation was not easy for many in the congregation. However, the decision to realign within the Anglican Communion had revealed some further cracks in the membership. Some harboured grief from previous painful experiences or disagreements. Others had moved in their theological approach or no longer held to a strong belief in the authority of Scripture. Still others had retained their membership of the congregation at St Thomas' for social or historical reasons. Whatever the reasons, people left us, so we had to count the considerable cost of standing firm on this point of principle.

There was also the pain of other church leader colleagues choosing to remain in the SEC. For many this was also a principled stand. They hope to bear witness to orthodox teaching in a liberal catholic denomination. They must be credited for that. We had done that for thirty-five years but could no longer do so. It was felt that it was time to leave behind being part of a broken system where trust in the bishops had failed, where obedience to Scripture was not expected and where meetings for governance had become depressingly political rather than joyful gatherings to celebrate what the Lord had done and would do in us. It might be that the Lord will use those who remain to bring reform and renewal in the years to come. Our observation at this point is that those who remain are more likely to become like the institution they serve, rather than that institution becoming more like them. Loyalty and obedience to the institution is taught and expected. We shall see how orthodoxy fares as we pray for those in the SEC who seek to stand firm in faith.

In the midst of the pain, there was some comfort. New people chose to join us, too, appreciating the stand that we had taken. We entered a fresh season, determined not to look back, but to look forwards and outwards.

Other congregations also decided to realign. In January 2019, the congregation of Westhill Community Church just outside Aberdeen under the Reverend Ian Ferguson's leadership voted by 87 per cent to leave the SEC. They then faced ongoing negotiations to secure the new church building that the congregation had paid for a few years ago. In December 2019, St Silas Church, Glasgow, began afresh, as an evangelical Anglican congregation under the care of Bishop Andy Lines.

This has been a long and hard road to travel and it was not chosen willingly. Those in leadership of the SEC have not always been transparent and, at times, have behaved in ways that have been, at best, misleading. Relationships have been strained and difficult decisions have not always been implemented well. We have learnt much on the way, both through the pain but also through the joy of standing firm together. We have enjoyed some of the sweetest fellowship in the whole of my service as a minister, with friends old and new. Like the time I sat with my dear friend, the aforementioned Ian Ferguson, by the River Tay in a little restaurant that, over the years, had become our operations room. Much to our surprise, in walked the Bishop of Edinburgh and another senior cleric. We were noticed and a pleasant conversation ensued. We could see the Lord's hand in that and many other events.

St Thomas' Church was finally relaunched in June 2019. Bishop Charlie Masters of the Anglican network in Canada joined us as we recommitted ourselves to the work of the gospel. We chose to mark the occasion by placing a plaque in a prominent place in the church. It reads:

On 2 June 2019 the people of St Thomas' Church reaffirmed their commitment to serve God, to worship him in accordance with Anglican practice and to gladly accept the Great Commission of the risen Lord. 'Therefore go and make disciples of all nations, baptizing them in the name of the Father and of the Son and of the Holy Spirit, teaching them to observe all that I have commanded you. And behold, I am with you always, to the end of the age' (Matthew 28:19–20).

12

Clear blue water:
leaving the Church of England
and alternative Anglicanisms

THE REVEREND DR PETER SANLON

No longer let false doctrine disgrace your pulpit. Be bold – be firm –
be decisive. Let Christ be all ... Leave the consequences with your
Divine Master. He will be with his faithful ministers to the end of
time.
(Letter to Henry Venn, in A member of the Houses of Shirley and
Hastings, *Selina, the Countess of Huntington*)[1]

Seeking clear blue water

Becoming an incumbent in the Church of England forces a minister to
ponder the long-term security of local ministry. One considers staffing
decisions, investments in buildings, the shifting demographics of a parish
and the impact of the wider denomination on local ministry. This is
especially painful for those evangelicals who can see that recent decisions
by the bishops of the Church of England and General Synod make it difficult to believe that the present reality – to say nothing of the future
trajectory – of the Church of England is a secure place for faithful gospel
ministries.

The gospel calls on people to repent their own and others' sin and place
their faith in Jesus. Many in the senior leadership of the Church of
England prefer to call on people to ignore sin and place their faith in
the secular culture's ideals. The first people to point this out are often the

evangelicals, as they value dynamism, growth and vibrancy in missional ministries. Unfortunately, they can be so focused on local church ministry that they ignore governance and polity. Canons, synods, episcopal ministry, liturgy – these are seen as, at best, irrelevant to work in the parish and, often, as a hindrance.

A number of factors are pushing evangelical ministers to re-examine their prejudice against polity. There are no answers to the current crisis from the older evangelical ministers, who espoused that view for decades. They reside in their posts, but neither offer solutions to little churches round the country, nor security to their own congregations beyond their retirements. Worse, the conservative evangelical world in the Church of England has been rocked by a series of long-festering abuse stories, which go to the heart of their leadership. All this raises doubts about whether we can afford to be so dismissive of polity, given part of its role is to offer security against abuses of power and personality.

With all this in mind, I am happy to share some of my experiences in leading a congregation out of the Church of England.

A classic car

Helping a congregation step out of the established church requires some kind of strategy and vehicle. It is not something one can do haphazardly. Another Church of England minister told me about the Free Church of England (FCE) in 2016. I was surprised that I had never heard of the denomination and so began reading its history. I wondered if it could be the help that my church needed.

Finding the FCE was like buying a house and, on going into the garage, discovering a tarpaulin, pulling it back and under it is hidden a classic car. The car is valuable but has been resting there for some years. It needs a new coat of paint, some parts need to be replaced. With the eyes of faith one can see how compelling it could become. Some loving care and attention, and it will be sweeping along roads all over the country, bringing the gospel to all and sundry.[2]

The FCE has a history – it is not a pristine model, ready to roll out of the garage, with a no-questions-asked insurance policy. The FCE is more like a classic car that needs to be nurtured into a roadworthy condition.

Some are put off by the fact that the FCE is not a new institution. For myself, I am more nervous about designing something from a blank sheet of paper, than I am about slowly strengthening and supporting an old idea. I believe that there is something Anglican about my instinct. The English Reformation was not a total fresh start – it was a preservation of all that could be kept and a reformation of that which demanded it. The instinct to start again *completely* afresh, is more anabaptist- or Enlightenment-driven, than Anglican.

The FCE has challenges and weaknesses, but they are the same as those that newer groups outside the established church will eventually face. I have found that experienced incumbents are alert to the benefits of working within a long-established structure – even if that means some goals require patience or need to be managed using less-than-perfect processes. All this is safer and humbler than imagining you can invent the ideal.

The FCE's story

The FCE played a key part in how our congregation exited the Church of England. There are other ways to leave it and alternative denominations to join. Before considering those, it may be helpful to hear more about the FCE.

Bishop Paul Hunt is an incumbent of a local church and bishop of the southern diocese of the FCE. He was baptized and grew up as a member of the FCE, so while Church of England Anglicans explore the FCE as a possible move for them, Bishop Paul never did that; it has always been his home. Given that, he was the obvious choice to invite to give a talk on the history of the FCE. People who heard him give that talk (in Tunbridge Wells, 2018) were struck by his introduction. He observed, 'The FCE is not a new church. We have a long history – indeed, as long as the history of the Church of England! Up until 1844, the FCE shares its history with the Church of England. Our history is your history.' This point is an important one to remember: it means that the Anglican instincts which took centuries to form and reach back not only to the Reformation but also beyond that to the patristic consensus, are the heritage of not only the Church of England but also the FCE. Members of clergy who left the

Church of England to serve in the FCE structure had, until they left, been willing to remain in the established church. When they left, quite understandably, they maintained their shared history, emotional affinities and ecclesial instincts.

The flashpoint that led to the FCE becoming a cousin of the established church was persecution by the well-known (and authoritarian) Anglo-Catholic, Bishop Phillpotts of Exeter (1830–1869). The Church Society and evangelicals more widely have written about the Gorham Case.[3] Bishop Phillpotts sought to deny the Reverend Gorham a parish on the basis that he denied baptismal regeneration, as understood by the Tractarian movement of the day. The animosity with which Bishop Phillpotts made his case (threatening even the then Archbishop of Canterbury with excommunication if any dared to offer Gorham a living), did much to immortalize the story.

Less well known was Bishop Phillpotts' similar treatment of a conservative evangelical minister, the Reverend James Shore. In 1832, he was appointed minister of Bridgetown Chapel, in the parish of Berry Pomeroy. Bridgetown Chapel had been built and furnished by the Duke of Somerset at the cost of £7,000. In today's money, that would be about £500,000. The building could seat a congregation of 700. The Duke and Bishop disagreed on the details of how to proceed with the licensing of the building for Anglican worship. The Duke was concerned to maintain a role in appointing ministers, while the Bishop wanted a financial fund from the Duke to be put in place to endow future stipends. They agreed on a compromise: a legal agreement was drawn up to the effect that another local minister would be patron until the Duke financed an endowment to pay stipends. On that basis the building was licensed for Anglican worship.

The first minister was the Reverend James Shore. He served as minister of Bridgetown, holding a licence as curate at Berry Pomeroy. That was a perfectly acceptable arrangement – except that, after some years, it transpired that the paperwork for Shore's licence had not been completed accurately. Bishop Phillpotts said that, technically, the Reverend Shore had been serving at the chapel for nine years without a licence. The Bishop ordered the Reverend Shore to cease ministry until he was granted a new licence. He did so – closing the doors of the church for five months. During that time, his people were offered ministry from a non-evangelical minister.

Eventually, the Duke asked the Reverend Shore if would he consider serving as a minister to his church, if it was outside the Church of England? The most detailed historical study of these events records, 'Although sincerely attached to the Anglican Church, Shore admitted that with pain and reluctance he was willing to secede from it out of concern for the continued spiritual welfare of his congregation, especially as they were now under a Tractarian incumbent.'[4]

Bishop Phillpotts warned the Reverend Shore that he could not serve as a minister anywhere without a licence. Despite this, on 14 April 1844, Shore resumed services at Bridgetown Chapel and called it the first congregation of the 'Free Church of England'.

The Bishop launched ecclesiastical legal proceedings against Shore, arguing that, while a minister could be deposed of Church of England orders, one could not elect to relinquish them. The case was heard by the church courts and, eventually, the Court of the Arches and the Privy Council. Speeches were made in defence of Shore in the House of Lords. *The Times* ran several articles urging people to support Shore, as a case of religious freedom and toleration.

All these efforts were to no avail. Shore was fined the sum of £186 14s. 2d. That equates to about £12,660. A warrant for his arrest was issued when payment was not forthcoming. As he descended from the pulpit in the Countess of Huntingdon's chapel at Spa Fields, the Reverend Shore was arrested. The extraordinary arrest and subsequent imprisonment in Exeter jail almost incited riots. Shore was unable to pay the fine demanded of him and, on principle, did not wish to in any case. His health began to decline in the parlous prison conditions, and a group of London evangelicals raised money by public appeals and paid his fine. As soon as it was paid, the Bishop said that he would not release the Reverend Shore until a further £124 (£8,407 today) was paid, to cover additional costs incurred. With no choice but to comply with these punitive demands, further money was raised and Shore was released.

When Shore got out of prison, 5,000 people gathered at Exeter Hall to hear him preach, before he resumed his ministry at Bridgetown.

The first FCE church, then, was established amid opposition to an authoritarian bishop, known for his uncharitable opposition to evangelicals. The story is one in which principles of religious freedom were at stake. Laypeople and the media worked to right an injustice and an evangelical preacher suffered in significant ways – all in order that he could offer his people secure evangelical ministry. It is bemusing that the Gorham case has become so celebrated within evangelical memory, but the Shore case has been all but forgotten. It is foundational for the FCE, but it is also instructive more widely.

There are other strands to the story of the FCE. In the mid- to late 1800s, the Tractarian movement gained influence in the Church of England. Evangelical ministers and the laity were concerned that the tacit (or sometimes explicit) support for baptismal regeneration, priestly view of ministers, sacrificial re-offering of Christ on an altar and so on were all destructive of the evangelical gospel. Recent research has argued that the Tractarian instincts were, indeed, incompatible with evangelical commitments. For example, Professor Steward summarized recent scholarship on the matter and concluded:

Since the 1930s, there has been a steady stream of commentators urging modern Christians to view Tractarianism (and its later expression of Anglo-Catholicism) as the natural offspring of an earlier evangelicalism so that some kind of 'détente', or better, collaboration might follow. But such advocacy is fraught with difficulty, and not only because (as this essay has shown) forms of evangelical Christianity (within and beyond Anglicanism) have almost from the first found fault with Tractarianism on biblical and doctrinal grounds, but also because of unfolding developments.[5]

The FCE was founded in opposition to Tractarian tendencies. Its ministers sought to engage in Anglican prayerbook ministry without embracing innovations that they believed would be more at home in the Roman Catholic Church than the Church of England. The English Reformers patently did not support liturgy affirming similar views of the mass, as people had been burnt at the stake for denying such beliefs. Tractarianism was an effort to make the words of the Book of Common Prayer mean things that the Reformers clearly did not intend. Today, evangelicals in the Church of England face an analogous problem: a fundamental distortion of words in the liturgy and Scripture to try and make them mean things (in this case, to do with sexuality and human flourishing) that cannot be a fair reading of the passages concerned.

After the Reverend Shore and others left to secure Anglican ministry outside the Church of England, one of the FCE's early leaders said:

> The body which we wish to see gathered and grow is the Church of England – that is to say, we will hold her doctrines, liturgy and general outline of government, but all freed from what we consider unscriptural and objectionable.[6]

As clergy attracted by the FCE vision left the Church of England, they found fellowship and solidarity with those who had been converted under the Calvinist Revival ministry of George Whitefield. While converts of Wesley's in time came to be organized into Methodism, those who took a more Reformed view of salvation found that they had greater common ground with FCE than Methodist congregations.

Bishop John Fenwick has painstakingly summarized many key aspects of the FCE story. He noted with regard to the fruit of the eighteenth-century evangelical Revival that, 'It was the smaller Calvinistic stream that was to be more closely associated with the origins of the FCE.'[7] The Revival was the most significant religious event of the eighteenth century and its passion for mission, spiritual reality and holiness of life remains a vital part of the FCE's story and vision.

Selina, the Countess of Huntingdon, was a leading benefactor of the eighteenth-century evangelicals – hosting prayer meetings and missions, and building homes for clergy and church buildings.[8] She hosted Venn, Wesley and Whitefield to preach on more than one occasion in Tunbridge Wells. In time, she funded the building of a church. That congregation began as part of her evangelical 'Connexion' of congregations. Papers found with Selina's last will and testament show that she wished her churches to band together in an alternative non-established alternative to the Church of England. Today, a monument still stands in the town announcing that near that spot, 'On 23rd July, 1769, George Whitefield preached the sermon at the opening of Emmanuel Church, Tunbridge Wells.' The ministry at Emmanuel began as part of Selina's Connexion, but it continued beyond her and Whitefield's lifetime. Thus, the first president of the FCE was the Reverend George Jones, who was the minister at Emmanuel from 1849 until 1888. As John Fenwick noted, 'There is a very real sense in which the FCE is a continuation of the Connexion, and hence a surviving expression of the heritage of Whitefield.'[9]

In 1844, the FCE formed a legal union with the Reformed Episcopal Church of America (REC). It had been seeking to develop a mission in England and it made sense to partner with the FCE to do that. One of the lasting benefits to the FCE was its appropriation of the REC's 'Declaration of Principles'. This short statement of faith insists that the FCE will interpret its liturgy and ministry in ways that are firmly evangelical and not Anglo-Catholic. It stands at the front of every FCE prayerbook and yearbook. The clergy and lay officers regularly assent to it, such as when they sign into convocation and synods. At a time when many Anglicans are confused about doctrine, it serves as an invaluable clarification of what the FCE understands to be evangelical Anglican doctrine.

By the summer of 1939, the FCE had fifty churches. Sadly, the war years led to its decline – the loss of buildings and ministers were difficult to recover from. By contrast, the Church of England had immense assets and resources to fall back on. In the years after the Second World War, the denomination charted a course not that different from evangelicalism more widely in the country – there was a decline in energy and distancing from the culture. The ministries of John Stott and Dick Lucas lifted Church of England evangelicals out of those ruts. The FCE, however, was untouched by their works. I asked Dick Lucas about his observations of ministry in the Church of England when he had been a curate, just after the war. He understood what I meant when I observed that the path of the FCE after those years, in many ways, was what would have been the story of Church of England evangelicals, had God not intervened.

Nevertheless, the FCE has survived. Humanly speaking, it has done so against all the odds. As evangelicals in the Church of England struggle with challenges that have as yet proved insoluble, the words of FCE Bishop Frank Vaughan come to mind. He wrote, in 1949, 'It is my conviction that God has been guiding and preserving the FCE for some as yet unrevealed purpose.'[10]

For many years, letterheads, banners and books produced by the FCE have described the denomination as 'evangelical, liturgical and episcopal'.

These three words capture something of the Anglican vision that the FCE has as its heritage, and which are attracting some to the FCE as a secure structure for future ministry. We shall now consider the value of each of these words for the present day.

Evangelical

Many evangelicals in the Church of England feel uncomfortable about the theological breadth of the established church. Many believe that the problems go back to ambiguities in the Book of Common Prayer's description of ministers as 'priests', the words in the baptism liturgy 'this child is regenerate' and the possible misreading of Communion as being open to Anglo-Catholic or sacramentalist practices. Regardless of whether these fears about the Church of England's position are fair or well-founded, that many conservative evangelicals feel their views to be under pressure from wider forces in the Church of England is undeniable. As it says in the FCE's 'Declaration of Principles', 'this church accepts the Book of Common Prayer of the Church of England, with such revisions as shall exclude sacerdotal doctrines and practices.'[11]

The FCE allays evangelical concerns by making use of a lightly edited Book of Common Prayer. At crucial points, it was altered to clarify the Protestant instincts of Thomas Cranmer and the other Reformers. Words declaring the baby 'regenerate' in baptism have been removed. The words of consecration in the Lord's Supper have a clause added to emphasize Cranmer's point that the Lord Jesus is present only in a 'heavenly and spiritual manner'. The Thirty-nine Articles, likewise, have been edited to make these views clear.[12] Such clarificatory alterations to the Book of Common Prayer have considerable impact in the FCE, as it is smaller than the Church of England and because all office holders regularly have to sign statements of adherence to doctrine and canons. These statements of assent are, for example, signed by all delegates to a synod as well as by ministers on ordination or appointment to a post. The form of words used is stricter and clearer in its expectations of conformity to FCE doctrine and liturgy than is the Church of England's words of assent used at ordinations.

The commitment to Protestant evangelical doctrine and practice is made most clear by the FCE's 'Declaration of Principles'. This is printed at the front of every prayer book, at the front of every yearbook and copies are sometimes displayed in church vestries. Everybody in the FCE is familiar with this, known simply as 'the Principles' – a short, one-page statement of the FCE's intent to uphold Protestant convictions at the points where conservative evangelicals feel that the Church of England has been lax. A history book, published under the authority of the FCE convocation, notes about the Principles:

> Adopted in 1873, they have been the foundation stone upon which, under God, the structure has been raised. They contain no new truth, no startling setting-forth of belief. These Principles have been the foundations of the belief of the Church since its earliest beginning.[13]

The Principles make use of material from the Church of Ireland and the Reformed Episcopal Church. In this it displays the wisdom of not seeking to reinvent the wheel or do theology from a blank slate. The statement opens by reminding readers that the evangelicalism the FCE aspires to is nothing less than the grand vision of the universal church. The FCE is 'a branch of the Holy Catholic Church of the Lord Jesus Christ.' Upholding evangelical doctrine does not seal one off in a holy huddle, it opens up the vistas of the great consensus of apostolic doctrine and ecclesial practice. The Principles make positive affirmations of upholding the Apostle's Creed, baptism and Communion – and the 'doctrines of grace' as found in the Thirty-nine Articles and elsewhere.

Alongside these warm-hearted, positive affirmations, the Principles make five negative clarifications. Many church statements have made use of negative prohibitions as the only effective way to guard against error, as mere positive affirmations run the risk of creating legal loopholes for theological Trojan horses. The use of negative statements to clarify the real intent of positive affirmations goes back to at least the Ten Commandments, and to Jesus himself. The negative second half of John 14:6 clarifies the meaning of the positive first half. Recent statements, such as the Nashville Statement, follow this tradition by pairing affirmations with denials.[14] So the Principles seek to guard the FCE's positive vision for evangelical doctrine by making five clarifications:

This Church CONDEMNS and REJECTS the following erroneous and strange doctrines as contrary to God's Word:

> First, That the Church of Christ exists only in one order or form
> of ecclesiastical polity;
> Second, That Christian Ministers are 'priests' in another sense
> than that in which all believers are 'a royal priesthood';
> Third, That the Lord's Table is an altar on which the oblation
> of the Body and Blood of Christ is offered anew to the Father;
> Fourth, That the Presence of Christ in the Lord's Supper is
> a presence in the elements of Bread and Wine;
> Fifth, That Regeneration is inseparably connected with Baptism.

For those evangelicals who have felt frustrated with the Church of England's ambiguity about the matters dealt with in the Principles, these statements are reassuring and welcome. From a position of clarity, charity can be shown to other denominations. Thus, the Principles close with the promise, 'This Church will maintain communion with all Christian Churches, and will set forward, so far as in it lieth, quietness, peace and love, among all Christian people.' Conservative evangelicals in the Church of England have felt themselves painted into a corner from which they come across as negative and critical. That is partly the result of serving in a denomination that lacks the clarity provided by the FCE's Principles. That warm-hearted charity expressed in its final clause is possible because of the commitment to evangelical doctrine guarded in the preceding clarifications.

Episcopal

The pastoral epistles assume oversight of churches, by those external to the local congregations. The significance of this has been well-chronicled by Roger Beckwith,[15] and is evidenced by verses such as Titus 1:5, 1 Timothy 5:19 and 2 Timothy 1:6. There are various ways to provide oversight that is external to a local church. Presbyterianism, for example, offers one alternative to the way in which this is handled in Anglicanism. In the Anglican tradition, bishops are one way to give expression to the biblical expectation of oversight of congregations.

Evangelicals in the Church of England have struggled with this crucial part of the Anglican heritage. Whether it is a desire to plant a church where one wishes or reluctance to have a revisionist bishop do a confirmation, the tensions between local evangelical churches and bishops are legion. Many evangelical churches look to their own self-appointed networks (such as New Wine or ReNew) or societies (the Church Society or Cross Links, for example) or para-church organizations (such as the UCCF, Proclamation Trust or Titus Trust, formerly the Iwerne Trust). As such organizations play a greater part in shaping and supporting ministers than bishops, a consequence is that the Church of England evangelical scene is dominated by the large churches. These are always, without exception, led by clergy drawn from a cadre of public-school men. With millions of pounds flowing annually through the various funds and charities associated with the large churches, it is little surprise that meaningful episcopal care is set aside in favour of what Mike Ovey nicknamed monarchical presbyter oversight. In such a system, a minister of a large Church of England church holds more power than any diocesan bishop over money, appointments and the selection and training of clergy. Recent revelations about the mismanagement of John Smyth and the Jonathan Fletcher abuse scandals have made younger evangelicals wary of unregulated large church monarchical presbyter leaders. There is a renewed interest in and desire to experience the value of a Reformed, biblical oversight.

Ideally, a bishop is an experienced presbyter. He can speak with members of a local church with knowledge and love of the minister and congregation. He has the authority to resolve problems in a way that is pastoral and wise. He should, in some ways, have his power checked. In the FCE, that is achieved by having more than one bishop, and the canons and by-laws shape his decisions.

Many Church of England evangelicals fear the excessive authority of bishops. In the FCE, most bishops remain ministers of local congregations, which fosters trust and realism between congregations and bishops. Crucially, the structure of the FCE is such that bishops remain accountable to the Convocation for their ministries. Bishops are voted into office and can be changed by the democratic mandate of the Convocation. The Convocation is the ruling body of the FCE. As it is made up of five voting members from each church, only one of whom is a minister, the oversight given to bishops is much more lay-led than in the Church of England. This commendable feature of the FCE flows from a realistic awareness of the problems concerning power, which, so often, are allowed to do damage in the evangelical large church and para-church contexts.

Liturgical

The Anglican way of worship is inescapably liturgical. Sir Roger Scruton spoke, the year before his death, of the importance of liturgy:

> In liturgy, language is used to evoke the eternal presence of God and his unchanging nature ... To find such words, is the task of a poet. Cranmer, Tyndale and Coverdale were all amply supplied with the poetic gift.[16]

The services crafted by Cranmer drew on patristic and medieval sources and he added a dash of vibrant English language. Many of the phrases used in the Book of Common Prayer have passed into the self-understanding of our nation.

Most evangelicals in the Church of England do not greatly value or use liturgy. A desire for freedom in worship, fear of appearing disconnected from culture, negative views of childhood church – all play their part in evangelicals of varied hues neglecting liturgy. Even in those parts of the established church that do value liturgy, the 'Common Worship' project has embedded irretrievable fluidity into liturgical practice.

The FCE continues to be a liturgical church. The Book of Common Prayer remains widely used and is repeatedly affirmed as our doctrinal and liturgical standard. The canons and Convocation continue to uphold the pre-eminent place of the Book of Common Prayer, ensuring that the FCE would not be a viable home for ministers who despise liturgy. While the FCE has not loosened liturgical norms to anything like the extent of the Church of England, the by-laws permit an FCE bishop to authorize non-Book of Common Prayer services as contextually required. Given that, the church I serve, Emmanuel Anglican Church, has our bishop's permission for some of its services to make use of the modern language An English Prayer Book.[17]

I have found that there is a deep interest in liturgy – among younger people, the unchurched and those of all classes. I have found it helpful to have short sessions in a service where parts of the liturgy are explained. Renewed commitment to liturgy has ensured that all our services are shaped by the gospel, and regular members are helped to learn off by heart key texts such as the Lord's Prayer, Apostle's Creed, Ten Commandments and Prayer of Humble Access. In a post-Christian culture, this is a valuable way to teach people. Alongside liturgical worship and preaching, the FCE is also committed to encouraging free and open prayer. The Principles describe the FCE as 'retaining a Liturgy which shall not be repressive of freedom in prayer'. In my own congregation, we have weekly and monthly prayer meetings and, during services, often have times of open prayer. The liturgy we use facilitates and encourages genuine prayer, outreach and worship.

Moves into the FCE

In recent years, ministers have realized that the FCE offers alternative structures for Anglican ministry. Having been a Church of England incumbent for five years, I could see that there were serious long-term challenges to continuing my ministry in the Church of England. I could point to documents that contain official teaching I uphold, but the facts on the ground, the trajectory, and the episcopal leadership were not things that I could accept faithfully. I considered seeking to get my PCC to pass a resolution to accept ministry from Bishop Rod Thomas. I arranged for him to visit to do a confirmation and to speak to our PCC. However, as I reflected on the situation, I realized that his role, as a bishop who served under the diocesan bishop, meant that, for all the effort it takes to pass a PCC resolution, he did not actually provide alternative oversight to that of the Church of England bishops. Essentially, instead, he simply provides an illusion of some respite from compromised oversight. The structure is such that a church cannot 'go under' the oversight of Bishop Rod; it can only 'receive his ministry' under that of the actual diocesan bishop.

In January 2017, therefore, I took out a licence in the Free Church of England, which allowed me to visit its synods and build relationships.

Crucially, it gave me, alongside my Church of England bishop, another bishop to care for me and offer genuinely independent episcopal oversight.

When, at the end of 2019, my Church of England church established a small church plant, we decided to shelter that under the auspices of the FCE. It met on Sunday evenings in a building that we rented, in a different part of the parish from our main building. At that point, there had been nothing going on in our Church of England ministry during that evening slot.

People opted for the FCE for two reasons. First, the laypeople involved in the decisions felt that the structures of the FCE were the most appealing. People with experience of business said that they felt reassured by us having structures around our new work – liturgy, canons, bishops. Second, there had been an FCE church in Tunbridge Wells previously. The church had been established by Countess Selina and the first sermon was preached by George Whitefield in the eighteenth century. The church, eventually, was in a grand building in a prominent part of the town. Sadly, it was demolished in the late 1970s to make way for an access road to a hospital, but that local historical link was appealing – perhaps for romantic reasons, perhaps for providential reasons.

For a year-and-a-half, I led the FCE congregation alongside the Church of England church, in much the same way that many evangelical churches have their minister oversee a sister congregation of a larger church. When the Church of England bishops issued their Advent 2018 guidance on using the service of baptism renewal (or baptism) as a celebration of a sex change,[18] I believed that it would be unfaithful for me to remain as a minister in a denomination where such things were permitted to be done with the sacraments. A right use of sacraments is a distinguishing feature of a Christian church.[19]

I began discussing arrangements for my departure with my Church of England diocese. At this point, I discovered that the FCE was very helpful. As a denomination with historic and legal links to the Church of England, my diocese understood how to relate to it. We were a known entity. I had kept my Church of England bishop aware of my licensing in the FCE, and planting the FCE church. All of this meant that the diocese was willing to discuss a reasonable and fair package for my departure. They recognized that I was leaving on the basis of my convictions about changes in the Church of England and they trusted me to leave the parish building, funds and data in good order. For their part, the diocese told me that they had a reasonable duty of care towards me and my family so, after some discussions, we agreed that I would take gardening leave for one month of my three months' notice, and my family could live in the vicarage as they would be able to for a Church of England incumbent, for a year from the date of my resignation. That, in effect, saved our church plant's housing costs for a year. As we had started out in a fragile, self-funding entre- preneurial venture, it was a gesture that was much appreciated. It also enabled us to stagger the house move and the church move – doing them both at the same time would have been very demanding.

I am aware that some who have left the Church of England without the presence of an historic denomination such as the FCE, have less pleasant stories to tell of how they were treated. I can commend the decency and fairness with which my diocese (Rochester) handled the process for us – it was a good separation.

We announced our resignation from the Church of England in February 2019 and Easter Sunday that year was my final day serving in the Church of England. The subsequent Sunday, we ran morning and evening services in a rented building, a few minutes' walk from the Church of England parish building.

We started out with a congregation of about twenty adults, and that number has since trebled, with most joining us from places outside the Church of England. In our first year we have seen one new profession of faith from an unchurched person and others say that their faith has been renewed by joining us. We have started a fortnightly youth club and members are involved in community work around our area. All those involved in setting up our little church have grown in faith and are thriving as they serve alongside one another. They are excited about the way we can pray and build towards a long-term mission in our town of Tunbridge Wells. I was struck that, in a recent membership class (the FCE is a membership, rather than parish model of church), one person men- tioned how reading the most recent statements issued by the Church of England bishops was no longer necessary. The problems that so held back our ministry in the Church of England for some time are simply not our concern any longer. We feel that we have preserved what matters about evangelical Anglican Christianity and jettisoned that which conformed to the culture.

The FCE is much smaller than the Church of England. Indeed, nothing can compete with the Church of England for sheer size, recognized names and historic assets of money and property, yet there have been signs of spiritual renewal and life.

The Reverend Jonatas Bragatto moved from Brazil – he was called as a missionary to England. His European citizenship meant that he could live and work in the UK and, via friends in Brazil who worship in FCE churches there (we have a missionary diocese in the country), he got in touch with FCE bishops in England. This led to Jonatas being appointed as a minister in Middlesborough. Jonatas comes from a ministry family and is a very good scholar of the history of the FCE. He brings a fresh cultural perspective to our labours in England. It was a delight to see pictures of new members of his church, and to hear how he is establishing new services and holding services of reception for new members.

When the Reverend Andy Palmer was interviewed for the job of senior minister at the Co-Mission church, Christ Church Balham, he explored with its lay leadership how the church could best guard its future. While already identifying as a confessionally Anglican church, Christ Church has never been in the Church of England. It was planted by Dundonald church in 2002 as part of the Co-Mission network. That means, while the church developed out of the ministry of Richard Coekin, who was ordained in the Church of England, the church managed all its buildings, costs and staffing outside Church of England provisions. Andy discussed with the lay leaders his concern that the church needed to have some form of genuine Anglican oversight, as a safeguard against abuses of power and to preserve succession of leadership. After exploring other options – such as coming under Bishop Rod Thomas in the Church of England or joining Anglican Mission, in England – Andy was drawn towards the FCE.

I met with his lay leaders to listen to their hopes and answer questions about the FCE. Bishop Paul Hunt of the FCE visited the church leaders and conversations were had with Richard Coekin. Richard explained to me that he saw no problem with Co-Mission churches joining the FCE. He said 'Co-Mission is not a church, it's a network. Some of our churches affiliate with the Church of England and I don't see why some can't choose the FCE as a wider denominational support, should they wish.' As a result of those cordial conversations, Christ Church explained on its website:

> As an affiliate member of the Free Church of England we are part of a family of churches working together to disciple the nations through local congregations. Like all Anglican churches, we hold to the doctrine of the early Councils of the Church, Thirty-nine Articles of Religion and the Book of Common Prayer. We seek to be contemporary in our style of corporate worship, whilst remaining conservative in theology. Our Senior Minister was ordained in the Church of England but now holds a licence in the Free Church of England, which is itself part of the worldwide GAFCON movement.
>
> We enjoy strong partnership with many other Bible-believing churches in the local area. As part of the Co-Mission network, whose Articles of Faith we subscribe to, we are working with churches across the city to seek to reach the unreached for Jesus by trying to plant and establish reformed evangelical churches in London.

Becoming part of the FCE means that Andy has a route to ordaining and training people for ministry that is Anglican, but outside the Church of England. One of his staff is beginning lay reader training and a former staff member is at Oak Hill College, training to be a presbyter in the FCE.

Christ Church has been on a journey of discovering more of the riches of Anglican heritage that are often neglected by conservative evangelicals. Andy told me that, with Bishop Paul's blessing, while they remain contemporary in style, they 'structure their services according to the Book of Common Prayer – with liturgical prayers of confession, collects, creeds, both Old and New Testament readings, and a Psalm sung to a modern tune.'

People mistakenly think that because the FCE holds firm to traditional doctrine regarding grace, the sacraments and ordination, and we value our Book of Common Prayer liturgy, that we cannot be adaptable for mission. The partnership with Christ Church is an example of how the FCE bishops have freedom to permit liturgical practice that varies from the Book of Common Prayer, while helping a congregation value liturgy it was previously less familiar with. Andy wrote up their story for *Evangelicals Now*, observing that he hoped the move into the FCE 'will help secure gospel ministry for generations to come.'[20]

Moves out of the FCE

I was aware when I joined the FCE that there had been a serious split of churches out of it back in the early 2000s. Disputes over centralization, property ownership and toleration of Anglo-Catholic practices had resulted in congregations departing the FCE and some legal disputes that remain unresolved to this day. Despite knowing that churches and ministers not only joined but also left the FCE, I felt the historical and legal links to the Church of England – together with its potential to help others – made it the best option for our context.

During the years that I held a licence in the FCE, I observed others join and leave. One example was the Reverend Julian Mann. He left the Church of England for many of the same reasons that I did, taking up a post as a minister in the FCE. He was to revitalize the FCE church in Morecambe. Within a few months, however, he resigned and left. He published his reasons for doing this:

In the past few years the current Bishop Primus, John Fenwick, has been introducing Anglo-Catholic practices into the FCE, especially in its northern diocese. Convocation, which is supposed to be the governing body of the FCE, does not seem to have been doing much to stop this ironic departure from the FCE's founding convictions. A 'Pastoral Letter and Statement' watering down the Declaration of Principles appeared on the FCE website last year signed by John Fenwick and the Bishop of the southern diocese, Paul Hunt. Convocation has not approved this letter but it is still there and John Fenwick has been insisting that FCE people in 'the 21st Century' must read the Principles in the light of it. Though I have been very concerned about this, the main reason I resigned as FCE minister of Emmanuel Church in the Lancashire coastal town of Morecambe Bay was to do with church growth and evangelism, which should be the priority for any evangelical. The FCE Central Trust closed the door on a suggested partnership with another evangelical church in Morecambe for a shared use of the Emmanuel building.[21]

I observed the Reverend Mann's departure with sadness. In the time since he left, the church building in Morecambe has been infested with insects and weeds. With hardly any congregation, it is unlikely that it will ever be revived.

Little did I expect at that time that I, too, would leave the FCE in 2021, having been licensed in it for a mere five years. As a member of the General Council of the FCE, I – and other officers – became concerned about potential financial and governance irregularities. When we asked the kinds of questions trustees would be expected to ask, Bishops Paul Hunt and John Fenwick were unwilling or unable to answer the queries. The concerns were reported to the Charity Commission and police and widely reported in the media.[22] In January 2021, the FCE was unable to sign off its accounts without reservations. In June 2021, the police called me to say that they agreed the questions ought to be answered, so their investigations would continue. As investigations did indeed continue and relationships were strained, my church felt that we had no choice but to withdraw from the FCE. We issued a public statement:

On 12th February a bishop, clergy and some laity emailed the General Council of the FCE to raise concerns about governance in the Free Church of England. Our rector was one of those who signed that letter.

Some of the matters arising have subsequently been reported on by *The Telegraph*. These articles make clear that serious matters are being considered by the Charity Commission and Police. To this date no satisfactory explanations have been given by Bishop John Fenwick or Bishop Paul Hunt. Whistleblowers who have raised alerts have been subjected to abuses of process and unjust treatment.

In light of this our Church Council met on 27th April. The proposal that our rector resign his licence in the FCE and our church leave the denomination was unanimously agreed. We will be seeking suitable ecclesial oversight and support for our church family and mission. This will of course take time to arrange but we are thankful to those who have already reached out to explore how they can support us in this period of transition. Meanwhile our day-to-day ministry continues unchanged, and we are thankful to God for his many blessings.

My church was not the only one to leave the FCE over these financial concerns – others continue to make preparations to leave, and one of those that left was the largest in the denomination, which was led by Bishop Josep Rosello. As the media reports made clear, Bishop Rosello had been excluded from the committees about which financial concerns had been raised. The members of his church felt similarly to mine and left the denomination. As a bishop with considerable gifts and church-planting experience, he may well be used by God to develop a new vision for mission or to support one of the other Anglican structures outside the Church of England. As my church is in a limbo state polity-wise, we value his ongoing pastoral support.

The important lesson from all this to those who feel that they must get clear blue water between themselves and the Church of England is to not be naive. Do not make the mistake of thinking that there are no problems or risks in alternative Anglican structures! It would be perverse to use those risks as a justification for inertia within the Church of England or to ignore serious doctrinal error there, but nobody can pretend that it is easy or risk-free to deal robustly with false teaching by stepping out from the Church of England. I continue to have a deep affection and love for the FCE and cherish both people in it and its history. I have no regrets about our decision to leave the Church of England for the FCE – the transition of a congregation out of the established church was greatly eased by the historic and legal relationship that still exists between them.

Alternative Anglicanisms

This means that my church must once again ponder with who it is to affiliate. We are in a season of prayer and seeking the Lord's will in the matter. Our congregation is growing, spiritually blessed and a joy to be part of. It is wonderful that we can consider our options from a position of spiritual and practical security. As noted, there is a limited number of options for any who opt to put clear blue water between themselves and the Church of England. Local circumstances and whether you are bringing a viable congregation with you are relevant. Our opting for the FCE was due in no small part to the historical links it has had with the town we serve in. There may be some kind of providential link you have that means a lot to you or key stakeholders.

Some leave the Church of England and lay aside Anglicanism itself as they do so. Others have founded or joined Presbyterian churches[23] or accepted a post in an FIEC church.[24] Polity is important but, given that its specific form is secondary to soteriology, it is a valid decision to change polity for the sake of security on more vital issues. Various people have done so with integrity. Those who wish to explore Anglican structures outside the Church of England could consider the FCE, of course, which has already been discussed in detail. The other current alternatives are the following.

- **The Church of England (Continuing)** This is a small denomination that was founded in 2019, in opposition to liturgical revision in the Church of England. Its constitution commits it to uphold the doctrine of the Thirty-nine Articles 'in their original, natural and intended usage'. Services are 'generally' according to the 1662 Book of Common Prayer and 'The Authorised Version of the Bible shall be the only version used.'[25] Episcopal governance is maintained and, as of 2021, the website listed four congregations. Three of these have church buildings and one meets in a community centre.[26]
- **The Evangelical Connexion** This group of churches includes five of the churches that split from the FCE in the early 2000s.[27] The name of the group is taken from the Countess of Huntington's description of her churches as a 'connexion' of congregations supporting one another. Currently the Connexion does not have a bishop – the churches have been governing one another via a coordinator – but as Anglicans who seek to uphold the founding vision of the FCE, they could welcome a bishop were a suitable one to come along.
- **GAFCON** The first Global Anglican Future Conference took place in Jerusalem in 2008. It operated as a de facto alternative Lambeth

Conference, drawing together representatives from the majority of Anglicans around the world. There have been subsequent conferences in 2013 and 2018. The conference has become a movement seeking to nurture orthodox Anglicanism worldwide. In 2019, Archbishop Foley Beach, primate of ACNA became the chair of GAFCON's Primates' Council. He brings considerable leadership ability and spiritual integrity to the movement, as it evolves step by step into an alternative home for Anglicans who need to distance their ministries from compromised national churches.

All of these alternative Anglicanisms face their own challenges in the UK. The FCE, Church of England (Continuing) and the Evangelical Connexion all struggle because of their small sizes, lack of resources and, to varying degrees, commitment to inherited traditions. I have friends in all of them, and they would all readily acknowledge the difficulties I have mentioned to be true.

GAFCON is clearly where the spiritual future of global Anglicanism lies – incredible advances and missions have been spearheaded in extremely challenging contexts. Work is advancing in the UK, but unique difficulties are posed. The deep influence of the Iwerne Camps on the formation and commitments of many senior conservative evangelical leaders in England means that, in the UK, there is a unique set of hostilities from conservative Anglicans towards charismatics. There is also an edge to the complementarianism commitments that goes beyond that which is found in other cultures which also restrict ordination to males.

GAFCON represents – in the eyes of the Church of England – a conservative strand of Anglicanism. In the eyes of most conservative evangelicals in the Church of England, however, GAFCON appears too liberal as it insists orthodox charismatics, Anglo-Catholics and evangelicals can work together, and it is open to women being ordained. Squaring this circle in England is difficult and has resulted in numerous launches of movements and ventures that have fizzled out (note the number of times 'Fellowships' of confessing evangelicals have been announced and then shelved).

It does, thankfully, look like GAFCON has got the movement off the ground in England and sought a way to hold the groups together. What that currently means is that Bishop Andy Lines leads GAFCON in the UK and is able to establish 'convocations' under his oversight. These work with the other convocations, but can also maintain their distinctives. So AMiE is complementarian and, in practice, less liturgical than most other GAFCON Anglicans; the Anglican Network in Europe is more liturgical and supportive of ordained women. While this approach accepts the uniquely English conservative divisions and shares resources in line with them, it has proven necessary and, in time, hopefully will lead to convocations evolving into healthy GAFCON dioceses. That will depend partly on evangelical Anglicans not only making difficult decisions about their relationship with a compromised national church but also stepping out of constituency ghettos that are unique to English Anglican conservative evangelicalism. The most difficult steps may need to be left to a future generation of leaders.

My hopes for the future

I have been following the Church of England story closely since 1997 when, as an enthusiastic seventeen-year-old I felt called by God to ordained ministry. At that time – and up until only a few years ago – I thought that the key issue of contention in the Church of England was the sexuality revisionism battle. To be sure, that is what it appeared to be from the media and church statements I pored over!

I do still believe that holding to orthodox teaching on sexuality debates is vital, but I don't think that what God is doing in churches in England today has much to do with enabling orthodox church ministers to uphold the Bible's teaching on sexuality. Rather, I think that, in the midst of this battle, and in the midst of others, God is sifting his church to see who genuinely loves Jesus and is willing to do ministry in ways that are Jesus-shaped and countercultural. With that in mind, my hope for the future is that churches around our nation will commit to doing God's work in God's way. For evangelicals, it will require a fresh outpouring of the Spirit and a radical re-evaluation of ministry praxis. The alternative Anglicanisms have none of the human worldly strengths and powers that reside in the Church of England. They all look small and weak in the eyes of the world. For those who become convinced that the established church has so compromised with culture that it can no longer credibly guard the message of redemption from sin, through faith and repentance in Jesus' death on the cross, God will provide lifeboats that can enable clear blue water to be placed between them and the Church of England. I can assure any who find themselves convicted that they must take that path, it will be incredibly painful and opposed by many. Friendships will be lost as others are gained. Still, the spiritual rewards and realities experienced will be immense. My personal hope is merely that others experience these spiritual blessings as Jesus guards his church.

Notes

1 Letter to Henry Venn, quoted in 'A member of the Houses of Shirley and Hastings', *The Life and Times of Selina Countess of Huntingdon*, Vol. 1, (London: William Edward Painter, 1839), pp. 225–226.

2 I am grateful to the Reverend J. Paice for challenging me to read about the history of the FCE and for contributing this analogy.

3 D. Phillips, 'Oxford Movement and the church', *Cross Way*, Autumn 2008, No. 110 (© Church Society, available online at: <www.essaycompany.com/essays/theology/oxford-movement-church-4838>, accessed December 2021).

4 G. Carter, *Anglican Evangelicals* (2nd ed.) (Eugene, OR: Wipf & Stock, 2015), p. 363. This entire chapter, which goes into considerable detail regarding the complex story of the Reverend Shore, is well worth reading.

5 K. J. Stewart, 'The Oxford Movement and evangelicalism: Initial encounters', *Themelios*, 44(3) 2019, pp. 503–516.

6 Thoresby's 1863 address, *FCE Magazine*, 1870, p. 164, cited in J. Fenwick, *The Free Church of England* (1st ed.; London: T&T Clark, 2004), pp. 52–53.

7 Fenwick, *The Free Church of England*, p. 16.

8 F. Cook, *Selina Countess of Huntingdon* (Edinburgh: Banner of Truth, 2001).

9 Fenwick, *The Free Church of England*, p. 53.

10 F. Vaughan, 'Memories and reflections of forty-five years in the ministry of the Free Church of England' (n.p., 1949).

11 The FCE's 'Declaration of Principles' is available online (at: <https://fcofe.org.uk/wp-content/uploads/2018/12/FCEDofP-pdf.pdf>, accessed December 2021).

12 Summary of edits made to the Book of Common Prayer are listed in Fenwick, *The Free Church of England*, pp. 231–237.

13 *A History of the Free Church of England* (The Free Church of England Publications Committee, 1960), pp. 72–73.

14 The Nashville Statement is available online (at: <https://cbmw.org/nashville-statement>, accessed December 2021).

15 R. Beckwith, *Elders in Every City* (Milton Keynes: Paternoster, 2003).

16 R. Scruton, 'The language of the Book of Common Prayer', Prayer Book Society Annual Conference, 20 September 2018 (available online at: <www.youtube.com/watch?v=k1kfqWcgwY4>, accessed December 2021).

17 An English Prayer Book (available online at: <www.churchsociety.org/resources/?q=&category=an-english-prayer-book&post_tag=all>, accessed December 2021).

18 'Pastoral guidance for use in conjunction with the Affirmation of Baptismal Faith in the context of gender transition', Advent 2018 guidance (available online at: <www.churchofengland.org/sites/default/files/2018-12/Pastoral%20Guidance-Affirmation-Baptismal-Faith.pdf>, accessed December 2021).

19 Article 19 of the Church of England's 'Thirty-nine Articles of Religion' and echoed in the Free Church of England's 'Declaration of Principles'.

20 A. Palmer, 'It's a free choice', *Evangelicals Now*, March 2019 (available online at: <www.e-n.org.uk/2019/03/uk-news/its-a-free-choice>, accessed December 2021).

21 J. Mann, 'The Free Church of England should do what it says on its evangelical tin', Virtueonline, 20 February 2020 (available online at: <https://virtueonline.org/free-church-england-should-do-what-it-says-its-evangelical-tin>, accessed December 2021).

22 'Former Archbishop's aide faces questions over "missing" £300,000', *The Telegraph*, 18 April 2021 (available online at: <www.telegraph.co.uk/news/2021/04/18/former-archbishops-aide-faces-questions-missing-300000>, accessed December 2021). Also, 'Aide to former Archbishop of Canterbury "tried to blackmail minister over racism claims"',

The Telegraph, 1 May 2021 (available online at: <www.telegraph.co.uk/news/2021/05/01/aide-former-archbishop-canterbury-accused-trying-blackmail-minister>, accessed December 2021).

23 The Reverend A. Grey, for example (see: <www.immanuelbrentwood.org/Groups/185844/Immanuel_Church_Brentwood/About_Us/Leadership/Leadership.aspx>) and the Reverend D. Moore (see: <www.chelmsfordpres.org.uk/about-us/whos-who>, both accessed December 2021).

24 Such as the Reverend C. Tinker (see: <www.cornerstone-church.co.uk/chris-t.html>, accessed December 2021).

25 The Church of England (Continuing)'s Constitution is available online (at: <https://s3-us-west-2.amazonaws.com/cofec/publications/journal35.pdf>, accessed December 2021).

26 The congregations of the Church of England (Continuing) can be found online (at: <https://cofec.org/congregations>, accessed December 2021).

27 The churches of the Evangelical Connexion of the Free Church of England can be found online (at: <https://ecfce.com/church-reports>, accessed December 2021).

Appendix 1

The Thirty-nine Articles of Religion of the Church of England

ARTICLES OF RELIGION

A TABLE OF THE ARTICLES

1 Of Faith in the Holy Trinity.
2 Of Christ the Son of God.
3 Of his going down into Hell.
4 Of his Resurrection.
5 Of the Holy Ghost.
6 Of the Sufficiency of the Scriptures.
7 Of the Old Testament.
8 Of the Three Creeds.
9 Of Original or Birth-sin.
10 Of Free-Will.
11 Justification.
12 Of Good Works.
13 Of Works before Justification.
14 Of Works of Supererogation.
15 Of Christ alone without Sin.
16 Of Sin after Baptism.
17 Of Predestination and Election.
18 Of obtaining Salvation by Christ.
19 Of the Church.
20 Of the Authority of the Church.
21 Of the Authority of General Councils.
22 Of Purgatory.
23 Of Ministering in the Congregation.

24 Of speaking in the Congregation.

25 Of the Sacraments.

26 Of the Unworthiness of Ministers.

27 Of Baptism.

28 Of the Lord's Supper.

29 Of the Wicked which eat not the Body of Christ.

30 Of both kinds.

31 Of Christ's one Oblation.

32 Of the Marriage of Priests.

33 Of Excommunicate Persons.

34 Of the Traditions of the Church.

35 Of the Homilies.

36 Of Consecrating of Ministers.

37 Of Civil Magistrates.

38 Of Christian men's Goods.

39 Of a Christian man's Oath. The Ratification.

Text from the Book of Common Prayer, the rights in which are vested in the Crown, is reproduced by permission of the Crown's Patentee, Cambridge University Press. (Available online at: <www.churchofengland.org/prayer-and-worship/worship-texts-and-resources/book-common-prayer/articles-religion>, accessed December 2021.)

Appendix 2
The Jerusalem Declaration

In the name of God the Father, God the Son and God the Holy Spirit:

We, the participants in the Global Anglican Future Conference, have met in the land of Jesus' birth. We express our loyalty as disciples to the King of kings, the Lord Jesus. We joyfully embrace his command to proclaim the reality of his kingdom which he first announced in this land. The gospel of the kingdom is the good news of salvation, liberation and transformation for all. In light of the above, we agree to chart a way forward together that promotes and protects the biblical gospel and mission to the world, solemnly declaring the following tenets of orthodoxy which underpin our Anglican identity.

1 We rejoice in the gospel of God through which we have been saved by grace through faith in Jesus Christ by the power of the Holy Spirit. Because God first loved us, we love him and as believers bring forth fruits of love, ongoing repentance, lively hope and thanksgiving to God in all things.
2 We believe the Holy Scriptures of the Old and New Testaments to be the Word of God written and to contain all things necessary for salvation. The Bible is to be translated, read, preached, taught and obeyed in its plain and canonical sense, respectful of the church's historic and consensual reading.
3 We uphold the four Ecumenical Councils and the three historic Creeds as expressing the rule of faith of the one holy catholic and apostolic Church.
4 We uphold the Thirty-nine Articles as containing the true doctrine of the Church agreeing with God's Word and as authoritative for Anglicans today.

5 We gladly proclaim and submit to the unique and universal Lordship of Jesus Christ, the Son of God, humanity's only Saviour from sin, judgement and hell, who lived the life we could not live and died the death that we deserve. By his atoning death and glorious resurrection, he secured the redemption of all who come to him in repentance and faith.

6 We rejoice in our Anglican sacramental and liturgical heritage as an expression of the gospel, and we uphold the 1662 Book of Common Prayer as a true and authoritative standard of worship and prayer, to be translated and locally adapted for each culture.

7 We recognise that God has called and gifted bishops, priests and deacons in historic succession to equip all the people of God for their ministry in the world. We uphold the classic Anglican Ordinal as an authoritative standard of clerical orders.

8 We acknowledge God's creation of humankind as male and female and the unchangeable standard of Christian marriage between one man and one woman as the proper place for sexual intimacy and the basis of the family. We repent of our failures to maintain this standard and call for a renewed commitment to lifelong fidelity in marriage and abstinence for those who are not married.

9 We gladly accept the Great Commission of the risen Lord to make disciples of all nations, to seek those who do not know Christ and to baptise, teach and bring new believers to maturity.

10 We are mindful of our responsibility to be good stewards of God's creation, to uphold and advocate justice in society, and to seek relief and empowerment of the poor and needy.

11 We are committed to the unity of all those who know and love Christ and to building authentic ecumenical relationships. We recognise the orders and jurisdiction of those Anglicans who uphold orthodox faith and practice, and we encourage them to join us in this declaration.

12 We celebrate the God-given diversity among us which enriches our global fellowship, and we acknowledge freedom in secondary matters. We pledge to work together to seek the mind of Christ on issues that divide us.

13 We reject the authority of those churches and leaders who have denied the orthodox faith in word or deed. We pray for them and call on them to repent and return to the Lord.

14 We rejoice at the prospect of Jesus' coming again in glory, and while we await this final event of history, we praise him for the way he builds up his church through his Spirit by miraculously changing lives.

GAFCON, Jerusalem Declaration, June 2008 (available online at: <www.gafcon.org/jerusalem-2018/key-documents/jerusalem-declaration>, accessed December 2021). Reproduced by kind permission of GAFCON (www.gafcon.org/about/jerusalem-declaration>).

Appendix 3

The Church of England Evangelical Council's (CEEC) Basis of Faith and Additional Declarations (Taken from the Constitution)

The Basis of Faith of the Council shall be:

1 As members of the Church of England within the one, holy, catholic and apostolic church we affirm the faith uniquely revealed in the holy Scriptures and set forth in the catholic creeds, of which the Thirty-Nine Articles of Religion are a general exposition. Standing in the Reformation tradition we lay especial emphasis on the grace of God – his unmerited mercy – as expressed in the doctrines that follow.

2 God as the Source of Grace – In continuity with the teaching of Holy Scripture and the Christian creeds, we worship one God in three persons – Father, Son and Holy Spirit. God has created all things, and us in his own image: all life, truth, holiness and beauty come from him. His Son Jesus Christ, fully God and fully man, was conceived through the Holy Spirit and born of the virgin Mary, was crucified, died, rose and ascended to reign in glory.

3 The Bible as the Revelation of Grace – We receive the canonical books of the Old and New Testaments as the wholly reliable revelation and record of God's grace, given by the Holy Spirit as the true word of God written. The Bible has been given to lead us to salvation, to be the ultimate rule for Christian faith and conduct, and the supreme authority by which the Church must ever reform itself and judge its traditions.

4 The Atonement as the Work of Grace – We believe that Jesus Christ came to save lost sinners. Though sinless, he bore our sins, and their judgement, on the cross, thus accomplishing our salvation. By raising Christ bodily from the dead, God vindicated him as Lord and Saviour and proclaimed his victory. Salvation is in Christ alone.

5 The Church as the Community of Grace – We hold that the Church is God's covenant community, whose members, drawn from every nation, having been justified by grace through faith, inherit the promises made to Abraham and fulfilled in Christ. As a fellowship of the Spirit manifesting his fruit and exercising his gifts, it is called to worship God, grow in grace, and bear witness to him and his Kingdom. God's Church is one body and must ever strive to discover and experience that unity in truth and love which it has in Christ, especially through its confession of the apostolic faith and in its observance of the dominical sacraments.

6 The Sacraments as the Signs of Grace – We maintain that the Sacraments of Baptism and Holy Communion proclaim the Gospel as effective and visible signs of our justification and sanctification, and as true means of God's grace to those who repent and believe. Baptism is the sign of forgiveness of sin, the gift of the Spirit, new birth to righteousness and entry into the fellowship of the People of God. Holy Communion is the sign of the living, nourishing presence of Christ through his Spirit to his people: the memorial of his one, perfect, completed and all-sufficient sacrifice for sin, from whose achievement all may benefit but in whose offering none can share; and an expression of our corporate life of sacrificial thanksgiving and service.

7 Ministry as the Stewardship of Grace – We share, as the People of God, in a royal priesthood common to the whole Church, and in the community of the Suffering Servant. Our mission is the proclamation of the Gospel by the preaching of the word, as well as by caring for the needy, challenging evil and promoting justice and a more responsible use of the world's resources. It is the particular vocation of bishops and presbyters, together with deacons, to build up the body of Christ in truth and love, as pastors, teachers, and servants of the servants of God.

8 Christ's Return as the Triumph of Grace – We look forward expectantly to the final manifestation of Christ's grace and glory when he comes again to raise the dead, judge the world, vindicate His chosen and bring his Kingdom to its eternal fulfilment in the new heaven and the new earth.

Additional Declarations (Taken from the Constitution)

1 (4.1.1.) We gladly proclaim and submit to the unique and universal Lordship of Jesus Christ, the Son of God, humanity's only Saviour from sin, judgement and hell, who lived the life we could not live and died the death that we deserve. By his atoning death and glorious resurrection, he secured the redemption of all who come to him in repentance and faith.

2 (4.1.2.) We acknowledge God's creation of humankind as male and female and the unchangeable standard of Christian marriage between one man and one woman as the proper place for sexual intimacy and the basis of the family. We repent of our failures to maintain this standard and call for a renewed commitment to lifelong fidelity in marriage and abstinence for those who are not married.

The Church of England Evangelical Council's (CEEC) Basis of Faith and Additional Declarations (Taken from the Constitution) (available online at: <www.ceec.info/basis-of-faith.html>).

Appendix 4
IVP's Statement of Faith

Echoing our history, and as part of our ongoing partnership, IVP is proud to share the same Statement of Faith as the UCCF. Everything we publish is overseen by our Publishing Board, to ensure that our books are in line with this Statement of Faith.

1 There is one God in three persons, the Father, the Son and the Holy Spirit.
2 God is sovereign in creation, revelation, redemption and final judgement.
3 The Bible, as originally given, is the inspired and infallible Word of God. It is the supreme authority in all matters of belief and behaviour.
4 Since the fall, the whole of humankind is sinful and guilty, so that everyone is subject to God's wrath and condemnation.
5 The Lord Jesus Christ, God's incarnate Son, is fully God; he was born of a virgin; his humanity is real and sinless; he died on the cross, was raised bodily from death and is now reigning over heaven and earth.
6 Sinful human beings are redeemed from the guilt, penalty and power of sin only through the sacrificial death once and for all time of their representative and substitute, Jesus Christ, the only mediator between them and God.
7 Those who believe in Christ are pardoned all their sins and accepted in God's sight only because of the righteousness of Christ credited to them; this justification is God's act of undeserved mercy, received solely by trust in him and not by their own efforts.
8 The Holy Spirit alone makes the work of Christ effective to individual sinners, enabling them to turn to God from their sin and to trust in Jesus Christ.

9 The Holy Spirit lives in all those he has regenerated. He makes them increasingly Christlike in character and behaviour and gives them power for their witness in the world.

10 The one holy universal church is the Body of Christ, to which all true believers belong.

11 The Lord Jesus Christ will return in person, to judge everyone, to execute God's just condemnation on those who have not repented and to receive the redeemed to eternal glory.

IVP's Statement of Faith (available online at: <https://ivpbooks.com/statement-of-faith>).